THE GREEK
COOKBOOK

THE GREEK COOKBOOK

SOPHIA SKOURA

translated and adapted
by HELEN GEORGES

CROWN PUBLISHERS, INC., NEW YORK

Published by Crown Publishers, Inc., 201 East 50th Street, New York, New York 10022.

CROWN is a trademark of Crown Publishers, Inc.

First published in the Greek language as E NEA MARYERIKI TIS SOPHIA SKOURA

Manufactured in the United Staes of America
Library of Congress Catalogue Card Number: 67-27043

ISBN 0-517-50339-5

15   14   13   12

CONTENTS

GLOSSARY

Avgolemono—The best-known Greek sauce. Made of eggs and lemon juice, and used to flavor soups, meats, and vegetables.

Baklava—A favorite Greek pastry. Crisp phyllo pastry filled with nuts and dripping with honey syrup.

Bourekia—Meats or vegetables wrapped in phyllo pastry. Smaller versions are called *bourekakia*.

Copenhagen—A dessert named in honor of King George I of Greece, who had been a Danish prince.

Dolmathes—Stuffed grape leaves. Filled with either meat or rice and served hot or cold, with or without avgolemono.

Feta—Best known of the Greek cheeses. Made of goats' milk.

Fide (Fidelo)—A very fine egg noodle. Sold here as fidelo, fidilini, etc.

Floyeres—Phyllo pastry having a long, flutelike shape.

Giouvetsi—Greek casserole.

Glyko—The word means "sweet" and is used to refer to spoon sweets.

Grapevine leaves—Used for preparing dolmathes. Sold in this country in jars, already prepared for use, just rinse before using.

Halvah—Dessert made with farina.

Imam baldi—A real treat of eggplant and trimmings. Legend has it that the *imam* (high priest) fainted in delight when served this. Other legends say he fainted at the cost of the amount of oil used.

Kasseri—A firm table cheese. Used as a grating cheese. You may substitute Parmesan or Romano cheeses, but these have a stronger flavor.

Kataife—Available in Greek pastry or specialty shops. Some people substitute shredded wheat for it with fairly good results.

Kefalotiri—A hard cheese very similar to Parmesan.

Kimino—Cumin seed. Not too well known but easily available in this country. You will find many uses for its unusual flavor.

Lathera—Foods braised in oil, and served in the same oil.

Mahlepi—An unusual spice. Must be ground before using. Found in specialty shops.

Mastiha—Mastic. Sometimes refers to the liqueur of the same name.

Mavrodaphne—A dessert wine. Available at most liquor shops.

Mizithra—A mild cheese similar to cottage and ricotta cheeses.

Mortadella—A salami.

Ouzo—A clear liquor flavored with aniseed. Very potent—few can drink it straight. Mix with cold water and it becomes cloudy.

Pantespani—Greek sponge cake.

Pastes Sardelis—Salt-packed anchovies, served cleaned, and with oil and vinegar.

Paximadia—Biscuits served with coffee or tea.

Phyllo—A strudel-like pastry dough available in specialty shops (see introduction to Phyllo chapter: "about Phyllo").

Pilafi—Cooked rice.

Renga—Smoked herring.

Retsina—National wine of Greece. Resinated drinks are quite unusual and one must acquire a taste for them. Don't feel bad if you cannot.

Rizi—Raw rice.

Skordalia—Famous Greek garlic sauce. Very, very powerful. Not to be eaten before a theatre engagement or any social event—unless everyone else has eaten it, too.

Tarama—Carp roe.

Trahana—A homemade noodle used in soups and stews. Now available commercially in specialty shops. Substitute semolina if trahana is unobtainable.

Vissino—Sour cherries in a delicious preserve.

Vissinada—Sour-cherry preserves mixed with iced water for a cool summer drink.

Zampon—Ham.

APPETIZERS

CANAPÉS

KASSERI* CANAPÉ ✠ KANAPE ME KASSERI

¼–½ pound Kasseri cheese
sliced white bread

3—6 slices mortadella* or other
 salami, chopped
chopped olives or pickles, or
 relish

Trim the crusts from the bread and cut into desired shapes with a cookie cutter or sharp knife. Top each piece with a thin slice of the cheese cut to fit the shape of the bread. Garnish the edges of the canapés with the mortadella or other salami, and the chopped olives, pickles, or relish.

ROQUEFORT CANAPÉ ✠ KANAPE ME TYRI ROKFOR

6 tablespoons Roquefort cheese
2 or more tablespoons sweet
 butter

sliced white bread or assorted
 crackers
pickle slices
capers

Soften the butter and gradually add the cheese to it; cream to make a smooth paste. Trim the crusts from the bread and cut to desired shapes. Spread the bread (or crackers) with the cheese mixture. Top each canapé with a slice of pickle and a caper.

EGG CANAPÉ   ✠   KANAPE ME AVGO

6 hard-cooked eggs
4–6 slices salami, chopped
bread rounds, trimmed of crusts,
   and/or assorted crackers

mayonnaise
parsley
pickle slices
capers
2 hard-cooked egg yolks

Slice 3 of the eggs and place one slice on a bread round or cracker. Top with a piece of pickle and a caper. Garnish the edges with chopped salami.

Slice the remaining eggs. Place each slice on a piece of bread or a cracker; squeeze a rosette of mayonnaise onto the center. Sprinkle with crumbled egg yolk and garnish with parsley.

ZAMPON* CANAPÉ 1   ✠   KANAPE ME ZAMPON 1

6 slices zampon
2 hard-cooked eggs, chopped
1 tablespoon mayonnaise or
   sweet butter

1 small pickle, chopped, or 1
   tablespoon relish
6 buttered bread rounds,
   crusts removed

Roll the zampon into horn shapes. Add the mayonnaise (or butter) to the chopped eggs, then add the chopped pickle or relish; mix well. Stuff the zampon horns with the filling, and place the horns on the bread rounds. Serves 6.

ZAMPON* CANAPÉ 2   ✠   KANAPE ME ZAMPON 2

zampon
crackers

cooked beet slices
pitted black olives

Cut the zampon to fit the shape of the crackers you are using. With a sharp knife, cut out small hearts and diamonds from the beet rounds; cut out small clubs and spades from the olives. Decorate the zampon canapés with these so they resemble playing cards.

TARAMOSALATA CANAPÉ ✠ KANAPE ME TARAMOSALATA

1 recipe taramosalata (see index)
pitted olives, or olives stuffed with anchovies

small sprigs parsley
bread, trimmed and cut into canapé shapes

1. Place an anchovy-stuffed olive in the center of each piece of bread. Squeeze a garland of taramosalata around the edges of the bread. Garnish with parsley.

2. Or cut small olives into slices. Using a pastry tube, place a large rosette of taramosalata in the center of each piece of bread. Tuck in the olive slices, to suggest leaves, around the rosettes. Garnish with parsley.

ANCHOVIES PACKED IN SALT ✠ SARDELIS PASTES

Wash the anchovies thoroughly under cool water; rub them gently between the fingers to remove all salt, and also the skin and fins. Rinse, and drain. Place in a bowl and cover with vinegar; let stand until ready to serve, then pour off the vinegar and replace it with a dressing of equal amounts of vinegar and oil—enough to just barely cover the anchovies. Serve directly from the bowl.

NOTE: These may be eaten in their entirety—bones and all—or the bones may be removed.

ANCHOVY CANAPÉ 1 ✠ KANAPE ME ANTSOUGIA 1

1 can flat anchovy fillets
1–2 cooked beets, chopped
bread, trimmed and cut into rectangles

5 hard-cooked egg whites, chopped
chopped olives
capers

Place an anchovy fillet lengthwise down the center of each piece of bread. On one side of it, put the chopped egg whites topped with a few capers; on the other side, put the chopped beets topped with the chopped olives.

ANCHOVY CANAPÉ 2   ✛   KANAPE ME ANTSOUGIA 2

1 can rolled stuffed anchovies   bread rounds or crackers
1 large cooked beet, chopped   about 4 tablespoons sweet butter

Put an anchovy in the center of the bread round or cracker. Make a garland of chopped beets around the anchovy, and a garland of butter threads around the beets. (Squeeze the butter through the writing tip of a pastry-decorating tube.)

ANCHOVY CANAPE 3   ✛   KANAPE ME ANTSOUGIA 3

1 can flat anchovy fillets and   pinch of dry mustard
  1 jar pitted olives, or 1 jar   bread rounds or crackers
  anchovy-stuffed olives   cooked chopped beets
1–2 tablespoons anchovy paste   chopped egg whites
6–8 tablespoons sweet butter

Mix some of the anchovy paste with the butter and mustard. Taste; add more anchovy paste or butter as needed. Spread this on the bread or crackers. Stuff the olives with pieces of anchovy (or use the prestuffed olives). Put an olive in the center of each bread round or cracker. Garnish around the edges with the beets and egg white.

RENGA* CANAPÉ   ✛   KANAPE ME RENGA

1 whole renga with its roe   pinch of dry mustard
oil   bread, trimmed of crusts and cut
lemon juice   into pieces, or crackers
                                            chopped parsley

Clean the roe and soften it by mashing with a little olive oil and lemon juice to taste. Add the mustard; blend well to make a paste. Spread on the bread or crackers and lay a piece of renga on top. Garnish with the parsley.

FOIE GRAS CANAPÉ   ✛   KANAPE ME FOIA GRA

Buy a can of foie gras. Cut into very small pieces. Spread over buttered bread rounds. Garnish with a garland of butter threads around the edges.

SALAMI CANAPÉ ✠ KANAPE ME SALAMI

salami
chopped egg white
sliced olives

bread, trimmed of crusts and cut
into canapé shapes, or crackers
chopped parsley

On a cracker or piece of bread, place a slice of salami cut slightly smaller than its base. On the edge of the bread, overlapping the salami slightly, place a garland of chopped egg white and some sliced olives; garnish with chopped parsley.

MORTADELLA* CANAPÉ ✠ KANAPE ME MORTADELLA

mortadella, cut to fit bread
   rounds or crackers
butter

hard-cooked eggs, chopped
chopped pickle, or pickle relish

Butter the bread rounds. Place the mortadella on top. Mound some chopped egg in the middle of the mortadella, surround with a garland of butter threads (as in Anchovy Canapé). Top with a bit of chopped pickle or pickle relish.

SHRIMP, LOBSTER, OR CRABMEAT CANAPÉ ✠ KANAPE ME YARIDES, ASTAKO, Y KAVOURIA

chopped shrimp, lobster, or
   crabmeat
mayonnaise
relish or chopped pickle

whole shrimp or pieces of lobster
   or crabmeat
bread rounds trimmed of crusts

Add one of the chopped seafoods to mayonnaise, using enough mayonnaise to make a smooth spread. Add the chopped pickle or relish to taste. Spread over the bread rounds. Top with a whole shrimp or chunk of lobster or crabmeat. Garnish the edges with pickle.

BLACK CAVIAR CANAPÉ ☩ KANAPE ME MAVRO HAVIARI

2 parts caviar
1 part sweet butter
chopped cooked beets

hard-cooked chopped egg whites
trimmed bread rounds, or
crackers

Mix the caviar with the softened butter. Spread on the bread or cracker bases. Garnish with the beets and egg whites.

TOMATO CANAPÉ ☩ KANAPE ME DOMATA

Spread mayonnaise on bread rounds. Place a piece of tomato in the center of each, and garnish with two slices of black olives and sprinkle chopped parsley over the mayonnaise.

RADISH CANAPÉ ☩ KANAPE ME RAPANAKIA

Clean and wash some radishes and cut them into rectangular slices. Cut a few radishes into round slices with the red skin showing. Place some green mayonnaise (see index for Green Sauce) on bread rounds. Put a round radish slice on each and surround with white radish slices, to suggest petals or rays. Between the "rays," place slices of black olives.

ALMOND CANAPÉ ☩ KANAPE ME AMIGDALA

Mix a little dried mustard and salt with softened butter. Spread this on bread rounds. Split salted almonds and lay these, like daisy petals, on the bread. Add chopped olives or beets for the center.

PISTACHIO CANAPÉ ☩ KANAPE ME FISTIKI

Spread softened cream cheese on bread rounds and sprinkle with chopped pistachio nuts.

WALNUT CANAPÉ   ☦   KANAPE ME KARITHIA

Prepare like Pistachio Canapé, above.

TARAMOSALATA   ☦   TARAMOSALATA 1
[TARAMA SAUCE] 1

6 ounces tarama*   2 or more lemons, juice only
6–8 slices white bread, trimmed   1 small onion, finely chopped
   of crusts   chopped parsley (optional)
1½–2 cups olive oil (finest   chives (optional)
   quality)

Put the tarama in a mixer or blender. Wet the bread and thoroughly squeeze out the excess water; add to the tarama. Add a little oil, and beat until thoroughly blended. Add the onions and continue to mix. Pour additional oil slowly into the tarama, beating constantly, to make a smooth, cream-colored paste. Add the lemon juice, a little at a time, to taste. The consistency and taste of the taramosalata are a matter of individual preference. Some people prefer it made with a little more bread; others like more lemon juice, some like less. No matter: the end result is always a tasty, rather thick, versatile diplike sauce. Serve it in a bowl, with crackers or crusty bread, onion slices, etc., to "go with." Or garnish with parsley and olives for a festive platter. Or use it as a salad dressing.

NOTE: Taramosalata is generally placed on the Greek table at the start of the meal and can be tasted at will throughout the meal.

TARAMOSALATA   ☦   TARAMOSALATA 2
[TARAMA SAUCE] 2

5 ounces tarama*   2–3 tablespoons lemon juice
¾ pound cold boiled potatoes,   1 tablespoon white vinegar
   mashed   chopped parsley (optional)
1½ cups (approximately) olive
   oil (finest quality)

Blend the tarama in a mixer or blender with a little of the oil for a few minutes. Add the potatoes and mix well. Add the oil alternately with the lemon juice and vinegar, blending constantly, until the mixture becomes a thick smooth paste. Garnish with parsley and serve in a bowl.

NOTE: You can vary the amounts of tarama and potatoes to make a paste to your taste (see Taramosalata 1, above).

HOT APPETIZERS

OREKTIKA TIS ORAS

''APPETIZERS OF THE HOUR''

EGG-CHEESE PUFFS   ✠   OREKTIKA ME AVGA KE TYRI

5 eggs
½ cup flour
1½ teaspoons baking powder
1 teaspoon salt

1 teaspoon minced parsley
1½ cups cubed kefalotiri*
    cheese
butter for frying

Beat the eggs well; add the flour sifted with the baking powder and the salt. Add the parsley and the cubed cheese. Mix together well. Brown the butter in a frying pan, and drop in the batter, a spoonful at a time, to fry. Keep the heat regulated so the puffs do not burn. When they are lightly brown, turn them carefully, with a slotted spoon, without piercing, and drain on absorbent paper. Serve hot.

EGG-AND-CHEESE CROQUETTES   ✠   KROKETAKIA ME AVGA KE TYRI

3 cups grated kefalotiri* cheese
1 teaspoon baking powder
½ teaspoon salt

5 egg whites
oil or butter for frying

Mix together the cheese, baking powder, and salt. Beat the egg whites until stiff but not dry. Slowly add the cheese mixture to the egg whites, beating constantly. The mixture should be very thick (if necessary, add a little flour until the mixture is the right consistency). Shape into croquettes about 1½ inches long. Fry in hot oil (or butter) to a light golden color. Drain on absorbent paper and serve hot.

SALTY BISCUITS ☩ ALMIRAH BISCOTAKIA

3 cups flour
3 teaspoons baking powder
1 teaspoon coarse salt
½ cup grated kefalotiri* cheese

⅓ cup sweet butter or other
  shortening
1 cup milk

Sift the flour together with the salt and baking powder into a bowl. Add the butter (or shortening), and knead lightly with the fingertips. Add the cheese and the milk, and work the whole together (the batter will be soft). Lightly flour a marble-top table (or a bread board) and your rolling pin. Roll out the dough about ½ to ¼ inches thick. Using the floured rim of a glass or cookie cutter, cut the dough into round shapes (about 1½ to 2½ inches in diameter). Place on a lightly buttered baking sheet and bake in a preheated 375° oven for about 15 minutes. Makes about 36 small biscuits.

SALTY BISCUITS ☩ ALMIRAH BISCOTA
WITH ANCHOVIES ME ANTSOUGIA

4 cups flour
5 teaspoons baking powder
3 teaspoons salt
½ cup shortening or sweet
  butter

1 cup milk
2 cans caper-stuffed anchovies
paprika

Sift the flour, salt, and baking powder into a bowl. Add the butter and knead lightly with the fingertips. Add the milk; knead to a soft dough. Lightly flour a bread board or marble-top table and rolling pin. Roll out the dough about ¼ to ½ inch thick. Cut out the biscuits with a floured cutter or glass. On each biscuit place an anchovy stuffed with a caper. Sprinkle with paprika. Place on a lightly buttered baking sheet and bake in a preheated 375° oven for 15 minutes. Makes 24 to 30 biscuits.

SALTY BISCUITS WiTH SALAMI ☩ ALMIRAH BISCOTA ME SALAMI

Make the dough as in Salty Biscuits with Anchovies. Roll out ¼ inch thick, and cut out as in that recipe. Place a piece of salami, cut to fit, on top of each piece of dough, and cover with another round of dough. Brush with beaten egg white. Sprinkle with a little kefalotiri* cheese. Bake on a lightly buttered baking sheet in a preheated 400° oven for 15 minutes. Serve hot. Makes 24 to 30 biscuits.

SALTY BISCUITS WITH FRANKFURTERS   ✠   BISCOTA ALMIRAH ME
("PIGS IN BLANKETS")   LOUKANIKA

Make biscuit dough as in Salty Biscuits with Anchovies. Cut the dough into small rectangles and roll them around cocktail frankfurters; seal the edges with a little egg white beaten with a few drops of water. Bake on a lightly buttered baking sheet in a preheated 375° oven for 15 minutes (or until golden). Serve hot. Makes about 24 Pigs in Blankets.

BATONS 1   ✠   MPATON SALE 1

3 cups flour   1 egg, separated
2 teaspoons salt   1 cup butter, melted, or oil
1 teaspoon baking powder

Sift the flour together with the salt and baking powder into a bowl. Add the egg yolk and the butter or oil, and knead to a soft dough. (If the dough is too thick, add a few drops of milk.) Break off small pieces of the dough and shape into batons or canes, each about as long as a finger. Place on a buttered baking sheet. Beat the egg white with a few drops of water and brush this on the canes. Bake in a preheated 400° oven for about 10 minutes.

BATONS 2   ✠   MPATON SALE 2

Make like Batons 1, above, but substitute ¾ cup grated kefalotiri* cheese for 1 teaspoon of the salt.

SALTY BRIOCHE   ✠   MPRIOS ALMIRAH

3 tablespoons butter   1 teaspoon baking powder
6 eggs, separated   ½ teaspoon salt
¾ pound kefalotiri*, grated   3 cups (approximately) flour

Cream the butter until very light in color. Add the egg yolks and beat well. Mix in the cheese, baking powder, flour, and salt. Beat the egg whites until stiff but not dry; add to the mixture and knead well. Pinch off small walnut-size pieces. Place on a lightly buttered baking sheet. Bake in a preheated 350° oven for 10 to 15 minutes. Serve hot. These may be reheated.

APPETIZERS WITH PUFF PASTE

CHOPPED MEAT OR LIVER PUFFS ✠ OREKTIKA ME SFOLIATA
KAI KIMA E SIKOTAKIA

1 recipe Puff Paste (see index)

1 recipe meat mixture for Piroski
(see index)
oil for frying

Make the puff paste as directed. Cut the dough into walnut-size pieces, and roll each out to a round. In the center of each circle, place a small amount of the meat mixture; turn the dough over it to enclose the meat, and seal the edges. Fry in deep fat until lightly brown, then remove with a slotted spoon and drain. Serve hot.

VOL-AU-VENTS ✠ VOLOVAN ME VOUTIRO
WITH SWEET BUTTER FRESKO

1 recipe Puff Paste (see index)
  or use half the recipe if smaller
  pastry containing more filling
  is desired)
1½ sticks sweet butter

4–5 hard-cooked eggs, chopped
5 slices zampon,* minced
1 teaspoon dry mustard
salt and pepper to taste
1 egg white, beaten

Prepare the puff paste, and roll out about ¼ inch thick. Cut into small circular shapes, 2½ to 3½ inches in diameter; place on a baking sheet. Cut out a second group of circles for the tops. In the center of these tops, make a small circular depression, being careful not to cut the dough all the way through. (These inside circles of dough will be removed later.) Brush the edges of the bottom circles with the egg white, but be careful not to spread the egg white all over, as it will prevent the dough from rising correctly. With the tines of a fork, carefully make ridges around the edges of both the top and bottom layers. Join the circles carefully.

While the patty shells are baking (in a preheated 350° oven until golden), cream the butter with the mustard, salt, and pepper. Add the chopped eggs and zampon, and mix well. When the shells are baked and partially cooled, carefully remove the centers from the top (this is the part that was indented earlier). Fill the shells and replace the centers, as lids for the shells.

VOL-AU-VENTS WITH CHOPPED MEAT ✠ VOLOVAN ME KIMA

1 recipe Puff Paste (see index)
1 pound chopped meat
Béchamel Sauce (see index)

grated Parmesan (or similar)
cheese

Prepare the puff paste, and shape it as in Vol-au-vents with Sweet Butter. Prepare and brown the chopped meat as in the recipe for Piroski (see index). Bake the shells and remove the lids; fill with the chopped-meat mixture. Do not top with the lids, but top with a tablespoon of béchamel and some of the cheese. Return the vol-au-vents to the oven until the tops are lightly browned. Serve hot.

VOL-AU-VENTS WITH BRAINS ✠ VOLOVAN ME MIALA

1 recipe Puff Paste (see index)
1–2 pairs Boiled Brains (see index)

½ recipe Thick Béchamel Sauce (see index)
salt and pepper to taste

Prepare the puff paste. Make it into shells, as in Vol-au-vents with Sweet Butter (see index). Bake the shells; cool them. Prepare the brains and cut into small pieces; season with salt and pepper, and mix into the béchamel sauce. Fill the shells with the brains mixture, and replace the lids. Serve hot.

CHOUX PUFFS WITH PARMESAN CHEESE ✠ SOU ME PARMEZANA

1 recipe Choux (see index)

THE FILLING
1 recipe Thick Béchamel Sauce
2 cups grated Parmesan cheese

Prepare and bake the puffs. Prepare the béchamel and add half the cheese to it. Split the baked and cooled puffs in half, and fill with the mixture. (You may prefer to fill them by forcing the mixture through a pastry bag into the side of the puff.) Brush with a little of the sauce, and roll in the rest of the cheese. Makes about 40 puffs.

FETA* OR PARMESAN PUFFS   ✠   OREKTIKA ME SFOLIATA KAI TYRI FETA E PARMEZANA

1 recipe Puff Paste (see index)
1 pound crumbled feta or
   grated Parmesan cheese

3—4 eggs
2 tablespoons minced onion
oil for frying

Prepare the puff paste. Beat the eggs lightly, and to them add the cheese and onion. Cut off small pieces from the puff paste and roll into rounds. Place a small amount of the cheese mixture in the center of each round and enclose the filling in the dough. Seal well. Deep-fat fry; drain. Serve hot.

PUFFS WITH SWEET BUTTER   ✠   SOU ME FRESKO VOUTIRO

1 recipe Choux (see index)

THE FILLING
6 hard-cooked eggs, chopped
1½ sticks sweet butter
3 tablespoons minced parsley
2 tablespoons dry mustard
2 tablespoons minced onion
salt and pepper to taste

Prepare and bake the puffs. While they are baking, mince the onions, set them aside in cold water for 10 minutes; drain. Cream the butter with the mustard and salt. Add the eggs, parsley, and onions. Mix well. Season with pepper. When the puffs are cool, split and fill them. Makes about 40 puffs.

PUFFS WITH ANCHOVIES   ✠   SOU ME ANTSOUGIA

1 recipe Choux (see index)

THE FILLING
¾ pound sweet butter
1 cup minced anchovy fillets
½ cup chopped gherkins
1 tablespoon dry mustard
salt to taste

Prepare the choux and bake the puffs. Meanwhile, cream the butter with the mustard and salt; add the anchovies and gherkins. Cool the puffs, cut in half and fill. Makes about 40 puffs.

PIROSKI   ✠   PIROSKI

THE CRUST	THE FILLING

THE CRUST
⅓ cup milk
3 packages granular yeast
4 cups flour
⅓ cup vegetable oil
4 egg yolks
1 teaspoon salt
oil for frying

THE FILLING
1 pound chopped meat
2 tablespoons butter
1 small onion, chopped
½ cup (approximately) tomato
   sauce
4–5 tablespoons grated
   Parmesan cheese
1 egg white, beaten with a few
   drops water
chopped parsley

Heat the milk to lukewarm, pour into a bowl; add the yeast. Mix with your fingers. Add a cup of the flour, and mix to form a ball. Cover the bowl, and set in a warm place. Let the sponge rise until double in bulk. Punch down. Add the vegetable oil, egg yolks, salt, and the remaining flour, mix well, then knead to make a stiff dough. (Add more water or flour, if necessary.) Cover and let rise again.

Meantime, brown the meat in the butter. Add the onion, and cook until light brown. Mix in the tomato sauce and parsley, and cook about 15 to 20 minutes. Stir in the grated cheese.

Lightly flour a bread board and turn the dough out onto it; knead until elastic. Divide into small pieces. Flatten these with your hands, or roll into thick round shapes. In the center of each, place a tablespoonful of the meat mixture. Fold over the dough to form a half-moon shape. Brush the edges with a little egg white, and pinch to seal. Flatten the piroski slightly and place on a buttered baking sheet. Set aside in a warm place to rise again, but for less time. Deep-fat fry until a deep golden color. Remove with a slotted spoon, drain, and serve hot. Makes about 15 to 18 piroski.

NOTE 1: These can be baked instead of fried. To bake, follow the directions above to the final rising, then brush the tops with egg white, and bake in a preheated 350° oven until golden brown.

NOTE 2: The filling can be of chicken, ham, fish, or hard-cooked eggs. For any of these, chop the filling and mix with Béchamel Sauce (see index), or mashed potatoes.

NOTE 3: You can also make sweet piroski by adding 3 tablespoons sugar when you add the salt. Fill the dough with marmalade and chopped glazed fruit. Bake as in Note 1 (above), and top with confectioner's sugar.

SALADS AND VEGETABLES

A General Note on Preparation: Greens should be cooked in a small amount of boiling salted water. Potatoes, carrots, beets, etc., are cooked in plain water and salt is added later in the cooking—salt added at the beginning of the cooking toughens the vegetable.

CABBAGE-TOMATO SALAD ✠ SALATA LAHANO-DOMATES

½–1 head cabbage
3–6 tomatoes
black olives
sprig parsley

⅓–½ cup oil
¼ cup (or less) vinegar or
    lemon juice

Clean the cabbage. Cut it in half. Shred. Place in a strainer and wash under running water for several minutes; drain well. Wash and slice half the tomatoes; cut the others into wedges. Mound the cabbage in the center of a round platter; surround with tomato slices. Place an olive in the center of the cabbage and circle it with tomato wedges. Place a sprig of parsley in the olive and scatter other olives on the cabbage. Just before serving, pour oil-and-vinegar dressing or oil-and-lemon dressing over it. Salt lightly. Serves 6.

NOTE: For an individual salad, wash a small tomato. Partially cut it into 4 wedges (do not cut all the way through). Place it on a small plate and surround with shredded cabbage. Top with parsley and an olive. Serve with oil-and-vinegar or lemon-and-vinegar dressing.

LETTUCE-TOMATO SALAD ✠ SALATA MAROULI-DOMATES

Prepare like Cabbage-Tomato Salad (above), using lettuce in place of cabbage.

COUNTRY SALAD ✠ SALATA HORIATIKI

10–12 small plum tomatoes
2–3 cucumbers
2 small onions
1 green pepper

½ pound feta cheese (more or
  less to taste)
salt and pepper to taste
olives

Clean and cut the tomatoes into bite-sized pieces. Cut the cucumbers. Mince the onions and peppers. Cut up the feta cheese. Place all these in a bowl, add olives. Season. Toss well. Serve with oil-and-vinegar dressing. Serves 6 to 8.

TOMATO-PEPPER SALAD ✠ SALATA PIPERIES-DOMATES

3–6 tomatoes
1 green pepper
oil

vinegar (optional)
parsley
salt to taste

Clean the tomatoes and cut into wedges. Do the same with the pepper. Season. Toss in a bowl. Serve with oil-and-vinegar dressing or omit the vinegar. Garnish with parsley. Serves 6.

LETTUCE SALAD ✠ SALATA MAROULIA

2 heads lettuce
3–4 boiled potatoes
3 hard-cooked eggs
1 tablespoon chopped dill or
  anise seed
2 tablespoons oil

2 tablespoons chopped scallions
4 teaspoons vinegar
1½ cups mayonnaise
4–5 olives
1 tablespoon chopped parsley

Wash and dry the lettuce. Save the hearts and tear the remaining leaves into pieces. Cut half the potatoes into small cubes; cut the rest into round slices. Slice 2 of the eggs; crumble the yolk of the third egg. Mix the lettuce, potato cubes, scallions, and the dill or anise seed together; blend the oil and vinegar and sprinkle over the salad. Let this rest for 5 to 10 minutes, then drain off dressing. Mix in half of the mayonnaise. Place the salad on a round platter and cover with the remaining mayonnaise. Surround with egg slices, potato slices, and olives, and sprinkle with parsley and crumbled egg yolk. Place in the refrigerator until ready to serve. Serves 6.

COOKED-GREENS SALAD   ✠   SALATA HORTA VRASMENA

2 bunches dandelion greens or   lemon
   chickory or endive or escarole   coarse salt
oil

Bring to a boil ample water with some coarse salt in a large pot. Wash the greens and pick them over; toss into the rapidly boiling water and boil in a covered pot over a very high heat (this retains the green color) until tender. Do not overcook. Boil for 20 to 30 minutes. Drain, and serve hot in individual vegetable dishes. Add oil and lemon to taste.

SQUASH SALAD   ✠   KOLOKITHAKIA SALATA

3 pounds (approximately) small   lemon
   squash   salt
oil

Buy small, fresh, tender squash. Clean and place in lightly salted rapidly boiling water. Cover and boil over a high heat for 30 to 45 minutes (or until tender). Remove from the pot with a slotted spoon. Arrange on a round platter or in a bowl. Serve whole. Pass the oil and lemon. Serves 6.

CABBAGE-CARROT-TOMATO SALAD   ✠   SALATA LAHANO-
                                                    KAROTA-DOMATES

½–1 cabbage   ¼ cup (or less) vinegar or
3–6 tomatoes   lemon juice
3–5 large, tender carrots,   salt to taste
   shredded   Calamata or black olives
⅓–½ cup oil   parsley

Shred the cabbage. Place in a strainer and wash under running water for several minutes; drain well. Wash the tomatoes and cut into wedges. Wash and scrape the carrots. Place the carrots in the center of a platter; surround them with a ring of cabbage and then with a ring of tomatoes, or put the tomatoes in the center and lay the carrots around them. Sprinkle with salt. Before serving, add a dressing of oil and vinegar or oil and lemon. Garnish with Calamata olives and parsley. Serves 6.

BEET SALAD   ✛   BATZARIA SALATA

12 or more medium-sized beets   vinegar (optional) or
oil (optional)   Skordalia Sauce (optional)

Select fresh tender beets and cut off the tops and roots. Wash the beets, without removing the skins, and boil in a large pot with ample water. Meanwhile, clean the beet greens with the stems; add to the pot after the beets have cooked 30 minutes. When the beets are tender (after about 45 minutes—test by piercing with a fork), remove the beets and strain the liquid. Peel the beets and cut them into round slices; chop up the beet greens. Mound the greens in the center of a platter and surround them with the beet slices. Pour oil and vinegar over all, and serve; or serve with Skordalia* Sauce (see index). Serve hot or cold. Serves 6.

BOILED CAULIFLOWER SALAD   ✛   KOUNOUPITHI VRASTO SALATA

1 head cauliflower (about 4   lemon juice
  pounds)   salt and pepper to taste
oil

Wash and clean the cauliflower, and cut it into 6 pieces. Drop into lightly salted boiling water. Boil over high heat until tender (from 30 to 45 minutes). Remove the cauliflower with a slotted spoon. Pour oil and lemon juice to taste over it. Season. Serves 6.

NOTE: The cauliflower can be boiled in very little water, stems down, floweret up (semisteamed). Add the salt when half cooked.

GREEN-BEAN SALAD   ✛   AMPELOFASOLIA SALATA

3 pounds (approximately) green   1 tablespoon chopped garlic
  beans   1 cup oil
½ cup parsley   ½ cup vinegar

Clean the green beans and wash them well. Drop into rapidly boiling water. Cover and cook over a high heat for about 20 to 30 minutes (or until tender). Remove from the heat; drain. Place in a bowl with the remaining ingredients; mix together and serve. Serves 6 to 10.

TOMATO-AND-CUCUMBER SALAD ✠ SALATA DOMATES KE AGOURIA

3–6 tomatoes
2–3 cucumbers
1/3–1/2 cup oil

1/4 cup (or less) vinegar
black olives
salt to taste

Clean the tomatoes and cut in half, then into wedges. Slice the cucumbers. Place on a platter, garnish with olives. Serve with oil and vinegar and salt. Serves 6.

POTATO SALAD ✠ PATATOSALATA

3 pounds potatoes
3/4 cup oil
salt and pepper to taste
1/3 cup vinegar or lemon juice
1 teaspoon grated onion

2–3 tablespoons chopped
   parsley
2–3 hard-cooked eggs, sliced
olives
parsley sprigs

Wash and scrub the potatoes, then boil until tender; cool, and slip off the skins. Slice or cut into pieces; place in a salad bowl. Beat together the oil, vinegar, (or lemon juice), salt, pepper, and onion until well blended; mix in the parsley. Pour the dressing over the potatoes and toss lightly. Garnish with egg slices placed alternately on the salad with olives and parsley sprigs. Serves 6 to 8.

EGGPLANT SALAD 1 ✠ MELITZANOSALATA 1

2–3 large eggplants
1 onion, finely grated
salt and pepper to taste

lemon juice or vinegar to taste
1 (or more) cups olive oil, as
   needed

Wash the eggplants and put into a pan (or wrap in aluminum foil) and bake until soft. Put the onions into cold water to soak and remove some of the strength. Remove the skins from the cooked eggplant and mash the pulp thoroughly. Drain the onion well and add to the eggplant. Add salt and pepper, and beat. Add lemon or vinegar alternately with the oil, and beating all the while, until you have a thick mixture. Serve in a bowl or as a side dish.

EGGPLANT SALAD 2   ✠   MELITZANOSALATA 2

3 large eggplants   ¾ cup (approximately) milk
salt and pepper to taste   lemon juice to taste
1–1½ cups olive oil   ½ cup grated Parmesan cheese

Prepare the eggplants as in Eggplant Salad 1, then add the salt and pepper, and mix well. Add alternately the oil, milk, and lemon juice to taste, mashing until you have a light mixture. Blend in the cheese. Serve in a bowl.

SOUPS

CABBAGE SOUP ✠ SOUPA ME LAHANO

2 cups shredded cabbage
½ cup butter or other shortening
1 cup chopped onions
12 cups water

½ tablespoon chopped dill
1 cup chopped frankfurters
salt and pepper
croutons (see index)

Select the white leaves from the cabbage and shred them finer than for salad. Cover with water (which is not part of the 12 cups listed above), boil for 5 minutes, and drain. In a skillet, brown the butter. Add the onions and sauté until they are a light golden color, *not dark*. Transfer them to a large pot with the 12 cups of water; bring to a boil. Add the dill, frankfurters, and cabbage, and season to taste. Cook for about 1 hour, or until the onions and cabbage are very soft. Serve hot with croutons. The soup will boil down to serve 6 to 8.

BEAN SOUP ✠ SOUPA FASSOLIA

3 cups dried white beans
2 medium onions
2–3 stalks celery
3–4 medium carrots

1 tablespoon chopped celery root
1 cup oil
1 tablespoon tomato paste
salt and pepper to taste

Wash the beans and soak them overnight in cold water. Rinse well. Place in a large pot and pour in enough water to cover the beans by about 1 inch. Bring to a boil. Pour off this water and replace it with fresh hot water. Chop the onions and the celery stalks, and cut the carrots into rounds. Add all the vegetables to the beans. Add the oil. Simmer for about 45 minutes. Add the tomato paste diluted with some of the liquid from the pot. Season to taste. Boil 20 minutes longer. Serve hot. Serves 6 to 8.

NOTE: This soup is thick, but it can be thinned with hot water if desired.

PURÉE OF BEAN SOUP ✠ SOUPA FASOLIA (KREMA)

4 cups dried white beans
water as needed
2–3 medium onions, chopped
2 tablespoons chopped celery
   root
2–3 carrots, finely sliced
1 cup oil

1 tablespoon cornstarch
   (optional)
salt and pepper to taste
2 lemons, juice only
croutons (optional)
lemon slices

Clean the beans. Soak them overnight in cold water, then drain. Place in a large pot with 3 to 4 quarts fresh water, and bring to a boil. As soon as the water boils, pour it off and replace it with fresh hot water. Add the vegetables, and cook until the beans begin to split (about 1 to 1½ hours). (If the soup cooks too rapidly, you may have to add more water while it is boiling.) Pass the soup through a strainer or blender, thinning it out with hot water if it is too thick; return to the pot. Add the oil and cook for 5 minutes longer, stirring constantly. Mix the cornstarch with the lemon juice, and stir it into the soup. Again bring it to a boil, and cook 5 minutes longer for it to thicken, stirring constantly. Serve plain or with croutons (see index). Serves 6 to 8.

NOTE: If you do not use the cornstarch, serve the soup after you add the oil. Pass the lemon slices.

CHICK PEA SOUP ✠ SOUPA REVETHIA

5 cups chick peas (garbanzos)
water
2 tablespoons baking soda
2–3 onions, chopped

1 cup oil
salt and pepper to taste
lemon slices

Soak the beans overnight in warm water in a ceramic bowl. Strain; dust with baking soda. Let stand for 15 minutes. Rinse with hot water. Rub a few at a time between your fingers to remove the skins (unless you have bought them without the skins). Wash well, put into a strainer; let the water run through them for several minutes. Put into a large pot with water to cover and bring to a boil. Skim off the froth as it rises. Add the onions, oil, salt, and pepper. Half cover; simmer until the beans split (about 1 to 2 hours). Serve hot with lemon slices. Serves 6 to 8.

LENTIL SOUP   ✠   SOUPA FAKEZ

3 cups lentils
12–15 cups hot water
1 cup oil
4–5 cloves garlic
1 onion, minced
2 stalks celery
2 medium carrots, minced

1 sprig rosemary
1½ pounds tomatoes, peeled
   and strained (or 1 1-pound-
   14-ounce can of tomatoes)
salt and pepper to taste
vinegar (optional)

Soak the lentils overnight in cold water. Rinse and place in a large pot with plenty of water. Bring to a boil. Drain off this water and replace it with the 12 to 15 cups hot water. Add the remaining ingredients except the tomatoes and salt and pepper. Simmer for 45 minutes, then add the tomatoes and cook for about 20 minutes longer (until the lentils are soft). Season. Serve hot. Serves 6 to 8.

NOTE: If the soup is too thick, add more water before adding the tomatoes. If the soup is too thin, add 1½ tablespoons flour mixed with 3 tablespoons vinegar, and cook for 5 minutes to thicken.

This soup is often served with vinegar at the table, to be added to taste.

PURÉE OF LENTIL SOUP   ✠   SOUPA FAKEZ (KREMA)

4 cups lentils
1 onion, minced
3–4 ripe tomatoes, cut into
   small pieces
3–4 carrots, diced
1 bay leaf

1 stalk celery
1 sprig rosemary
4 tablespoons sweet butter
salt and pepper to taste
croutons (optional)
vinegar (optional)

Soak the lentils overnight in cold water. Rinse, then put into a large pot with about 4 quarts of water and bring to a boil. When it has boiled for about 5 minutes, drain off the water and replace it with 4 quarts of fresh hot water. Add the vegetables and rosemary. Cover, and cook at a slow boil until the lentils are very tender and soft (about 1 hour). Pass the soup and vegetables through a strainer or blender, and return to the pot. Add water, if necessary; add salt and pepper. Cook for about 5 minutes longer. Remove from the heat. Add the butter, stirring it in gently. Serve with croutons (see index) and vinegar if desired. Serves 6 to 8.

SOUP WITH FARINA ✠ SOUPA ME SIMIGDALI

8 cups meat stock
5 tablespoons farina

salt to taste
2 tablespoons butter

Bring the stock to a boil in a large pot. Add the farina, a little at a time, stirring constantly so it does not lump. Cover, but check it frequently because this mixture swells. Boil about 10 to 15 minutes. Add the salt. Skim off any froth. Remove from the heat, stir in the butter. Serve hot. Serves 6.

VEGETABLE SOUP ✠ HORTOSOUPA

2 pounds potatoes
2–3 onions
4–5 carrots
1 bunch celery
1½ pounds (approximately) ripe
   tomatoes (or 1-pound-14-ounce
   can of whole tomatoes)

10 cups water
1 tablespoon coarse salt
dash of pepper
2 tablespoons shortening or oil
croutons (optional)

Wash, clean, and chop the potatoes, onions, carrots, and celery. Add to the water and boil for 20 minutes. Add the salt and tomatoes (if you are using ripe tomatoes, pierce them with a fork) and cook for 30 to 45 minutes. Remove from the heat. Pass all the vegetables through a strainer or purée machine or blender, then return to the pot. Add a little pepper and stir in the shortening or serve the soup and add oil at the table. Serve with croutons (see index). Serves 6.

TOMATO SOUP WITH OIL ✠ DOMATOSOUPA ME LATHI

2 pounds ripe tomatoes
1 stalk celery
1 carrot, chopped
1 onion, minced
2–3 whole cloves garlic

8 cups water
¾ cup oil
1 cup sesame seed, stars,
   or other small pasta
salt and pepper to taste

Wash the tomatoes. Cut them into large pieces and add to the water with the celery, carrot, onion, and garlic. Boil for 30 minutes. Pass through a strainer or purée in a blender, return the purée to the pot, add the oil, and cook for 5 minutes longer. Stir in the pasta. Bring the soup to a boil, then cover it. Lower the heat, simmer for 20 minutes. Add salt and pepper to taste. Remove from the heat and let stand for 10 minutes. Serves 6.

ONION SOUP ✠ KREMITHOSOUPA

½ cup butter or vegetable oil
1½ cups sliced onions
10 cups broth
salt to taste

croutons (see index)
¾ cup (approximately) grated
    Parmesan cheese

Brown the butter. Add the onions, and cook to a light golden color. Add the broth and salt, and boil for about 15 minutes. (The broth will reduce to about 8 cups.) Serve hot in deep plates, with 10 to 12 croutons in each. Sprinkle with cheese. Serves 6.

TOMATO-NOODLE SOUP ✠ DOMATOSOUPA ME FITHE

¾ pound ripe tomatoes
6 cups water
1 cup fide* (fine noodles)

4 tablespoons butter
salt and pepper to taste

Pass the tomatoes through a strainer. Add to the water and boil for 20 minutes Add the noodles; stir 3 to 4 minutes. Reduce the heat. Add salt and pepper; let simmer over low heat. As soon as the soup boils, remove from the heat. Add the butter and serve. Serves 6.

PURÉE OF GREEN BEAN SOUP ✠ SOUPA FASOLAKIA FRESKA (KREMA)

6 tablespoons vegetable
    shortening
2 medium onions, minced
4 cups cleaned chopped green
    beans
½ cup chopped carrots

2 teaspoons chopped parsley
12 cups meat stock
4 tablespoons flour
salt and pepper to taste
2 tablespoons sweet butter
croutons (optional)

Put half of the vegetable shortening into a large pot, heat; sauté the onions until they are a light golden color. Add the beans, carrots, and parsley, and sauté them also. Add 10 cups of the stock. Cover the pot and cook at a low boil until the vegetables are tender (about 45 minutes). Pass the soup through a strainer or blender, then return to the pot. In another smaller pot, heat the remaining shortening, then slowly add the flour, stirring until well blended. Add the remaining hot broth and continue to stir until the sauce thickens, then season with the salt and pepper. Remove the sauce from the heat and swirl in the butter. Return the bean purée to the heat, bring to a quick boil, then stir in the sauce. Mix well and serve hot, with croutons (see index) if desired. Serves 6 to 8.

NOTE: If the soup is too thick, thin it by adding more hot broth.

GREEK EASTER SOUP ✠ MAYERITSA

entrails (liver, heart, lungs, intestines) of a very young spring
lamb
4 tablespoons butter
1 medium onion, chopped
2 tablespoons chopped scallion

2 tablespoons chopped dill
salt and pepper to taste
meat broth
½ cup raw rice
2–3 eggs
2 lemons, juice only

Wash the entrails in plenty of water. Scald them in boiling water for about 2 to 3 minutes. Cool, then cut into small pieces. Melt the butter in a pot. Sauté the onion until a very light golden color, then add the scallion and the cut-up meats, turning the latter 5 or 6 times. Add the dill, salt and pepper, and enough broth to cover. Bring the whole to a boil and cook, covered, until the meat is tender (1½ to 3 hours). About 20 minutes before it is done, add the rice, and more broth if necessary. When the rice is tender, remove the pot from the heat.

Beat the eggs as in Avgolemono Soup; add the lemon juice, beating it in well. Slowly add some of the hot liquid from the pot, stirring constantly. After the egg-lemon mixture is well blended, pour it into the soup; stir. Serve hot. Serves 4.

NOTE: The broth is usually made from the lamb's head, breast, or shoulder, but you can use any meat stock.

CREAM OF RICE SOUP ✠ SOUPA KREMA RIZI

10 cups meat stock
1⅓ cups raw rice
3 egg yolks
salt and white pepper to taste

1 cup milk, scalded
3 tablespoons sweet butter
croutons (optional)

Bring the stock to a boil. Add the rice; stir for a few minutes to separate the grains. Half cover the pot and cook until the rice is very soft (about 30 minutes). Put the soup and rice through a strainer or blender, then pour into a clean pot. Bring to a boil and cook for 3 minutes, stirring constantly. Beat the egg yolks with the salt and pepper, and to them add the hot milk very slowly, beating constantly. Pour this mixture into the soup and mix in well. Stir in the butter. Serve hot, with or without croutons (see index). Serves 6 to 8.

NOODLE SOUP ✠ SOUPA FITHES

For 4 cups of broth, use ¾ cup uncooked noodles (fidelo* or other very fine egg noodles). Cook until the noodles are tender (about 10 minutes). Serve with lemon. Serves 4.

CREAM OF POTATO SOUP ✠ PATATOSOUPA

1 pound potatoes
1 cup sliced onions
6 cups water
2 cups milk, scalded

salt and pepper to taste
3 tablespoons sweet butter
croutons (optional)

Peel and wash the potatoes and cut them into small pieces. Boil them in the water with the onions until they are very soft (about 30 minutes). Pass the mixture through a strainer, or purée in a blender, then return it to the pot. Stir in the milk, salt, and pepper, and mix well. Cook for 20 to 30 minutes, until the soup is thick (it should have the consistency of a light cream sauce), then remove it from the heat. Stir in the butter, and serve plain or with croutons (see index). Serves 6.

AVGOLEMONO SOUP ✠ AVGOLEMONO SOUPA

6–8 cups any meat stock
2–3 whole eggs (or yolks only)
1–2 lemons, juice only

1 tablespoon cornstarch or flour
(optional)

Heat the stock. Beat the eggs well. (Egg whites bind faster than the yolks, and they may be eliminated. However, we have always used whole eggs; when well beaten, they are no trouble. Or you may, if you prefer, beat the yolks and whites separately, then mix them together and proceed as follows.) Slowly add the lemon juice to the eggs, beating constantly (about 3 to 5 minutes). To this mixture, slowly add about 1 cup hot stock, mixing constantly, then pour into the pot of soup. Continue to stir the soup or gently shake the pot until the soup thickens slightly (about 3 minutes longer). Serve hot. Serves 6 to 8.

NOTE: If you prefer a thicker soup, slowly add the cornstarch or flour to the eggs while you are beating them. The addition of the thickener is not recommended for any soup made with pasta or rice.

TRAHANA* SOUP ✠ SOUPA TRAHANAS

12 cups water
coarse salt

3 cups trahana
3–4 tablespoons butter

Put the water and a little salt into a large pot and bring to a boil. Slowly add the trahana, stirring constantly until the water boils again. Lower the heat and cook until the trahana are soft and the soup is thick (about 45 minutes). Remove from the heat. Stir in the butter, and serve hot. Serves 6 to 8.

FISH SOUP WITH TOMATOES ✠ PSAROSOUPA ME DOMATA

3 pounds whole fish (bass, cod, blackfish, or any other fatty fish)
3 quarts water
salt and pepper to taste
2–3 carrots
2–3 medium onions

2–3 stalks celery
1½ pounds ripe tomatoes
¾ cup oil
6 tablespoons (approximately) raw rice (more if desired)
croutons (optional)

Clean the fish, wash it, season lightly with salt and pepper; set aside to drain. Put the carrots, onions, and celery into a large pot; add the water; bring to a boil. Add the whole tomatoes, pierced in several places with a fork; cook for 45 minutes. Add the fish and oil. When the fish has cooked (20 to 30 minutes), remove it to a platter, handling it carefully to avoid breaking. Put the soup through a strainer, then return it to the heat. Add the rice, stirring it as it begins to cook. Remove the pot from the heat when the rice is tender (after 20 or 30 minutes). Serve hot. Serves 6 to 8.

NOTE: The fish can be served as a side dish, or used in salads, or put back into the soup. Or the rice may be eliminated altogether and the soup served with croutons (see index).

BORSCHT ✠ BORS SOUPA

3 pounds soup beef
2½ quarts water
⅓ cup butter
1½ cups finely sliced onions
½ cup vinegar
1 tablespoon tomato paste diluted with 1 cup water

½ cup chopped carrots
1 cup diced potatoes
1 tablespoon chopped parsley
2 cups shredded cabbage
coarse salt
salt and pepper to taste
1 cup cooked cubed beets

Wash the meat. Simmer in enough water to cover. Add a little coarse salt and cook about 1½ hours or until tender. Remove from the heat. Remove the meat from the bones and cut the meat into walnut-size pieces. Meanwhile, keep the broth hot. Put the butter in a deep pot, and sauté the onions in it until they are a light golden color. Add the vinegar and the tomato paste to the onions, and bring to a boil. Add all the vegetables except the beets, and cook for 10 minutes. Then add the broth and the meat chunks, and salt and pepper to taste, and simmer, covered, over low heat until the vegetables are half tender (about 15 minutes). Add the beets; cook 15 minutes longer. Serve hot. Serves 6 to 8.

CONSOMMÉ 1   ✠   KONSOME 1

1½ pounds lean beef
1½ pounds neck or shoulder
   of beef
¾ pound beef bones (or chicken
   parts, including wings, neck,
   and feet)
3 quarts water
½ tablespoon coarse salt

2 medium onions
3 tablespoons chopped celery
   root
1 bunch parsley, chopped
1 tablespoon chopped leek
5–6 peppercorns
½ cup Mavrodaphne* wine

Cut the meat into small pieces, wash them, and place in a large pot with the water. (If you are using chicken feet, be sure to scald them and remove the skin before using.) Wash and crack the bones, and add to the pot; add the salt. Bring the water to a boil, skimming off the froth as it rises. Add all the other ingredients except the wine. Cover the pot. Cook over low heat for 3 hours or more, until the meat is very soft and mushy. Remove the soup from the heat, put the whole through a coarse strainer, then pass the broth through a fine cheesecloth. Cool. Skim off all the fat. Serve cold in a cup, or reheat and serve hot. Add the wine just before serving. Serves 8 to 10.

NOTE: For a deeper-colored soup, grate one of the onions, with its skin on, before adding it to the soup.

CONSOMMÉ WITH CROUTONS 2   ✠   KONSOME ME KROUTON 2

Prepare Consommé as above. For the croutons, use day-old bread. Trim away the crusts and cut the bread into cubes. Heat the butter in a pan until it smokes, and toss the cubes of bread (a few at a time) in it; fry until a light golden color. Drain on absorbent paper. Use as needed.

CONSOMMÉ WITH POACHED EGGS 3   ✠   KONSOME ME AVGA POSE 3

Prepare Consommé as above. Serve over a poached egg in a deep dish. Garnish with parsley.

CONSOMMÉ WITH PEAS 4   ✠   KONSOME ME BIZELIA 4

Prepare the consommé as above. Serve in a deep dish containing a tablespoon of cooked peas. Sprinkle with chopped parsley.

CONSOMMÉ WITH CHICKEN 5   ✠   KONSOME ME PSAXHNO KOTTAS 5

Prepare the consommé as above. Serve over 1 tablespoonful of chopped chicken breast in a deep dish.

TRIPE SOUP   ✠   SOUPA PATSAS

2 pounds honeycomb tripe	2 lemons, juice only
4–8 lamb's feet	pepper to taste
4–6 cloves garlic (optional)	vinegar (optional)
coarse salt	oil (optional)
2–3 eggs	

Clean, scrape, and wash the tripe and feet. Scald in boiling water; cool. Cut the tripe into small pieces, place in a large pot with the feet, cover with plenty of water; bring to a boil, skimming off the froth as it rises. Lower the heat. Add the garlic, and cook at a slow boil for 1 to 2 hours, adding a little coarse salt just before the meat is tender. Remove the pot from the heat; strain the broth and reserve. Remove and discard the bones from the feet; cut the meat into 3 or 4 pieces; return to the broth.

Prepare the avgolemono as follows: Beat the eggs very well. Slowly add the lemon juice to them, beating all the while. Add a little hot broth from the pot, stirring constantly, then pour the mixture back into the soup. Add pepper just before serving. Serves 6 to 8.

NOTE: This soup, very light in color, can be served not only hot but cold. For the latter, let it jell, then cut into squares or diamonds for serving. When it is served hot, some people prefer it mixed with oil and vinegar, instead of avgolemono.

EGGS AND
EGG SPECIALTIES

EASTER EGGS   ✠   KOKINA AVGA

One of the nicest Greek customs is the use of red eggs for the Easter celebration. It is unthinkable to set an Easter table without these eggs, for they add to the celebration and happy atmosphere.

To prepare:

Carefully wash and dry each egg. Set a large pot of water to boil. Add a red dye or food coloring and ¾ cup of vinegar to the water, and boil for a few minutes. Slowly lower the eggs into the pot, and when the water comes to a boil, lower the heat. Let the eggs simmer for 15 minutes, then remove them carefully from the pot. If you plan to cook more eggs, add an additional 2 tablespoons vinegar to the water. Wipe cooked eggs with an oil-soaked cotton ball, then wipe each egg with a clean dry cloth. Place on a platter. Serve cold.

OMELET WITH VEGETABLES   ✠   OMELETA ME LAHANIKA
AND FETA CHEESE   KE FETA

½ cup cooked peas, fresh or
   canned
½ cup cooked diced carrots
5 tablespoons butter
5 eggs

salt and pepper to taste
3 tablespoons milk or water
½ cup feta* cheese, sliced or
   crumbled

If you are using canned peas and carrots, drain them and rinse with fresh water. Put 2 tablespoons of the butter in a pan, add the vegetables; sauté for 2 or 3 minutes. Add salt and pepper. Put the remaining butter into another frying pan, and heat. Beat the eggs with the milk (or water); pour into the pan and let cook. As soon as the omelet is set, top with the vegetables and cheese. Fold in half, and serve immediately. Serves 3 to 4.

SUNNY-SIDE-UP EGGS WITH TOMATOES 1

✠

AVGA MATIA ME
SALTSA DOMATAS

1½ pounds ripe tomatoes
5 tablespoons butter
6 eggs

salt and pepper to taste
1 tablespoon chopped parsley

Drop the tomatoes into boiling water for 2 minutes, then carefully peel off the skins. Remove the seeds and the soft insides and cut into small pieces. Place the pieces in a frying pan with a little salt. Cook over low heat, meanwhile mashing into a pulp. Add the butter, and while it browns, break the eggs into a shallow dish. Lightly salt and pepper them, and gently ease them into the pan. To set the eggs, baste them with some of the hot butter from the pan. When cooked to your taste, serve with the sauce in which they were cooked, and garnish with parsley. Serve immediately with fried potatoes. Serves 3.

SUNNY-SIDE-UP EGGS WITH TOMATOES 2

✠

AVGA MATIA ME
SALTSA DOMATAS

Cook as above. Serve the eggs on a slice of toast, top with the sauce. Garnish with parsley.

EGGS AU GRATIN

✠

AVGA O GRATEN

8–10 hard-cooked eggs
salt and pepper to taste
1 recipe Béchamel Sauce (see index)

1 cup grated kefalotiri* cheese
3–4 tablespoons toasted bread crumbs
3–4 tablespoons butter, melted

Cut each egg into 8 pieces. Lightly salt and pepper them. Prepare the béchamel. Mix together half of the sauce, the eggs, and ¾ cup of the cheese. Butter a small pan. Spread a thin layer of béchamel over the bottom and sprinkle this with a little cheese. Add the egg mixture and spread evenly. Add the remaining sauce and spread this carefully over the eggs. Sprinkle with the remaining cheese and then the bread crumbs. Drizzle melted butter over the top. Bake in a preheated 350° oven 15 to 20 minutes, or until golden brown. Let stand 10 minutes before serving. Serves 6.

POULTRY LIVER OMELET 1   ✜   OMELETA ME SIKOTAKIA POULION

5 tablespoons butter or
  shortening
1 cup chopped poultry livers

salt and pepper to taste
6 eggs
3 tablespoons milk or water

Melt the butter in a frying pan. Fry the livers, for 4 to 7 minutes, covering them so they do not dry out. Meantime, beat the eggs with the milk (or water), and season with salt and pepper; pour over the livers. Stir at first, then lower the heat and cook until the eggs are set. Serve immediately. Serves 3 to 4.

POULTRY LIVER OMELET 2   ✜   OMELETA ME SIKOTAKIA POULION

Prepare the livers as above. Remove from heat to a dish and keep hot. Beat the eggs and cook the omelet as usual, then place the livers in the center, and fold over. Serve immediately. Serves 3 to 4.

SAUSAGE OMELET 1   ✜   OMELETA ME LOUKANIKA

5 sausages (any kind)
4 tablespoons butter
  (approximately)

5 eggs
6 tablespoons milk or water
salt and pepper to taste

Dip the sausages into hot water and dry them; cut into ½-inch-thick slices; fry until they are cooked but not dry and hard, using butter as needed. Break the eggs into a bowl, add salt and pepper, and milk (or water); mix well. Remove the frying pan from the heat and add the well-beaten eggs; stir gently. Return the pan to low heat, and cook until the eggs are set. Turn out onto a round platter. Serve immediately. Serves 2 to 3.

NOTE: The kind of sausage used will determine how much water you will need. If pork sausage is used, pour off the fat as it accumulates and use less butter for frying the eggs. Frankfurters may take more butter.

SAUSAGE OMELET 2   ✜   OMELETA ME LOUKANIKA

Prepare the sausages as above. Remove from heat to a dish and keep hot. Beat the eggs and cook the omelet as usual. Place the sausages on the omelet and fold over. Serve immediately. Serves 2 to 3.

CHEESE OMELET ✠ OMELETA ME TYRI

5 eggs
½ teaspoon salt
½ teaspoon pepper
3 tablespoons milk or water

½ cup grated Parmesan cheese
   (Gravieri or kefalotiri*)
5 tablespoons butter

Beat the eggs with the salt and pepper and milk (or water). Add the cheese and mix well. Brown the butter in a frying pan. Remove from the heat. Add the eggs. Stir gently, then tilt the pan to spread the mixture evenly. Cook on low heat until the eggs are set. Fold the omelet in half, and slide onto a plate. Serve immediately. Serves 2.

CHEESE-POTATO OMELET ✠ OMELETA ME PATATES

1 pound potatoes
½ cup butter
5 eggs
3 tablespoons milk or water

dash of pepper
½ cup grated Parmesan cheese
1 tablespoon chopped parsley

Pare the potatoes and cut into thin, even slices; wash and drain. Melt half the butter in a large frying pan and spread the potato slices in an even layer in it. Fry gently but do not let brown. Add the remaining butter. Beat the eggs with the milk (or water), add the pepper and cheese; mix well. Pour over the potatoes. Lower the heat and cook slowly, stirring very little, until the eggs are set. Remove from the heat. Turn a platter upside down on the pan and turn the pan over quickly so the whole omelet drops onto the platter. Garnish with parsley. Serve immediately. Serves 2 to 3.

CHEESE-SQUASH OMELET ✠ OMELETA ME KOLOKITHAKIA

Prepare like Cheese-Potato Omelet (above), but substitute squash for the potatoes.

TOMATO OMELET ✠ OMELETA ME DOMATA

1½ pounds ripe tomatoes
salt and pepper to taste

4 tablespoons butter
6 eggs

Wash and peel the tomatoes, scoop out the seeds and discard. Cut into small pieces. Place in a frying pan with a little salt and pepper and cook until reduced to a pulp. Add the butter, and while this is browning, beat the eggs with salt and pepper. Add to the pan. Lower the heat and stir gently. Allow to cook until set to your taste. Remove from the heat. Gather the tomatoes from the edges of the pan, spread on the top of the omelet; fold in half. Serve immediately with fried potatoes. Serves 3.

HAM OMELET ✠ OMELETA ME ZAMPON

8 eggs
4 tablespoons milk or water
salt and pepper to taste

6 tablespoons butter
6 slices ham

Beat the eggs with the milk (or water) and the salt and pepper. Heat 3 tablespoons butter in a frying pan and pour in half the mixture. When the omelet has set, remove from the heat. Place 3 slices of ham on the omelet and fold it in half. Keep hot on a platter. Prepare a second omelet like the first, using the balance of the mixture and ham. Garnish with cooked carrots and spinach. Serves 4 to 6.

HAM SOUFFLÉ ✠ SOUFLE ZAMPON

5 tablespoons butter
8 tablespoons flour
1½ cups milk, scalded

1 cup chopped ham
1 teaspoon salt
6 eggs, separated

Melt the butter in a small saucepan. Add the flour and stir to make a smooth paste. Slowly add the scalded milk, stirring constantly until the sauce thickens. Remove from the heat. Cool. Add the ham and the salt; mix well. Beat the egg yolks until very thick. Beat the whites until stiff. Fold the yolks, then the whites, into the sauce, and pour immediately into a buttered form. Bake in a preheated 350° oven about 30 minutes. Serves 6.

CHEESE SOUFFLÉ ✠ SOUFLE TYRI

4 tablespoons butter
6 tablespoons flour
1 cup milk, scalded

1 teaspoon salt
1 cup grated kefalotiri* cheese
6 eggs, separated

Melt the butter in a saucepan. Add the flour, and stir to a smooth paste. Slowly add the milk, stirring constantly to make a thick sauce. Mix in the salt. Remove the pot from the heat; add the cheese. Mix well. Beat the yolks until very thick; add to the mixture. Cool. Beat the whites until stiff, and fold in gently into the cheese mixture. Pour immediately into a buttered mold and bake in a preheated 350° over for 20 minutes. Leave in the oven until ready to serve. (This will stay puffed for 3 to 4 minutes.) Serves 5 to 6.

FISH SOUFFLÉ ✠ SOUFLE PSARI

5 tablespoons butter
7 tablespoons flour
1⅓ cups milk, scalded

1 teaspoon salt
1 cup chopped cooked fish
7 eggs, separated

Melt the butter in a small pot; add the flour. Stir to blend well. Slowly add the milk, and stir until you have a thick, creamy sauce. Remove from the heat. Add the salt and fish and blend in well. Beat the egg yolks until very thick; add to the fish mixture. Beat the egg whites until stiff, then fold gently into the sauce. Pour into a buttered mold and bake immediately in a preheated 350° oven for about 30 minutes. Serve immediately. Serves 8.

SHRIMP SOUFFLÉ ✠ SOUFLE GARIDES

Make like Fish Soufflé, above, but use 1 cup chopped boiled shrimp in place of the fish.

LOBSTER SOUFFLÉ ✠ SOUFLE ASTAKO

Make like Fish Soufflé, above, but substitute 1 cup chopped boiled (or canned) lobster for the fish.

SPINACH SOUFFLÉ ✠ SOUFLE SPANAKI

1 cup raw spinach, chopped	1 cup milk, scalded
salt and pepper	7 eggs, separated
5 tablespoons butter	4–5 scallions, white parts only,
7 tablespoons flour	chopped

Clean and wash the spinach. Select only the tender leaves and chop these to measure 1 cup. Season lightly with salt and pepper, and place in a strainer. Let drain for 1 hour. In a small pot, melt the butter. Add the flour, stirring constantly to a smooth paste. Add the hot milk and stir to make a thick sauce. Add a little salt and pepper. Remove from heat. Add the spinach and the scallions to the sauce. Beat the egg yolks until very thick. Beat the whites until stiff. Fold the yolks into the sauce, then fold in the whites. Pour into a buttered mold. Bake immediately in a preheated 350° oven for about 30 minutes. Serve immediately. Serves 6 to 8.

SQUASH SOUFFLÉ ✠ KOLOKITHAKIA SOUFLE

1½ pounds squash	1 teaspoon baking powder
½ cup butter	4 eggs, separated
½ cup milk, scalded	¼–½ pound grated Parmesan
½ cup toasted bread crumbs	salt and pepper to taste

Wash and peel the squash. Bring to a boil in a pot of water; cook about 10 minutes or until tender. Chop finely or mash. Brown the butter in a pot. Add the squash and mix well; mix in the hot milk. Mix together the bread crumbs and baking powder; add to the squash. Beat the egg yolks and add them with the cheese to the squash. Season with salt and pepper. Beat the whites until stiff, and fold gently into the mixture. Pour immediately into a buttered mold. Bake in a preheated 350° oven for 30 minutes. Serve immediately. Serves 6 to 8.

POTATO SOUFFLÉ   ✠   PATATES SOUFLE

3 pounds potatoes   4 eggs, separated
3 tablespoons butter   1 cup grated kefalotiri* cheese
1 cup warm milk   salt and pepper to taste

Boil the potatoes in their skins until tender. While they are still hot, remove skins, and purée potatoes by passing through a sieve or food mill. Melt the butter in a pot. Add the puréed potatoes and mix well. Add the milk and continue to stir. Beat the egg yolks until thick and add to the potatoes. Remove from the heat immediately. Add the cheese. Beat the whites until stiff. Cool the potatoes slightly, then fold the whites into them. Pour into a buttered mold and bake immediately in a preheated 350° oven for 20 to 25 minutes. Serves 6 to 8.

NOTE: This can be made in individual ramekins.

VANILLA SOUFFLÉ   ✠   SOUFLE VANILIAS

4 tablespoons butter   1½ cups milk
6 tablespoons flour   5 eggs, separated
6 tablespoons sugar   2 teaspoons vanilla

Melt the butter. Slowly add the flour, and blend it in with a wooden spoon. Put the sugar into a pot with the milk and heat to scalding but do not boil. Remove from the heat and pour into the flour; stir quickly to make a thick cream (this may be returned to the heat for a few minutes if necessary). Partially cool. Beat the egg yolks with the vanilla until very thick. Beat the egg whites until stiff but not dry. Add the yolks to the cream mixture; stir well. Fold in the beaten whites. Pour into a buttered glass baking dish or into 6 or 8 individual buttered ramekins.

Bake immediately in a preheated 300° oven for about 20 minutes. Serve hot, sprinkled with powdered sugar. Serves 6 to 8.

ORANGE OR TANGERINE SOUFFLÉ   ✠   SOUFLE PORTOCALIOU E
                                                    MANDARINOU

Prepare like Vanilla Soufflé, above, but substitute 1 tablespoon grated orange or tangerine peel for the vanilla.

RICE

BOILED RICE   ✠   PILAFIA

There are two methods of cooking rice:

1. Pour the rice into a large pot of boiling water, stir with a fork to separate the grains; cover. Cook, uncovered, over high heat until the rice is done (12 to 20 minutes). Pour in a cup of cold water to stop the cooking; drain, rinse with cold water.

2. Measure the rice and liquids to be used—allow 1 cup rice for each 2½ cups liquid—and put the rice and cold liquid into the pot together. Cook, covered, until the rice is tender (12 to 20 minutes). Remove from the heat. Uncover the pot, put a clean towel over it, and put the lid back over the towel. Let stand for 10 minutes, or until all the liquid has been absorbed.

NOTE: 1 cup uncooked rice will make 3 cups cooked rice.

PILAF WITH TOMATO SAUCE   ✠   PILAFI ME SALTSA DOMATA

1–2 onions, chopped	1 tablespoon chopped celery
¾ cup butter	1 tablespoon chopped parsley
2 cloves garlic, chopped	3 cups raw rice
1½ pounds ripe tomatoes, peeled and strained	salt and pepper to taste

Sauté the onions in half the butter until a light-golden color. Add the garlic, and cook until soft but not brown. Add the tomatoes, celery, parsley, and salt and pepper. Simmer for half an hour. Pass the sauce through a strainer, or purée in a blender, then return it to the pot. Cook until thick. Prepare the rice as directed in Boiled Rice (see index). Brown the remaining butter and pour it over the rice, mixing it in. Pack the rice into a mold, then turn it out onto a platter. Serve hot, with the sauce poured over the rice. Serves 8 to 10.

PILAF WITH WHITE SAUCE AVGOLEMONO ✠ PILAFI ME ASPRI SALTSA AVGOLEMONO

9 cups broth or water
4 cups raw rice
¼ cup butter
¼ cup flour
1 cup hot broth
1 cup milk

3 egg yolks
1 lemon, juice only
¾ cup butter
½ pound grated Parmesan
    cheese

Put the broth (or water) into a large pot and bring it to a boil. Add the rice, and stir with a fork. Cover, and cook until the grains are separate and soft (about 15 minutes). In another pot, melt the butter. Add the flour and stir in well. Slowly add the hot broth and milk, and cook until the sauce thickens, stirring constantly to prevent lumping or burning. Remove from the heat. Beat the egg yolks with the lemon juice and add to the sauce, slowly, stirring constantly. Return the sauce to the heat, continuing to stir until thickened. Remove from the heat, add the butter and half the cheese. Pack the rice into a mold. Turn out on a platter. Pour the sauce over the rice. Sprinkle the remaining cheese over it. Serve hot. Serves 10 to 15.

PILAF WITH GLAZED TOMATOES ✠ PILAFI ME DOMATES GLACE

4 cups raw rice
9 cups broth or water
parsley

THE GLAZED TOMATOES
cherry tomatoes
¼ pound (approximately) butter
    for each ½ pound of tomatoes
½ cup sugar for each ½ pound
    of tomatoes

Prepare the rice as in Pilaf with White Sauce Avgolemono (see index). Pack into a tube pan and keep hot.

Meanwhile, remove the stems from the tomatoes and wash and drain them well. Butter a baking dish and put the tomatoes into it. Melt the butter and pour it over the tomatoes; sprinkle with the sugar. Bake in a preheated 350° oven for 15 to 25 minutes.

Turn the rice out of the mold onto a platter. Fill the center with the baked tomatoes and pour the sauce from the tomatoes over the rice. Garnish with parsley and serve.

PILAF TAS KEBAB   ✠   PILAFI TAS KEBAB

2 pounds leg of lamb or veal   salt and pepper to taste
1¼ cups butter   1 cup water
3 medium onions, chopped   3 cups raw rice
½ cup white wine
1½ pounds ripe tomatoes,
     peeled and strained or
     1 tablespoon tomato paste
     diluted with 1 cup water

Cut the meat into 2-inch cubes. Wash and wipe dry. Brown the meat in two-thirds of the butter. Add the onions and brown these too. Add the wine, tomatoes (or tomato paste), salt, and pepper. Cook for about 5 minutes. Add the water. Cook until the meat is tender and about 1 cup sauce remains.

Cook the rice as directed in Boiled Rice (see index). Melt the remaining butter and add it to the rice. Place the meat and the sauce in the bottom of a tube pan or solid mold. Add the rice and pack lightly. Turn out onto a platter so the meat is on top; the sauce will run down the sides of the rice. Serves 6 to 10.

PILAF WITH SHRIMP   ✠   PILAFI ME GARIDES

1½ pounds shrimp   1½ pounds ripe tomatoes,
salt to taste   peeled and strained, or
1 medium onion   1 tablespoon tomato paste
2–3 stalks celery   diluted in 1 cup water
1½ cups oil   2½ cups raw rice
1 medium onion, chopped

Wash the shrimp and put into a large pot. Add enough water to cover. Add salt and the whole onion and celery, and bring to a boil. Cook for about 5 minutes. Remove the shrimp with a slotted spoon and reserve the liquid. Shell and devein the shrimp. Heat the oil in a large pot. Sauté the chopped onions until light golden. Add the shrimp, turning them 2 or 3 times. Add the tomatoes (or tomato paste). Cook for about 5 minutes, then remove the shrimp. Set aside and keep warm.

Measure the liquid in which the shrimp were boiled, allowing 2½ cups for each cup of rice. Add the liquid to the pot with the tomato sauce. Bring to the boil and add the rice. Stir for the first few minutes to prevent sticking. Cook about 12 to 15 minutes until the rice is tender but has not absorbed all of the liquid. Add two-thirds of the shrimp. Mix well. Remove the pot from the heat. Cover with a clean towel and cover the towel with the lid. Let stand 5 to 10 minutes, until all the liquid is absorbed. Mold the rice into a pyramid shape. Garnish with the remaining shrimp. Serves 6 to 10.

PILAF WITH LOBSTER   ✠   PILAFI ME ASTAKOS

1 lobster (about 2–3 pounds)   1½ cups white wine
1¼ pounds ripe tomatoes,   2 tablespoons chopped parsley
   peeled and strained   salt and pepper to taste
1 cup oil   2 cups raw rice
1 medium onion, grated   4 tablespoons butter
4 cloves garlic, grated

Boil the lobster. Remove the meat from the shell and cut into small pieces. Reserve 1 cup of the liquid. Put the tomatoes into a pot. Add the oil, onion, and garlic. Cook 2 to 3 minutes. Add the wine, parsley, salt, pepper, and the cup of liquid reserved from the lobster. Simmer, covered, until the sauce thickens (20 to 30 minutes). Add the lobster meat and simmer 2 to 3 minutes. Cook the rice (see index for method, or as directed on the package), then add the butter and stir it through. Pour the lobster with the sauce into a mold. Add the rice and pack lightly. Turn out onto a platter. Serve hot. Serves 6.

ATZEM PILAF   ✠   ATZEM PILAFI

3 pounds lamb, cut into 1½-   salt and pepper to taste
   inch cubes   8 cups water
½ pound butter   4 cups raw rice
1 onion, chopped
1½ pounds ripe tomatoes,
   peeled and strained, or
   1 tablespoon tomato paste
   diluted with 1 cup water

Wash and dry the meat. Brown two-thirds of the butter in a large pot. Add the meat and brown it on all sides. Add the onions and continue to cook until they become a light golden color. Add the tomatoes or diluted tomato paste, and the salt, pepper, and water. Cover the pot and simmer until the meat is tender (about 1 hour). Put the meat into a casserole and keep it warm. Strain the sauce; measure it. Add water if necessary to make 8 to 9 cups. Pour into a large pot and bring to the boil. Add the rice. Stir at the start to prevent sticking. Cover and simmer until most of the liquid is absorbed (20 to 30 minutes). Remove from the heat. Add the meat and mix well. Brown the remaining butter and pour it over the rice. Cover the pot with a clean towel, then cover the towel with the pot lid. Let stand for 5 minutes. Serve hot. Serves 6 to 10.

PILAF WITH MUSSELS   ✠   PILAFI ME MITHIA

3 pounds mussels
1¼ cups oil
1 onion, chopped
½ cup white wine
1 tablespoon tomato paste
   diluted with 1 cup water

salt and pepper to taste
2–3 cups rice
water as needed

Scrub the mussels; wash well. Put into a large pot with about 1 inch of water, cover, and cook until the shells open (5 to 10 minutes). Remove the mussels from the shells and set aside.

Heat the oil in a large pot. Sauté the onion in it until golden. Add the mussels and sauté them 3 minutes. Remove from the heat, add the wine. Keep hot!

Put the diluted tomato paste, salt, and pepper into a large pot. Add water (2 cups for each cup of rice used) to the pot and bring to a boil. Add the rice, stir a few minutes. Cover the pot. Simmer until the rice is tender but has not absorbed all the liquid (about 15 minutes). Remove from the heat, add the un-shelled mussels, mix well. Cover with a towel, then with the pot lid. Let stand 5 minutes. Then serve. Or: Remove the rice from the heat, cover with a towel and lid; let stand for 5 minutes. Serve with mussels in their shells poured over the top. These are shelled as they are eaten. Serves 6 to 10.

RICE AU GRATIN   ✠   RIZI O GRATEN

3½ cups chicken or beef broth
4 tablespoons butter
1½ cups raw rice
salt and pepper to taste
1½ cups grated kefalotiri*
   cheese

3–4 eggs
1 cup chopped ham
2–3 tablespoons toasted bread
   crumbs

Boil the broth with 2 tablespoons of the butter. Add the rice, stirring it so it doesn't stick. Add salt and pepper. Cover the pot and simmer until the liquid is absorbed (about 15 minutes). Add two-thirds of the cheese, mix well, then remove from the heat. Half cool. Beat the eggs lightly and add to the rice. Add the ham and mix in well with a fork. Butter a baking pan. Put the rice in and spread it evenly. Sprinkle with the remaining cheese and then the bread crumbs. Melt the remaining butter and drizzle it over the top of the rice. Bake in a preheated 350° oven about 15 minutes, or until golden brown. Serves 4 to 6.

SPINACH AND RICE ✠ SPANAKORIZO

4½ pounds spinach
1¼ cups oil
1 medium onion, chopped
1 tablespoon tomato paste
   diluted with 2 cups water

salt and pepper
1 cup rice
water as needed
lemon wedges (optional)

Wash and clean the spinach thoroughly. Cut each leaf in half or thirds. Heat the oil and fry the onion lightly. Toss in the spinach; stir several times until it wilts. Add the tomato paste, salt, and pepper. Cover, and cook over medium heat about 45 minutes. (Add water if needed, but remember that spinach throws off water while cooking.) Bring to a boil. Add the rice, stirring at first, cover, and cook until the rice is almost tender (about 15 minutes). Remove from the heat before all liquid is absorbed. Remove the lid, cover the pot with a clean towel, and replace the lid. Let stand about 10 minutes. Mix lightly and serve. Serves 6.

NOTE: You may eliminate the tomato paste and serve with lemon wedges.

MAKARONIA, SPAGETO, PASTITSIOS

MACARONI AND SPAGHETTI ✠ MAKARONIA KE SPAGETO
(BASIC RECIPE)

packaged macaroni or spaghetti

¼–½ pound butter for each pound

Cook the macaroni (or spaghetti) according to the directions on the package. Place the butter in a medium-size pot (it will rise and spill over if the pot is too small); heat until it is brown and smoking. Pour over the macaroni. Serve with grated cheese and Tomato Sauce (see index).

MACARONI WITH CHOPPED MEAT ✠ MAKARONIA ME KIMA

2 pounds macaroni
2 pounds chopped meat
3 tablespoons butter
1 medium onion, chopped
1½ pounds ripe tomatoes,
   peeled and strained, or 1½
   tablespoons tomato paste
   diluted with 2 cups water

salt and pepper to taste
2 pieces of stick cinnamon
2–3 cloves
1 tablespoon chopped parsley
grated cheese

Cook the macaroni as directed on the package. In the meantime, put the meat, butter, and onion in a pot to brown. Stir to break up the chopped meat. Add the tomatoes or diluted tomato paste, salt, pepper, cinnamon, cloves, and parsley. Cook for 1 hour or until the liquids are absorbed and a thick sauce remains. Remove cinnamon and cloves.

Put the macaroni on a platter, sprinkle with cheese; pour the sauce over the top and sprinkle with more cheese. Serve hot. Serves 6.

MACARONI AND CHOPPED MEAT IN PASTRY ✝ MAKARONIA SE FORMA ME KIMA

1 pound chopped meat
1 onion, chopped
6 tablespoons butter
½ pound ripe tomatoes, peeled
   and strained, or 1 tablespoon
   tomato paste diluted with 1
   cup water
salt and pepper to taste
½ pound thick macaroni
2 egg whites
1 cup grated Parmesan cheese
4 phyllo sheets (see index: About
   Phyllo)
melted butter

THE BÉCHAMEL SAUCE
8 tablespoons butter
10 tablespoons flour
4 cups hot milk
2 egg yolks, lightly beaten
salt and pepper to taste

Brown the meat and onion with 3 tablespoons of the butter, breaking up the meat with a wooden spoon during the process. Add the tomatoes (or paste) and seasoning, and cook over low heat for about 20 minutes, or until the liquid is absorbed. Meanwhile, cook the macaroni as directed on the package; drain. Brown the remaining butter in another pan and pour it over the macaroni. Beat the egg whites lightly and add.

To prepare the béchamel, melt the butter and add the flour slowly to it, blending in well. Add the hot milk, stirring it in rapidly with a clean wooden spoon until the sauce thickens. Remove the sauce from the heat; blend in the egg yolks. Pour over the macaroni. Sprinkle with cheese.

Butter a round cake pan and spread 2 phyllo sheets into it (let the sheets extend over the pan; do not trim them). Brush with the melted butter. Spread half the macaroni on the phyllo, top with the chopped meat; add the rest of the macaroni, and fold the edges of the phyllo up over it. Use the 2 remaining phyllo sheets for the top: butter each and trim to fit the pan. Bake in a preheated oven at 375° for about 20 minutes or until brown. Cool; turn out onto a platter. Serves 4 to 6.

LENTEN MACARONI ✝ MAKARONIA ME SALTSA NISTISIMI

Cook and strain the macaroni (see basic recipe). Allow about 1 pound for 3 to 4 servings. Pour ½ to ¾ cup hot oil over the top (Greeks use oil, not butter during Lent). Serve with Tomato Sauce 2 (see index), substituting oil for the butter in that recipe.

MACARONI WITH TUNA SAUCE ✠ MAKARONIA ME SALTSA TONNOU

2 pounds macaroni	1 cup oil or ¾ cup butter
5–6 Pastés Sardines	2 cloves garlic, chopped
1¼–1½ pounds ripe tomatoes, peeled and strained, or 1½ tablespoons tomato paste diluted with 2 cups water	salt and pepper to taste
	1 bay leaf
	½ cup canned tuna
	2 tablespoons chopped parsley
	½ cup grated Parmesan cheese

Prepare the macaroni according to the directions on the package.

Wash the sardines thoroughly, first in cool water, then in vinegar. (These sardines are packed in salt.) Remove the skins and fins, if any, by rubbing gently with the finger tips. Remove the center bone. Cut sardines into small pieces (the bones are very small and many Greeks leave them in.) Put the tomatoes or diluted tomato paste into a pot with the oil or butter. Bring to a boil, and add garlic, salt, pepper, and bay leaf. Cook until the sauce thickens. Remove the bay leaf. Add the tuna, sardines, and parsley and cook 5 to 8 minutes longer. Remove from the heat, add cheese. Stir well. Pour over the macaroni and serve. Serves 6.

MACARONI AU GRATIN ✠ MAKARONIA O GRATEN

1½ pounds thick macaroni	THE BÉCHAMEL SAUCE
½ cup butter	5 tablespoons butter
3 eggs, separated	½ cup flour
½ pound kefalotiri* cheese, grated	3 cups milk
	toasted bread crumbs
	salt and pepper to taste

Parboil the macaroni for about 8 minutes. Drain. Melt the butter and pour three-fourths of it over the macaroni. Lightly beat the egg whites and mix them with the macaroni. Sprinkle with half of the cheese and mix it in.

Prepare the béchamel sauce (see index for method). Add the 3 well-beaten egg yolks and half the remaining cheese. Butter a medium-size pan and sprinkle with the bread crumbs. Spread half the macaroni in the pan, and cover with a layer of béchamel. Top with the rest of the macaroni and the remaining béchamel. Sprinkle the rest of the cheese over the top. Drizzle the balance of the melted butter over the cheese. Bake in a preheated 350° oven for 30 minutes or until golden brown. Serves 6.

BAKED SPAGHETTI   ✠   SPAGETO STO FOURNO

2 pounds spaghetti
2 pounds ripe tomatoes, peeled
  and strained
¾ cup butter

salt and pepper to taste
2–3 cups water
½ pound Parmesan cheese,
  grated

Parboil the spaghetti according to the directions on the package. Put the tomatoes into a baking pan. Melt the butter and add to the tomatoes. Add salt, pepper, and water. Place in a preheated 375° oven and bake for 15 to 20 minutes. Add the spaghetti, stir; return to the oven and bake for 10 to 15 minutes longer. Serve with the grated cheese. Serves 6.

SPAGHETTI WITH ZAMPON   ✠   SPAGETO ME ZAMPON

1 pound spaghetti
¾ cup butter
3 eggs
¾ cup undiluted evaporated
  milk

1 cup grated kefalotiri* or
  Parmesan cheese
1½ cups chopped zampon*
1 cup cooked peas
bread crumbs
pepper

Cook the spaghetti as directed on the package; drain. Brown the butter and pour -thirds of it over the spaghetti. Sprinkle with half of the cheese; mix in the ham peas. Butter a baking pan. Pour in the spaghetti and spread evenly. Beat the eggs in a deep bowl. Slowly add the milk, beating continuously. Mix in the remaining cheese. Pour this over the spaghetti. Sprinkle with toasted bread crumbs. Season with pepper to taste. Drizzle on the remaining butter. Bake in a preheated 350° oven about 30 minutes or until golden brown in color. Serves 6.

NOTE: If you are using canned peas, drain and rinse them well before adding.

SPAGHETTI WITH SWEET BUTTER   ✠   SPAGETO ME FRESKO VOUTIRO
AND PARMESAN CHEESE   KE PARMEZANA

2 pounds spaghetti
¾ cup sweet butter

½ pound grated Parmesan
  cheese

Cook the spaghetti as directed on the package. Drain. Melt the butter and pour over the spaghetti. Serve with grated Parmesan cheese. Serves 6 to 8.

SPAGHETTI AND CHICKEN LIVERS ✠ SPAGETO ME SIKOTAKIA POULION

½ pound chicken livers
4 tablespoons shortening
1 pound spaghetti
3 tablespoons sweet butter
¾ cup grated Parmesan cheese

3 eggs
¾ cup grated gravieri or
    Gruyère cheese
pepper

Wash the chicken livers and cut into small pieces. Place in a small pot or frying pan with the shortening to brown, and cook for about 3 to 4 minutes. Cook the spaghetti as directed on the package, drain. Return to the pot and mix the spaghetti with half of the butter. Butter a baking pan. Spread half of the spaghetti in it. Sprinkle half of the Parmesan cheese on top. Put the livers on the cheese, cover with the remaining spaghetti, and sprinkle with the rest of the Parmesan cheese.

Beat the eggs in a small bowl. Add the gravieri or Gruyère cheese and pepper to taste. Pour this over the spaghetti. Melt the remaining butter and drizzle over the top. Bake in a preheated 350° oven for about 20 minutes or until golden. Serves 6.

SPAGHETTI SHRIMP BAKE ✠ SPAGETO ME GARIDES STO FOURNO

2 pounds spaghetti
2 pounds shrimp
ccarse salt
¼ cup vinegar
1 cup excellent oil
¾ cup chopped onion
½ cup Retsina*
1 pound ripe tomatoes, peeled
    and strained, or 1 tablespoon
    tomato paste diluted with 2
    cups water

½ cup parsley
1 green pepper, chopped
salt and pepper to taste
6–8 cherry tomatoes
sugar
¼ cup oil (for the top)

Wash the shrimp. Fill a pot with water (just enough water to cover shrimp), add some coarse salt, and the vinegar, and bring to a boil. Add the shrimp. Cook for 15 minutes. Remove from the heat. Drain, shell, and clean the shrimp. Cut each shrimp into 2 to 3 pieces. In a wide pot, heat the oil and sauté the onions until a light golden color. Add the wine, tomatoes (or diluted tomato paste), parsley, green pepper, and salt and pepper. Cook the sauce until it begins to thicken, then add the shrimp. Cook for about 3 minutes; remove from the heat. In the meantime, cook the spaghetti as directed on the package; drain. Add to the sauce and mix well. Butter a roast pan and pour the spaghetti into it, spreading it evenly. Wash the cherry tomatoes and remove the stems. Place them on top of the spaghetti. Sprinkle with a little sugar and drizzle with a little oil over them. Bake in a preheated 300° oven for about 15 to 20 minutes. Serves 6 to 8.

MACARONI PASTITSIO WITH FETA CHEESE

MAKARONIA PASTITSIO
ME TYRI FETA

1½ pounds macaroni
1 cup melted butter or oil
5 eggs
½ cup evaporated milk

¾ pounds feta* cheese (hard),
    cut into small pieces
¾ pound phyllo* pastry
butter for brushing the phyllo

Boil the macaroni. Drain, and pour in melted butter. Beat the eggs in a large bowl, and add the milk and cheese. Pour over the macaroni and mix well. Butter a pan and in it spread 7 to 8 phyllo sheets, brushing each one with melted butter. Pour in the macaroni, spreading it evenly. Fold phyllo over the filling, and butter the top. Place 4 to 5 phyllo sheets on top, buttering each. Trim all edges that extend over the sides of the pan. Butter the top layer well. Score into 4 to 5 strips. Cook in a pre-heated 350° oven for 30 minutes, or until the pastry begins to brown; remove, from the oven, and cut through the strips. Cut the strips into diamonds, squares, or triangles. Serves 6 to 8.

MACARONI PASTITSIO WITH CHOPPED MEAT

MAKARONIA PASTITSIO
ME KIMA

1½ pounds macaroni
1 cup butter or oil
2 eggs, separated
1¾ pounds chopped meat
½ pound kefalotiri* or
    Parmesan cheese, grated
1 medium onion, chopped
½ cup white wine

1½ pounds ripe tomatoes,
    peeled and sieved, or 1
    tablespoon tomato paste,
    diluted with 1 cup water
salt and pepper to taste
1 piece of stick cinnamon
1 cup bread crumbs
1 recipe Béchamel Sauce (see
    index)

Parboil the macaroni in a generous amount of salted water for 6 minutes; drain. Brown half of the butter and pour it over the macaroni. Beat the egg whites (reserve the yolks for the béchamel), and add to the macaroni. Sprinkle with half of the cheese. Brown the remaining butter (but keep about 2 tablespoons aside to use later), with the chopped meat and onion. Add the wine, the tomatoes (or diluted tomato paste), salt, pepper, and cinnamon, and simmer until all the liquid is absorbed. Remove from the heat, remove the cinnamon, and add half of the remaining cheese and half of the bread crumbs. Mix well.

Prepare the béchamel. Butter a pan and sprinkle with bread crumbs. Spread half of the macaroni evenly in it, and cover with the chopped meat. Add the remaining macaroni. Pour the béchamel over the top. Sprinkle with the remaining cheese, then with the rest of the bread crumbs. Drizzle the remaining melted butter over the top. Bake in a preheated 350° oven for 30 minutes, until golden brown. Serves 6 to 8.

MACARONI PASTITSIO   ✠   MAKARONIA PASTITSIO
WITH PHYLLO PASTRY   ME PHYLLO

1½ pounds thick macaroni   1½ pounds ripe tomatoes,
1 cup butter   peeled and strained, or 1
2 eggs   tablespoon tomato paste
¼–½ pound kefalotiri,* grated   diluted with 1 cup water
1¾ pounds chopped meat   salt and pepper to taste
1 medium onion, chopped   1 piece of stick cinnamon
½ cup white wine   ¾ pound phyllo* pastry
                                          butter for brushing the phyllo

Cook the macaroni in salted water; drain. Melt 1/3 cup butter and pour over the macaroni. Beat the eggs lightly and mix them with the macaroni. Sprinkle with half of the cheese. Brown the remaining butter, chopped meat, and onion in a large pot; stir the chopped meat to break it up. Add the wine, the tomatoes (or diluted tomato paste), salt, pepper, and cinnamon; simmer until all the liquid is absorbed. Remove the cinnamon. Butter a deep pan. Line with 7 to 8 sheets of phyllo—allow the sides to overlap the pan—brushing each with melted butter. Divide the macaroni into 3 portions and the meat into 2. Put one layer of macaroni on the phyllo, a layer of chopped meat, then another layer of macaroni again, a second of meat, and top with the macaroni. Fold the phyllo over the filling and brush with butter. Top with the remaining phyllo, brushing each sheet with butter; trim the excess with a sharp knife. Brush the top phyllo with butter, sprinkle lightly with water; score into 4 or 5 strips. Bake in a preheated 350° oven for 30 minutes, or until golden brown. Remove from the oven, cut the strips apart, and then cut them crosswise into serving pieces. Serves 6 to 8.

LASAGNA PASTITSIO ✠ LAZANIA PASTITSIO

1 pound lasagna (flat variety)
1 cup butter
2 egg whites
½ pound Parmesan cheese, grated
1 pound chopped veal
1 onion, chopped
salt and pepper to taste
1 pound ripe tomatoes, peeled and strained

THE BECHAMEL SAUCE
4 tablespoons butter
5 tablespoons flour
4 cups milk, scalded
salt and pepper to taste
2 egg yolks

Set a large pot of water to boil with a little coarse salt. Add the whole lasagna (do not break). Stir and cook until just tender (about 9 minutes; they must be under-cooked). Remove from the heat. Add 3 to 4 cups cold water; drain. Return to the pot. Melt 1/2 cup butter and pour over the lasagna. Beat the egg whites lightly and add to the lasagna. Sprinkle with 3 tablespoons cheese; mix again. Set aside 3 tablespoons of the remaining butter and brown the balance of the butter with the chopped meat and onion. Stir to break up the meat well. Add salt and pepper; add the tomatoes; simmer until all the liquid has been absorbed.

To make the béchamel, melt the butter, add the flour slowly, stirring con-stantly. Blend the scalded milk slowly into the butter and flour and stir over low heat until it becomes a smooth sauce. Remove from the heat. Add salt and pepper. Beat the egg yolks very well and blend into the sauce. Stir again until smooth.

Divide the macaroni, chopped meat, and sauce into 2 portions each. Butter a baking pan and sprinkle with bread crumbs. Spread in half the lasagna and sprinkle with some of the cheese. Add half the chopped meat, spreading it evenly. Spread on the rest of the lasagna. Sprinkle with cheese, add the remaining chopped meat, and finally the béchamel. Sprinkle the top with cheese, then with bread crumbs. Drizzle the remaining butter over the top. Bake in a preheated 350° oven for 30 minutes, or until the crust is a deep golden brown. Serves 6 to 8.

STUFFED AND ROLLED SPECIALTIES

YEMISTA

| STUFFED ARTICHOKES | ✠ | ANGINARES YEMISTES |

12–15 large, tender artichokes
3 tablespoons butter
2 pounds chopped meat
2 onions, minced
1 tablespoon tomato paste
    diluted with 1½ cups water
salt and pepper to taste

½ cup grated kefalotiri* cheese
1 recipe Béchamel Sauce (see
    index smaller recipe)
2 zweiback, crushed, or bread
    crumbs as needed
melted butter as needed

Cut the stems from the artichokes so they can stand up. Peel off any bruised outer leaves; cut the tips off all the remaining leaves. Scoop out each 'choke, leaving a small hole in the center. Rub the cut portions with lemon. Boil the artichokes in salted water until tender but not soft (about 35 to 40 minutes). Drain well and place on a platter.

To make the stuffing, melt the butter in a pot; add the meat and onions. Stir to break up the meat; brown well. Add the tomato paste and salt and pepper. Simmer until all the juices are absorbed (about 30 minutes).

Fill the artichokes and place in a buttered pan, and pour the béchamel sauce over them (allowing about 1 tablespoonful of sauce for each filled 'choke). Sprinkle with the cheese, and the bread crumbs or zweiback. Brush with melted butter; bake for 15 to 20 minutes in a 350° oven. Allow 1 or 2 'chokes per serving.

STUFFED TOMATOES
WITH MAYONNAISE

8–10 tomatoes
salt and pepper to taste
½ cup sliced boiled potatoes
¼ cup chopped cooked squash

½ cup chopped cucumber
1 recipe mayonnaise (see index)
chopped parsley
10 Calamata olives

Select small firm round tomatoes. Wash them. Cut the tops off and reserve. Scoop out the centers (discard the seeds but reserve the pulp). Salt and pepper the tomato cases and turn upside down to drain for 1 to 2 hours.

Salt and pepper the potatoes, squash, tomato pulp, and cucumbers and mix together with two-thirds of the mayonnaise. Carefully fill the tomatoes with this mixture; top each with 1 tablespoon mayonnaise. Garnish with a garland of parsley and an olive. Refrigerate, and serve cold. Serves 4 to 5.

NOTE 1: The tomatoes may also be stuffed with shrimp, lobster, or anchovies, but are more refreshing stuffed with vegetables.

NOTE 2: You may also stuff peppers in this fashion.

TOMATOES STUFFED WITH RICE

DOMATES YEMISTES ME RIZI

12–15 tomatoes
1½ cups oil
1 cup chopped onion
1 cup raw rice
salt and pepper to taste

1 cup chopped parsley
½ cup water
⅓ cup bread crumbs
1½ pounds potatoes

Select large, round tomatoes. Cut off the tops, reserving them, and scoop out the insides, discarding only the seeds. Salt and pepper the tomato cases and place on a platter. Pass the tomato pulp through a strainer. Rinse and drain the chopped onion. Heat half the oil in a pan, and sauté the onions until golden brown; add the rice, browning it slightly. Add half the strained tomato pulp, salt, pepper, parsley, and water, and simmer until the rice is partially cooked (about 7 minutes). Remove from the heat. Stuff the tomatoes three-quarters full with this mixture, replace the tops, and place them in a pan. Drizzle with the remaining oil and sprinkle with the bread crumbs. Peel and slice the potatoes thinly, and salt and pepper them. Put them in-between the tomatoes; pour the remaining tomato pulp over the top. Bake in a preheated 350° oven for 45 minutes to 1 hour. Serves 6 to 8.

STUFFED TOMATOES WITH EGGS ✠ YEMISTES DOMATES ME AVGA

2 pounds small round potatoes
½ pound kefalotiri* cheese
6 large round tomatoes
salt and pepper to taste
2–3 tablespoons chopped
  parsley

1 cup fine-quality vegetable or
  olive oil
6 eggs
3–4 tablespoons bread crumbs

Clean the potatoes; boil until just tender; cool. Peel them and place on a platter. Cut 6 very thin slices from the cheese and grate the rest. Wash the tomatoes and cut off the tops; scoop out the pulp and pass it through a strainer; reserve. Salt and pepper the tomato cases and turn them upside down to drain. Sprinkle the potatoes with the parsley and put them into the tomatoes, then place the stuffed tomatoes in a shallow pan. Drizzle some of the oil over the top, and sprinkle with part of the grated cheese. Pour the remaining oil and tomato purée into the pan. Bake in a preheated 350° oven for 15 minutes. Remove from the oven.

Spoon up some of the oil from the pan and baste the tomatoes with it, then put a slice of cheese on each tomato, and break an egg—be careful not to break the yolk—on top. Sprinkle the eggs with salt, pepper, the rest of the cheese, and the bread crumbs. Return to the oven to bake for another 15 minutes at 300°. Serve immediately. Serves 6.

TOMATOES STUFFED WITH CHOPPED MEAT ✠ DOMATES YEMISTES ME KIMA

10 large tomatoes
salt and pepper to taste
1½ pounds chopped meat
2 onions, chopped
½ cup butter

½ cup wine
2 tablespoons chopped parsley
½ cup water
½ cup bread crumbs
½ cup grated kefalotiri* cheese

Wash the tomatoes and cut off the tops, but reserve them. Scoop out the centers and pass the pulp through a strainer. Salt and pepper the tomato cases. Put the chopped meat, onion, and half the butter into a pot, mix well, and brown. Add the wine, tomato pulp, salt, pepper, parsley, and water. Cover and simmer for 1 hour or until all the liquids have been absorbed. Remove from the heat. Add three-fourths of the bread crumbs and three-fourths of the cheese. Mix well. Stuff the tomatoes with this mixture. Cap with the tops. Place the stuffed tomatoes in a shallow pan. Drizzle with the remaining butter; sprinkle with a little grated cheese, bread crumbs, and more butter. Bake 20 to 30 minutes in a preheated 350° oven. Serves 10.

NOTE: If you wish, fill the tomatoes only three-quarters full, top them with Béchamel Sauce (see index) and sprinkle with cheese and bread crumbs. Drizzle with butter; bake as above.

TOMATOES STUFFED WITH EGGPLANT   ✠   DOMATES YEMISTES ME MELITZANA

12–15 tomatoes
2 cups cubed eggplant
flour as needed
oil as needed
½ cup raw rice
½ cup bread crumbs

½ cup feta cheese, cut into
  chunks
4 teaspoons chopped parsley
4 teaspoons chopped onion
salt and pepper to taste
3 hard-cooked eggs, sliced

Wash the tomatoes and cut off the tops; reserve them. Scoop out and set aside the pulp but discard the seeds. Salt and pepper the tomato cases and let them drain.

Immerse the eggplant cubes in cold water as you cut them; drain well. Roll them in flour and fry in plenty of oil; remove with a slotted spoon to a bowl, and add to them the rice, bread crumbs, cheese, and parsley. Sauté the onion in the same oil in which you fried the eggplant and add it to the bowl; season, and add half the tomato pulp; mix well. Stuff the tomatoes with this mixture, top with a slice of egg; cap with the tomato tops. Place the tomatoes in a shallow baking pan; drizzle over them the oil from the frying pan and the remaining tomato pulp. Bake in a preheated oven at 350° for about 40 minutes. Serve as a main course (allow 2 per serving) or as a vegetable (allow 1 per serving).

STUFFED EGGPLANTS   ✠   MELITZANES YEMISTES

eggplants (allow 1 per serving)
grated cheese (1 tablespoon per
  eggplant)

½ cup melted butter
¾ pound ripe tomatoes, peeled
  and strained

Clean the eggplants and boil for 15 minutes in lightly salted water. Remove from the pot and drain well. Cut a thin slice from the side of each eggplant and carefully scoop out the pulp; cut this into small pieces and measure it.

For each cup eggplant pulp use the following:

THE FILLING

½ cup toasted bread crumbs
¼ cup chopped parsley
½ cup pine nuts
1 cup grated cheese

¼ cup butter, melted, or oil
3 eggs
salt and pepper to taste

Mix the filling ingredients with the eggplant pulp and blend well. Carefully stuff the eggplant shells. Sprinkle with cheese and a few bread crumbs. Pour on the ½ cup melted butter, and then pour on the tomatoes. Bake in a 350° oven for 30 to 45 minutes.

EGGPLANT STUFFED ✠ WITH CHOPPED MEAT

MELITZANES YEMISTES
ME KIMA

3 pounds long, narrow eggplants
½ pound chopped meat
1 small onion, minced
1⅓ cups oil
1 pound ripe tomatoes, peeled
    and cut up

salt and pepper to taste
½ cup minced parsley
water as needed
1 cup raw rice
4—5 tablespoons toasted bread
    crumbs

Wash and clean the eggplants; scoop out a hollow in each, but do not remove all of the inside. Throw the eggplant cases immediately into salted boiling water, and parboil for 15 to 20 minutes. Remove; place in a strainer to drain. Put the oil into a wide pot, add the meat and onion; mix with a wooden spoon to break up the meat, and let the whole brown. Add the leftover eggplant, tomatoes, salt, pepper, parsley, and a ½ cup water; cook for 15 minutes. Add 1 cup hot water; as soon as it boils, add the rice, and stir it with a fork. Cover the pot; cook for 10 minutes longer; remove from the heat. Stuff the eggplants with this mixture, filling them not quite to the top (remember: rice swells in cooking), and sprinkle bread crumbs over the top. Line the eggplants up in a shallow baking pan, and sprinkle with the rest of the bread crumbs and the remaining oil. Pour 1/3 cup water into the pan. Bake for 30 to 45 minutes in a preheated oven at 350°. Serve hot. Serves 6.

SQUASH STUFFED WITH RICE 1 ✠ KOLOKITHAKIA YEMISTA ME RIZI

3 pounds medium zucchini
    squash
1 cup chopped onions
1⅓ cups oil or 1 cup butter
1 cup water
1 cup chopped parsley
1 cup raw rice, washed

salt and pepper to taste
½ cup grated cheese
¼ cup toasted bread crumbs
2 eggs, separated
2 lemons, juice only
water as needed

Cut the stems from the squash, and scrape off the skins. Wash and scoop out the flesh, leaving a quarter-inch shell. Brown the onions with half the butter or oil, and add 1 cup water, the parsley, rice, salt, and pepper. Cook slowly until all the liquid is absorbed (about 15 to 20 minutes). Remove from the heat. Add the cheese and bread crumbs, and cool slightly. Fold in the lightly beaten egg whites. Stuff the squash with this mixture; put in the pot. Pour over them the remaining oil or butter and another 1 to 2 cups water. Cover, and simmer until only a small amount of liquid remains.

Beat the egg yolks very well. Add the lemon juice, and beat continuously. Slowly add the liquid from the squash to the egg-yolk mixture and pour it over the squash. Cook over very low heat, shaking the pot gently, until the mixture thickens. Serve hot. Serves 6 to 8.

SQUASH STUFFED
WITH RICE 2
✠
KOLOKITHAKIA YEMISTA
ME RIZI

Prepare like Squash Stuffed with Rice 1, but omit the avgolemono sauce and substitute for it 1½ pounds ripe tomatoes, peeled and strained. Add half the tomatoes to the rice while it is cooking; pour the rest of the tomatoes over the squash after they are stuffed. Cook until tender and only the oil remains.

SQUASH STUFFED
WITH CHOPPED MEAT
✠
KOLOKITHAKIA YEMISTA
ME KIMA

2¾–3 pounds medium zucchini
   squash
1 pound chopped meat
1 medium onion, chopped
1 cup butter
¾ pound ripe tomatoes, peeled
   and strained
salt and pepper to taste

2 tablespoons minced parsley
water as needed
½ cup raw rice
½ cup grated cheese
½ cup toasted bread crumbs
2 eggs, separated
2 lemons, juice only

Prepare the squash as for Squash Stuffed with Rice 1 (see index). Brown the chopped meat and onion in half the butter, and crumble it with a wooden spoon. Add the tomatoes, salt, pepper, parsley, and ½ cup water. Boil for 15 minutes. Add 1 cup hot water, and as soon as it boils, add the rice. Cover; simmer for 10 minutes. Remove from the heat. Add the cheese and bread crumbs. Cool the mixture slightly, then add the lightly beaten egg whites. Mix well. Stuff the squash with the mixture and place carefully in a pot. Add the remaining butter, and 1 more cup water. Bring to a slow boil, and cook until only a small amount of liquid remains. Beat the egg yolks with the lemon juice. Add some liquid from the pot, beating constantly. Pour the sauce into the pot. Shake the pot constantly until the sauce thickens. Serve hot. Serves 6.

DOLMATHES

STUFFED GRAPE LEAVES   ✠   DOLMATHES YALANTZI

1—1½ pounds tender grape-
  vine leaves
1½ pounds onions
1 cup oil
1¼ cups raw rice
½ cup chopped parsley
2 tablespoons chopped dill
½ teaspoon chopped fresh
  mint leaves

salt and pepper to taste
1 lemon, juice only
water as needed
lemon wedges (optional)
pine nuts (optional)
raisins (optional)

If possible, buy the prepared gravevine leaves, wash them in clear cold water before using. If you are using fresh leaves, tenderize them first, as follows:

Cut the stems from the leaves with a sharp knife or scissors. Wash the leaves thoroughly, then throw them into a pot of rapidly boiling water. Boil for about 2 to 3 minutes, or until the leaves soften. Remove from the water and spread on a platter or tabletop.

To prepare the filling, peel and chop the onions. Put in a strainer and run cold water through them; drain. Sauté in the oil to a very light golden color. Add the rice; brown lightly. Add 1½ to 2 cups water, and the parsley, dill, mint leaves, salt, and pepper. Cook for 5 to 7 minutes, until the rice absorbs the liquid but is only half cooked (watch it carefully so it does not stick to the pot).

When filling the leaves, keep the shiny side of the leaf on the outside. Put 1 teaspoonful of filling in the center of the leaf and fold the sides up over it, covering it, then roll it up like a cigar. Lay the stuffed leaves in a pot (open side down so they do not swell open) in even, tight rows. When one layer is completed, make a second layer on top of the first, or a third layer, if necessary. Lay a plate directly on the top layer of dolmathes. Add enough water to the pot to half cover the stuffed leaves, and add the lemon juice. Cover the pot; cook until the liquid has been absorbed and only a slight amount of oil remains (this should take about 45 minutes). Serves 6 to 8.

NOTE: Although these are usually served cold with wedges of lemon, they can also be served hot with Avgolemono Sauce (see index). During the cooking, you may add pine nuts, and/or raisins.

STUFFED GRAPE LEAVES   ✠   DOLMATHES AVGOLEMONO
WITH CHOPPED MEAT   ME KIMA

1½ pounds (approximately)	2 eggs, separated
grape leaves	salt and pepper to taste
2 pounds chopped meat	water as needed
½ cup raw rice	5 tablespoons butter
½ cup chopped parsley	2 lemons, juice only
2–3 medium onions, chopped	1 tablespoon cornstarch

Prepare the grape leaves as in Dolmathes Yalantzi (see index), or buy them ready to use.

Mix together the meat, rice, parsley, onions, egg whites, and salt and pepper. Stuff the leaves as instructed in the recipe for Dolmathes Yalantzi. Place them in a large pot and cover with water; add the butter. Cover the dolmathes with a plate to hold them in place. Cover the pot. Simmer for 1 hour, or until about 1½ cups liquid remain; remove from the heat.

Beat the egg yolks very well; add the lemon juice and cornstarch, beating them in thoroughly. Slowly pour in the liquid from the pot, beating all the while. Pour the sauce over the dolmathes, then return the pot to low heat and gently shake it for 3 or 4 minutes, until the sauce thickens. Let stand for 3 to 5 minutes, then serve. Serves 6 to 8.

LETTUCE DOLMATHES   ✠   DOLMATHES ME FILO
WITH CHOPPED LAMB   MAROULION KAI KIMA

2–3 heads lettuce	2 eggs, separated
1½ pounds chopped lamb	½ cup butter
2 medium onions, chopped	salt and pepper to taste
2 tablespoons chopped parsley	water
1 tablespoon chopped dill	1–2 lemons, juice only
½ cup raw rice	1 cup milk

Select lettuce with leaves suitable for stuffing. Clean carefully and separate the leaves. Bring a pot of water to a boil, add the leaves, a few at a time, cook just until they wilt. Remove immediately and spread on a platter. If they are too large, cut them in half before stuffing.

Place the chopped meat, onions, parsley, dill, rice, egg whites, 2 tablespoons of the butter, salt, and pepper in a bowl. Knead well to mix. Place about 1 teaspoon of the mixture on a leaf and bring up the sides toward the center, then roll up like a cigar. Place the stuffed leaves, the open side down, in layers in a pot. Add a little salt and pepper and the rest of the butter, and enough water to half cover. Lay a plate on the dolmathes; cover the pot. Simmer slowly and when they have absorbed almost all the water, add the milk. Allow to cook a few minutes longer until approximately 1 cup liquid remains. Beat the egg yolks, add the lemon juice to them, then blend in the liquid from the pot. Return the sauce to the pot. Shake over low heat for 2 to 3 minutes. Serve hot. Serves 6 to 8.

CABBAGE DOLMATHES WITH AVGOLEMONO SAUCE

✠

LAHANO DOLMATHES ME SALTSA AVGOLEMONO

5–6 pound cabbage	**THE AVGOLEMONO**
2¼ pounds chopped pork	1 tablespoon cornstarch
½ cup raw rice	1 cup cold milk
2 medium onions, chopped	1–2 lemons, juice only
1 tablespoon chopped parsley	1 cup liquid from the pot
2 tablespoons chopped dill	
2 eggs, separated	
salt and pepper to taste	
½ cup butter	

Select cabbage with leaves suitable for stuffing. Clean carefully, and separate the leaves. Bring a pot of water to a boil and add the leaves, a few at a time; boil for 5 minutes (just to soften the leaves). Remove from the water and set aside.

Mix together the meat, rice, onions, parsley, dill, egg whites, salt, and pepper; knead well. Put 1 teaspoonful of the mixture into the center of each leaf (if the leaf is too large, cut it in half, or even in thirds, if necessary), bring the sides up over the filling, and roll the leaf up like a cigar. Place the dolmathes, open sides down, in closely packed layers in a pot; season lightly with salt and pepper. Melt the butter and pour it in, add enough hot water to cover the dolmathes, and lay a plate on top of them. Cover the pot. Cook over medium heat for 1 hour or until 1 cup of liquid remains. Remove the pot from the heat; strain off the liquid and reserve it.

Prepare the avgolemono. First mix the cornstarch with the milk. In a separate bowl, beat the egg yolks; add lemon juice to taste, beating it in well. Add the milk slowly, beating continuously, then slowly add the hot liquid from the dolmathes. Pour the sauce back into the pot and shake it over low heat for 2 to 3 minutes (until the mixture cooks). Serve hot. Serves 6 to 8.

EGGPLANT "LITTLE SHOES"   ✠   MELITZANES PAPOUTSAKIA

8–10 eggplants
oil for frying
¾ pound chopped meat
½ cup chopped onion
1 pound ripe tomatoes, peeled
   and strained
salt and pepper to taste

1 tablespoon chopped parsley
½ cup Thick Béchamel Sauce
   (see index)
½ cup grated kefalotiri*
   cheese
½ cup bread crumbs
1 cup butter

Select medium-size eggplants. Wash and cut in half lengthwise. Scoop out the centers, leaving a rim about ¼ to ½ inches thick. The eggplants should resemble an empty trough. Fry them one at a time in oil (being careful not to burn them) and place in a pan. Strain the oil from the frying pan into a pot. Add the chopped eggplant pulp, chopped meat, and the onions to it, and brown them, stirring the meat to break up the chunks. Add the tomatoes, salt, pepper, and parsley. Cook over low heat until all the liquid has been absorbed. Stuff each eggplant half with this mixture. Cover with béchamel sauce. Sprinkle with grated cheese and bread crumbs. Melt the butter and pour it over the eggplants. Bake in a preheated oven for 15 to 20 minutes at 325°–350° until golden brown. Serves 8.

SQUASH "LITTLE SHOES"   ✠   KOLOKITHAKIA PAPOUTSAKIA

Clean 8 to 10 medium-size squash. Scrape the outsides. Parboil them in salted boiling water for about 6 minutes, then cut in half lengthwise. Scoop out the centers but leave a rim ¼- to ½-inch. Now proceed exactly as for Eggplant Little Shoes. Serves 8.

BAKED SPECIALTIES

AU GRATINS

SPINACH AU GRATIN ✠ SPANAKI O GRATEN

3 pounds spinach
7 tablespoons butter
¼ – ½ pound kefalotiri* cheese, grated
toasted bread crumbs
3 eggs either hard-cooked or raw (optional)

THE BÉCHAMEL SAUCE
1 can evaporated milk
1 can water
¼ cup butter
½ cup flour
1 egg, beaten
salt and pepper to taste

Clean and wash the spinach; cut each leaf into 3 or 4 pieces, and drop into rapidly boiling water. Let the spinach boil for 3 or 4 minutes, then strain it; press out all excess fluid and return it to the pot. Melt 5 tablespoons of the butter, pour it over the spinach.

To prepare the sauce, pour the evaporated milk and water (measured in the milk can) into a pot; scald and keep hot. Melt the ¼ cup butter in another pot. Blend in the flour. Add the hot milk, stirring constantly until the mixture is smooth and thick. Season with the salt and pepper. Cool slightly, then stir in the beaten egg, blending it in well.

Spread a thin layer of the béchamel in a buttered pan; sprinkle with a little cheese. Spread in the spinach; sprinkle with more cheese. Spread the rest of the béchamel over all; sprinkle with the remaining cheese and then with the bread crumbs. Melt the remaining 2 tablespoons butter and drizzle over the casserole. Bake in a preheated 400° oven for about 20 minutes.

NOTE: You may add the hard-cooked eggs to this, if you like. Slice them and place them on the spinach before adding the final layer of sauce. Or beat the un-cooked eggs and mix them with the spinach before you layer that into the casserole.

CAULIFLOWER AU GRATIN ✠ KOUNOUPITHI O GRATEN

3 pounds (approximately)
  cauliflower
½ cup butter
3 eggs
salt and pepper to taste

1 recipe Thick Béchamel Sauce
  (see index)
½ pound kefalotiri* cheese,
  grated
toasted bread crumbs

Cut the cauliflower into large pieces, wash, and put into boiling water. Cook until tender but not soft (about 15 minutes). Remove from the pot. Drain. Break into small pieces with a fork. Melt the butter and pour half of it over the cauliflower. Beat the eggs lightly; add to the cauliflower. Add the salt and pepper, and mix well. Prepare the béchamel sauce. Butter a baking dish. Alternately spread a layer of sauce and a layer of cauliflower in it, ending with a thick layer of sauce. Sprinkle first with the cheese, then with the bread crumbs. Drizzle the remaining butter over the top. Bake in a preheated 375° oven for about 20 to 30 minutes. Remove from the oven and cool for 20 minutes. Cut into square pieces and serve. Serves 6.

ARTICHOKES BÉCHAMEL ✠ ANGINARES BESAMEL

8–10 artichokes
½ pound feta* cheese
1 cup chopped cooked ham or
  chicken, or mortadella
1 recipe Thick Béchamel Sauce
  (see index)

1 cup grated Parmesan cheese
⅓ cup melted butter
2–3 tablespoons toasted bread
  crumbs

Clean the artichokes as you would for stuffing them (see index). Rub with lemon and place in salted water. Boil until tender (about 45 minutes). Drain. Prepare the béchamel. Break up the feta cheese and mix it with the meat. Add ½ cup of the béchamel; mix well. Sprinkle the mixture with half of the Parmesan cheese and mix in. Line up the artichokes in rows in a buttered baking pan, and drizzle some of the melted butter over them; fill them with the meat-and-cheese mixture. Cover the top with the remaining béchamel, then sprinkle with the rest of the Parmesan. Top with the bread crumbs, drizzle on the melted butter, and bake in a preheated 350° oven for about 20 minutes or until the cheese and sauce take on a golden color. Serves 4 to 5 or 8 to 10, depending on the size of artichokes.

ARTICHOKES AU GRATIN ✠ ANGINARES O GRATEN

1 lemon, juice only
coarse salt
8–10 small globe artichokes
½ cup butter, melted
salt and pepper to taste

1 recipe Thick Béchamel Sauce
(see index)
2 cups grated kefalotiri* cheese
3–4 tablespoons toasted bread
crumbs

Add some coarse salt and the lemon juice to a large pot of water; bring to a boil. Meanwhile, clean the artichokes (which see in index); put them into the boiling water. Cover the pot, and cook over high heat until they are tender (35 to 45 minutes); remove with a slotted spoon. Cut them into cubes, pour half the melted butter over them, and season. Prepare the béchamel sauce.

Butter a small pan and spread a thin layer of the sauce in it; sprinkle generously with the cheese. Spread the artichokes evenly on top and sprinkle additional cheese over them. Pour the remaining béchamel over the whole, then top with the rest of the cheese and the bread crumbs. Drizzle the remaining butter over the top. Bake in a preheated 350° oven for about 20 minutes or until golden brown. Serves about 6.

SQUASH AU GRATIN ✠ KOLOKITHAKIA O GRATEN

3 pounds small squash
(zucchini)
1 cup vegetable or olive oil
flour
1 recipe Thick Béchamel Sauce
(see index)

1½ cups grated kefalotiri*
cheese
toasted bread crumbs
3 tablespoons butter, melted
salt and pepper to taste

Select tender squash. Scrape the skin, wash. Cut into small slices. Season with salt and pepper. Heat the oil in a frying pan. Dip the squash into the flour, shaking off the excess, and fry until rosy. Prepare the béchamel.

Butter a medium pan. Spread in it a thin layer of béchamel, sprinkle with cheese. Cover with a layer of squash. Continue to spread these layers alternately, ending with a thick layer of béchamel. Sprinkle with the cheese and then the bread crumbs. Drizzle the melted butter over the top, and bake in a preheated 325° oven for 20 to 30 minutes.

HAM BÉCHAMEL ✠ ZAMPON BESAMEL

½ cup vegetable shortening
1⅓ cups flour
4 cups milk, scalded (not boiled)
2 egg yolks, well beaten

1 cup grated kefalotiri* cheese
6 ham steaks (¼–½" thick)
salt and pepper to taste
melted butter

Melt the shortening in a pot. Add the flour, and blend in well. Remove from the heat and add the scalded milk. Return to low heat and stir until the sauce is thick and smooth. Remove again from the heat, add the egg yolks, and season lightly with the salt and pepper. Butter a baking pan. Spread half the sauce smoothly in it, and sprinkle with half of the cheese. Place the ham steaks on top and cover them with the remaining sauce; sprinkle the remaining cheese over them. Drizzle on the melted butter. Bake in a preheated 400° oven for about 20 minutes. Serve immediately or the sauce will fall and the casserole will not look attractive. Serves 6.

MOUSSAKAS

MOUSSAKA POTATOES ✠ MOUSAKAS PATATES

3 pounds potatoes
1⅔ cups oil
salt and pepper to taste
½ cup chopped onion
1½ pounds tomatoes, peeled
    and strained, or 1½ table-
    spoons tomato paste diluted
    with 1 cup water

½ head garlic (6–8 cloves)
½ cup chopped parsley
1 cup grated cheese
bread crumbs

Clean and peel the potatoes; cut them into thin round slices. Fry in the oil, then season with salt and pepper. Sauté the onions to a light golden color in the pan in which you fried the potatoes, and add to them the tomatoes (or diluted tomato paste), garlic, parsley, and salt and pepper; cook for about 20 minutes, until you have a thick sauce. Remove from the heat. Add to the sauce ¾ cup of the cheese and 3 tablespoons bread crumbs.

Oil a medium-size baking pan lightly. Spread a layer of the potatoes in it; cover them with part of the sauce. Top with another layer of potatoes and another layer of sauce. Continue this process until all the potatoes and sauce are used; sprinkle with the remaining cheese and additional bread crumbs; dribble a little oil over the top, and bake in a preheated oven at 375° for about 30 minutes. Serves 6 to 8.

POTATOES AND SQUASH MOUSSAKA ✠ MOUSAKAS PATATES KOLOKITHAKIA

Prepare like Moussaka Potatoes (above) but substitute squash for half the potatoes called for in the recipe.

POTATO AND SQUASH BAKE ✠ PATATES KE KOLOKITHAKIA STO FOURNO

Prepare like Potatoes and Squash Moussaka (above), but cut the potatoes and squash into thinner slices, and do not fry them before the baking process.

MOUSSAKA POTATOES AND CHOPPED MEAT ✠ MOUSAKAS PATATES KE KIMA

3 pounds potatoes
butter or oil for frying
1½ pounds chopped meat
1 medium onion, chopped
3 tablespoons butter
1–1¼ pounds ripe tomatoes, peeled and strained, or 1 tablespoon tomato paste diluted with 1 cup water

1 recipe Béchamel Sauce (see index)
salt and pepper to taste
1 tablespoon parsley
1 cup grated Parmesan cheese
toasted bread crumbs

Clean and peel the potatoes. Cut into thin slices and fry them in the butter (or oil). Brown the chopped meat and onions in the 3 tablespoons butter, stirring to break up the meat. Add the tomatoes (or diluted tomato paste), salt, pepper, and parsley. Cover, and simmer until all the liquids have been absorbed. Remove from the heat. Add one-third of the cheese and 3 to 4 tablespoons bread crumbs; mix well. Butter a baking pan; sprinkle with bread crumbs. Spread half the potatoes into the pan and sprinkle with cheese. Spread the chopped meat evenly over it. Layer the remaining potatoes on top and sprinkle with more cheese. Cover with béchamel sauce, sprinkle with the rest of the cheese and then with bread crumbs. Drizzle melted butter on top. Bake in a preheated 350° oven 30 to 40 minutes, or until golden. Serves 6.

ARTICHOKES WITH CHOPPED MEAT ✠ ANGINARES ME KIMA

1½ pounds chopped meat
1 onion, chopped
3 tablespoons butter
1½ pounds ripe tomatoes,
    peeled and strained, or 1
    tablespoon tomato paste,
    diluted with 1 cup water
salt and pepper to taste
6–8 artichokes
1 lemon, juice only
¾ pound fresh peas
3 tablespoons butter
¼–½ pound grated Parmesan
    cheese
¾ pound phyllo* pastry
butter for brushing the phyllo

THE BÉCHAMEL SAUCE
1 can evaporated milk
1 can water
3 tablespoons butter
1 cup flour
2 egg yolks

Put the chopped meat, onions, and butter together in a pot to brown, stirring with a wooden spoon to break up the meat. Add the tomatoes (or diluted tomato paste), and salt and pepper; simmer, covered, until all the liquid is absorbed.

Clean the artichokes and rub them with lemon juice (see index for method); boil in salted water for about 15 minutes, then add the peas, and cook until tender (about 30 minutes). Drain; remove the artichokes, and cut them into small pieces; mix these with the peas. Melt the butter and pour it over these vegetables.

To prepare the béchamel, mix together the evaporated milk and water; scald but do not boil. Melt the butter in another pot, and add the flour, stirring constantly. Slowly pour in the hot milk, stirring continuously until the sauce becomes smooth and thick. Remove it from the heat and cool it slightly. Beat the egg yolks and add them to the sauce, blending well.

Butter a medium-size pan and spread 6 to 8 phyllo sheets (see index: About Phyllo) over it, one at a time, brushing each with melted butter. Do not trim the overhang. Spread half the artichoke mixture onto these, then sprinkle with part of the cheese and cover with half the béchamel. Spread the chopped meat evenly over this layer, and cover with the rest of the artichoke mixture. Sprinkle with the remaining cheese, and then spread the balance of the béchamel on it. Fold the phyllo up over this, buttering the sheets well so they do not stick. Spread 4 to 5 phyllo sheets over all, one at a time, brushing each with butter before adding the next; trim off the excess. Brush the top phyllo sheet with more butter. Score the pastry into square- or diamond-shaped serving pieces. Bake in a preheated 350° oven for 40 minutes. Serves 6 to 8.

SQUASH MOUSSAKA   ✠   MOUSAKAS KOLOKITHIA
WITH CHOPPED MEAT   ME KIMA

3 pounds zucchini squash
salt and pepper to taste
oil for frying
flour
¼ pound butter
1 onion, chopped
1½ pounds chopped meat
1½ pounds ripe tomatoes,
    peeled and strained, or 1
    tablespoon tomato paste
    diluted with 1 cup water

toasted bread crumbs
1 recipe Béchamel Sauce (see
    index)
2 eggs
¼–½ pound grated kefalotiri*
    cheese
2–3 tablespoons melted butter

Clean and wash the squash. Cut lengthwise into thin pieces; season lightly with
salt and pepper. Heat the oil. Dip the squash strips in flour. Shaking off the excess;
fry until rosy, then place on platter. Melt the ¼ pound butter in a pot, add the
onions; sauté until golden. Add the chopped meat, breaking it up with a wooden
spoon; brown thoroughly. Add the tomatoes (or the diluted tomato paste), salt, and
pepper, and simmer until all the liquids have been absorbed and only the oil remains.
Remove from the heat and add ½ cup bread crumbs. Prepare the béchamel sauce;
blend the 2 eggs into it.

Butter a medium-size pan, sprinkle with bread crumbs, and spread on half of the
squash. Sprinkle with cheese. Add a layer of chopped meat on top, then the remaining squash. Top with the béchamel. Sprinkle with cheese and then with bread
crumbs. Drizzle with the melted butter. Bake for 30 to 40 minutes in a preheated
350° oven. Serves 6.

EGGPLANT MOUSSAKA ✠ MOUSAKAS MELITZANES

½ cup butter or vegetable oil
1½ pounds chopped meat
2 tablespoons chopped onions
½ cup white wine
1½ pounds ripe tomatoes,
    peeled and strained
2 tablespoons chopped parsley
salt and pepper to taste

3 pounds eggplants
oil for frying
1 recipe Béchamel Sauce (see
    index)
1 cup bread crumbs
½ cup grated Parmesan cheese
2–3 tablespoons melted butter

Place half the butter (or oil) in a frying pan. Add the chopped meat and the onions. Stir to crumble the meat; brown. Add the wine, tomatoes, parsley, salt, and pepper, and bring to a boil. Lower the heat and simmer until the liquids are absorbed. Wash and dry the eggplant. Cut into thin slices. Fry in the remaining butter (add oil if needed). Place the fried eggplant slices on a platter. Prepare the béchamel.

Arrange half of the eggplant slices in even rows in a medium-size baking pan. Sprinkle with half the bread crumbs. Add half of the cheese to the chopped meat, mixing it in well; spread this on top of the eggplant. Add another layer of eggplant, then cover with the béchamel. Sprinkle the remaining cheese on top, then the remaining bread crumbs. Drizzle with melted butter. Bake for 30 to 40 minutes in a preheated 350° oven until lightly browned. Serves 6.

NOTE: This can also be made in individual baking dishes.

VEGETABLE SPECIALTIES

LATHERA

This section of typically Greek foods presents a very heavy diet. It is distinguished from other cooking by its use of oil and butter—and more oil and more butter. The foods are cooked until all the liquids except the fat are absorbed, and the meats or vegetables are literally swimming in the remaining oil or butter. For this reason, only the very best olive oil or butter should be used. Do not substitute margarine or other oils unless you are satisfied with less than perfect results.

This is not a section for dieters, young children, elderly people, or people with stomach problems. However, because of the excellent taste, many will be tempted to risk indigestion.

It is best not to serve more than one of these dishes at any one meal. Other vegetables or salads served with these delights should be very light.

FRIED EGGPLANT ✠ MELITZANES TIGANITES

Purchase round eggplants. Cut them into slices. Soak for 10 minutes in salted water. Heat a mixture of oil and butter in a deep frying pan. Lightly flour the eggplant slices and fry until golden. Serve with skordalia* (see index).

FRIED SQUASH ✠ KOLOKITHAKIA TIGANITA

Clean and wash as much squash as desired. Cut into medium slices, flour lightly, and fry in hot oil. Serve alone with skordalia* (see index) as a main dish, or as a vegetable to accompany a meat dish.

PEAS LATHEROS ✠ ARAKAS LATHEROS

4½–5 pounds peas
4 scallions
1¼ cups oil or 1 cup butter
1½ pounds ripe tomatoes,
   peeled and strained, or 1
   tablespoon tomato paste
   diluted with 2 cups water

3 tablespoons chopped dill
salt and pepper to taste
water as needed

Shell, wash, and drain the peas. Chop the white part of the scallions into small pieces and the green part into large pieces. Heat the oil in a large pot. Add the scallions and cook until soft but not browned. Add the peas and brown very lightly. Add the tomatoes (or the diluted tomato paste), dill, salt, and pepper. Add enough water to half cover the peas. Cover the pot. Cook over medium heat until only the oil remains and the liquid has been absorbed (about 45 minutes) Serves 6 to 9.

NOTE: You can make this without the tomatoes, if you wish. In that case, add just enough water to half cover the peas.

SQUASH LATHERA ✠ KOLOKITHAKIA LATHERA

3 pounds zucchini squash
1¼ cups oil
2 medium onions, chopped
1½ pounds ripe tomatoes,
   peeled and strained, or 1
   tablespoon tomato paste
   diluted with 1 cup water

2–3 cloves garlic, chopped
2 tablespoons chopped parsley
salt and pepper to taste
water as needed

Clean and wash the squash, cut each into 4 or 5 round slices. Heat the oil in a pot and sauté the onions until lightly browned. Add the tomatoes (or diluted tomato paste) and the garlic; bring to a boil. Add the squash, parsley, salt, pepper, and ½ cup water. Cover the pot. Simmer until all the liquid has been absorbed and only the oil remains as a sauce (about 45 minutes). Serves 6.

NOTE: You may fry the squash first, if you wish. In that case, use half of the oil for the onions and the other half for the squash, and cook the sauce for 15 to 20 minutes before adding the fried squash and the parsley. Do not add more water. Cook for about 20 minutes more, or until the liquid is absorbed and only the oil remains.

EGGPLANT IMAM BALDI ✠ MELITZANES IMAM BALDI

3 pounds small oblong eggplants
salt
2½ cups (approximately) oil
3 cups thinly sliced onions
5–6 cloves garlic, chopped
1½ pounds ripe tomatoes,
   peeled and strained

1 cup chopped parsley
salt and pepper to taste
2 tablespoons Parmesan cheese
2 tablespoons toasted bread
   crumbs

With a sharp knife, slash each eggplant lengthwise, being careful not to cut all the way through and leaving at least a half inch on both ends uncut. (Do not cut away the stem). Salt the cut and place the eggplants in a pot of salted water for 15 minutes. Drain, and rinse in clear water. Wipe dry. Fry the eggplants in ample oil and place them, split side up, side by side in a baking pan.

In the oil used for the frying, sauté the onions until golden. Add the garlic, tomatoes, parsley, salt, and pepper. Cook for 20 minutes, or until all the liquids are absorbed. Remove from the heat. Stuff this mixture into the cut in the eggplants; sprinkle with cheese and bread crumbs. Drizzle a little oil over them and bake for 30 minutes in a preheated 350° oven. Serves 6.

NOTE: This can also be made on top of the stove. After the eggplants are stuffed, place them side by side in a wide pot, add 2 to 3 tablespoons oil and 1 cup water, and cook over low heat for about 45 minutes.

FRIED EGGPLANT IN SAUCE ✠ MELITZANES TIGANITES ME SALTSA

about 3 pounds long eggplants
coarse salt
oil for frying

1½ pounds ripe tomatoes,
   peeled and strained

With a sharp knife, slash the eggplants lengthwise in 2 or 3 places; but do not cut off the stem. Fill a large pot with water, add a little coarse salt, and bring to a boil. Add the eggplants. Cook over high heat until tender but not soft. Remove and let drain.

Heat the oil in a frying pan. Lightly flour the eggplants, and fry them in the hot oil until golden brown. Remove to a platter. To the same oil, add the tomatoes; cook down to make a thick sauce. Add the eggplants to the sauce, reheat, and serve. Serves 6.

EGGPLANT POTTED WITH BUTTER ✠ MELITZANES KATSAROLAS VOUTIROU

3 pounds eggplant
¾ cup butter
3–5 cloves garlic, chopped
3 tablespoons parsley, chopped

1½ pounds ripe tomatoes,
     peeled and strained, or 1
     tablespoon tomato paste
     diluted with 1 cup water
salt and pepper to taste
1 cup water

Peel the eggplants, cut into 1½-inch cubes, and soak in lightly salted water for 15 minutes. Drain, and squeeze gently. Brown the butter in a large pot. Add the eggplant cubes and turn 2 to 3 times, to brown lightly on all sides. Add the garlic; cook until golden. Add the parsley, the tomatoes (or diluted tomato paste), salt, pepper, and 1 cup water. Cover. Simmer until all the liquid is absorbed and only the oil remains (30 to 45 minutes). Serves 6.

PEAS AND ARTICHOKES LATHEROS ✠ ARAKAS ME ANGINARES LATHEROS

3 pounds peas
6 medium artichokes
1 lemon
1¼ cups oil or 1 cup butter
5 scallions, chopped

1½ pounds ripe tomatoes,
     peeled and strained, or 1
     tablespoon tomato paste
     diluted with 2 cups water
2 tablespoons chopped dill
salt and pepper to taste
water as needed

Shell and wash peas. Drain. Clean the artichokes (see index), rub each one with lemon, and place in a pot of salted water. Squeeze half the lemon into this and let stand. Pour the oil into a pot, add the scallions; cook until soft but not browned. Add the tomatoes or the diluted tomato paste and bring to a boil. Add the peas. Rinse the artichokes and place them upside down (stem side up) on the peas. Add the dill and 1 cup hot water. Cover the pot. Cook over medium heat (about 30 to 40 minutes) until all the liquids are absorbed and only the oil remains as a sauce. Serves 6.

NOTE: You may omit the tomatoes, if you wish. In that case, substitute 2 cups water and the juice of another lemon.

EGGPLANT YIAXNI ✠ MELITZANES YIAHNI

3 pounds long thin eggplants
1¼ cups oil
1 medium onion, chopped
4–5 cloves garlic, chopped
1½ pounds ripe tomatoes,
   peeled and strained, or 1
   tablespoon tomato paste
   diluted with 2 cups water

salt and pepper to taste
3 tablespoons parsley
1 cup water

Peel the eggplants and cut each into 4 or 5 thick round slices. Put them into a pot of cold salted water and soak for 20 minutes. Heat the oil in a deep pot and sauté the onions and garlic until lightly golden. Add the tomatoes (or diluted tomato paste) and cook for 10 minutes. Drain the eggplants, squeeze them gently to remove the excess fluid, and add them to the pot. Add the salt, pepper, parsley, and water. Cover the pot. Simmer about 30 minutes to 1 hour until all the liquid has been absorbed and only the oil remains. Serves 6.

NOTE: Or you may fry the eggplant first, using half of the oil; use the rest to sauté the onions and garlic, then proceed as above.

CAULIFLOWER STIFADO ✠ KOUNOUPITHI STIFADO

6 pounds cauliflower
6 small white onions
1¼ cups oil
3–4 cloves garlic, split
   lengthwise

1 tablespoon tomato paste
   diluted with 2 cups water
½ cup vinegar
½ tablespoon rosemary
1 bay leaf
6 peppercorns

Wash the cauliflower and break into flowerets. Skin and wash the onions; drain. Heat the oil in a pot and lightly brown the whole onions. Add the garlic and cook until golden. Add the diluted tomato paste, vinegar, rosemary, and bay leaf, and cook for 30 minutes. Bring a large pot of salted water to a boil; add the cauliflower. Cook for 5 minutes, then drain and add the cauliflower to the sauce. (Add a little water if necessary.) Add the peppercorns. Cover the pot. Simmer until all the liquid has been absorbed and only the oil remains (about 30 to 45 minutes). Serves 6 to 8.

CAULIFLOWER KAPAMAS, CALAMATA STYLE ✠ KOUNOUPITHI KAPAMAS, KALAMATIANO

6 pounds cauliflower
2 lemons, juice only
1¼ cups oil
1 medium onion, chopped

1 tablespoon tomato paste
salt and pepper to taste
2 cups water

Wash the cauliflower well and break it into flowerets; drain. Place on a platter and pour lemon juice over all. Heat the oil in a frying pan and fry the pieces, one at a time, then carefully transfer these to a large pot. Fry the onions lightly in the same frying pan. Add the tomato paste and 1 cup water, stir, and bring to a boil. Cook for about 3 minutes, then pour the sauce into the pot with the cauliflower. Place over medium heat, bring to a boil. Add the second cup water. Continue to cook until all the liquid has been absorbed and only the oil remains (about 30 to 45 minutes). Serves 6 to 8.

OKRA IN OIL ✠ BAMIES LATHERES

3 pounds okra
salt and pepper to taste
½ cup vinegar
1¼ cups oil or butter
4–5 cloves garlic
1 medium onion, chopped

1¼ pounds ripe tomatoes,
     peeled and strained, or 1
     tablespoon tomato paste
     diluted with 2 cups water
water as needed

Wash the okra several times; clean carefully and remove the stems without cutting into the okra. Place them in a pan. Salt lightly, add the vinegar, and place in the sun for about 2 hours.

Heat the oil in a frying pan. Add the garlic and onion, and sauté until golden. Add the tomatoes (or tomato paste). Cook for 5 minutes. Rinse the okra well; discard the vinegar. Add okra, salt, pepper, and about 1 cup water to the tomatoes. Cover the pot. Simmer until the sauce is absorbed and the oil remains (45 minutes to 1 hour). Serves 6 to 8.

NOTE: After soaking the okra, you may rinse and fry it in half of the oil; use the rest of the oil as above. Then add the okra and 1 cup water to the sauce and cook for about 30 minutes.

GREEN BEANS IN OIL ✠ FASOLAKIA PRASINA YIAHNI

3 pounds green beans
1½ cups oil
2 medium onions, minced
1½ pounds ripe tomatoes,
   peeled and strained, or 1
   tablespoon tomato paste
   diluted with 2 cups water

2 tablespoons minced parsley
salt and pepper to taste
water as needed

Wash the beans and break them in half or slice them lengthwise. Place in a large pot of cold water. Heat the oil in a large pot and sauté the onions in it until soft and limp; add the tomatoes (or diluted tomato paste), and bring to a boil. Drain the beans and add them to the pot. Add the parsley, salt, pepper, and enough water to barely cover the beans. Cook over medium heat until the liquid is absorbed but the oil remains (30 to 45 minutes). Serves 6.

OVEN-BAKED GIANT BEANS ✠ FASOLAKIA YIYANTES STO FOURNO

2 pounds dried giant white
   beans
2 cups oil
1 head garlic, cleaned
3 medium onions, chopped
1 tablespoon chopped celery
½ cup minced parsley
salt and pepper to taste

1 cup hot water
1¾ pounds ripe tomatoes,
   peeled and strained, or 1
   tablespoon tomato paste
   diluted with 1½ cups water
water as needed

Wash the beans, place in water, and soak them overnight. Drain them, then place in a pot of fresh cold salted water; cook for 45 minutes; drain. Meanwhile, place the oil, garlic, and onions in a baking pan and bake in a preheated 350° oven until golden. Add the beans, celery, parsley, salt, pepper, and hot water. Bake 30 minutes longer. Remove from oven, stir the beans, pour in the tomatoes (or diluted tomato paste). Return to oven and bake until only the oil remains. Serves 6.

POTTED GIANT BEANS   ✛   FASOLAKIA YIYANTES YIAHNI

2 pounds dried giant white
  beans
2 cups oil
3–4 medium onions, chopped
½ cup chopped parsley

1¾ pounds ripe tomatoes,
  peeled and strained, or 1
  tablespoon tomato paste
  diluted with 1½ cups water
salt and pepper to taste

Wash the beans and soak them overnight. Drain, then put into a pot and cover with fresh cold, salted water. Bring to a boil; pour off all the water. Add the oil, onions, parsley, salt, and pepper; stir over medium heat until the onions are golden. Add 2 cups hot water. Cover and simmer for 1 hour. Add the tomatoes (or diluted tomato paste); stir. Cook until the beans are tender and only the oil remains (about 30 minutes). Serves 6.

BRIAM   ✛   BRIAM

2 pounds tomatoes
1 pound potatoes
1 pound small squash
1 pound eggplant
1 pound okra
vinegar
salt and pepper to taste

½ cup chopped onion
1 tablespoon chopped garlic
2 tablespoons chopped green
  pepper
2 tablespoons chopped parsley
1½ cups oil

Wash and peel the tomatoes and chop them into small pieces; spread half of them in a baking pan. Peel and wash the potatoes; and slice them into rounds. Do the same to the squash and eggplant. Clean the okra and sprinkle with a little vinegar. Lightly salt and pepper the tomatoes in the pan; spread the potatoes, squash, eggplant and okra over them. Add a little more salt and pepper. Mix the onion, garlic, green pepper, and parsley together and sprinkle over the vegetables. Top with the remaining tomatoes. Pour the oil over the surface. Bake in a 250° oven for 1½ to 2 hours, adding a little water if necessary. Serves 6 to 8.

BAKED POTATOES OREGANO ✠ PATATES STO FOURNO RIGANATES

3 pounds potatoes
¾ cup oil
1 lemon, juice only

pinch of oregano
salt and pepper to taste

Peel and wash the potatoes, and grate them coarsely. Place in a pan and add the oil and the lemon juice. Sprinkle a little oregano and salt and pepper over the potatoes and bake in a 350° preheated oven for 45 minutes. Serves 6.

POTATOES YAXNI ✠ PATATES YIAHNI

3 pounds potatoes
¾ cup oil
2 onions, chopped
1¼ pounds tomatoes, peeled
    and sieved, or 1 tablespoon
    tomato paste diluted with
    1 cup water

2–3 carrots, scraped and sliced
2–3 cloves garlic
2 tablespoons chopped celery
salt and pepper to taste
water as needed

Peel and wash the potatoes, and cut them into pieces (4 if the potatoes are large; 3, if medium; 2, if small). Place in a bowl of cold water. Heat the oil in a pot and add the onion; sauté to golden brown. Add the tomatoes (or diluted tomato paste), the carrots, garlic, celery, salt, pepper, and 1 cup water. Cook for 5 minutes, then add the potatoes. They should be half covered with the liquid; add water if necessary, to reach the proper level. Cover. Simmer until all the sauce has been absorbed and only the oil remains (about 45 minutes). Serves 6.

VEGETABLE CROQUETTES

SQUASH CROQUETTES OR PATTIES ✠ KOLOKITHOKEFTETHES

2 pounds small squash
1 tablespoon butter
3 tablespoons chopped onion
1 cup grated kefalotiri* or
  Parmesan cheese
1 cup toasted bread crumbs

1 tablespoon chopped parsley
2 eggs
salt and pepper to taste
flour
oil for frying

Clean and wash the squash. Boil in lightly salted water until soft; drain well. Mash and set aside. Melt the butter in a pan, and sauté the onions until limp and golden but not browned. Add the onions, cheese, bread crumbs, parsley, eggs, and salt and pepper to the squash, and mix well. If the mixture is too soft, add more bread crumbs. Let it stand for 10 minutes, then shape into croquettes or patties. Roll in flour, fry until golden.

EGGPLANT CROQUETTES ✠ MELITZANOKEFTETHES KROKETES

eggplants
cracker meal
oil for frying

THE MIXTURE
1½ cups bread crumbs
2 eggs
½ cup grated kefalotiri* or
  Parmesan cheese
1 teaspoon baking powder
2 tablespoons chopped parsley
salt and pepper to taste
1 teaspoon chopped onion

Wash the eggplants and pierce in several places with a fork. Boil in lightly salted water until tender; drain well. Remove the skin and mash the pulp; measure it. Mix 2 cups of eggplant pulp with the amount of ingredients listed above and blend well. Shape into croquettes or patties. Roll in cracker meal, and fry until golden brown.

PHYLLO ENTREES

PITTES

SPINACH PIE WITH EGGS ✠ SPANAKOPITTA ME AVGA

3 pounds spinach
1 medium onion, chopped
½ cup chopped scallions
1 cup butter
½ cup chopped dill
½ cup chopped parsley
salt and pepper to taste

½ cup evaporated milk
4–5 eggs
¾ pound phyllo* pastry
melted butter as needed
½ pound feta* cheese, coarsely
   crumbled

Wash the spinach in plenty of water and cut it into small pieces; place in a bowl. Salt it lightly; stir to spread the salt evenly. Take the spinach, a handful at a time, and squeeze out the excess water; place it in another bowl. Sauté the onion in half the butter until it is a light, golden color; add the scallions and cook until they wilt. Add the spinach; stir until all the vegetables take on a light color. Stir in the dill, parsley, salt and pepper; cover the pot and cook until all the water thrown off by the spinach is absorbed. Remove from the heat; turn into a bowl, and immediately add the milk (to cool the spinach). Beat the eggs in another bowl and add the cheese to them; add to the cooled spinach; mix well.

Line a pan with 8 sheets of phyllo (see index: About Phyllo), brushing each sheet with the melted butter before topping it with the next sheet. Do not trim the overhanging sections. Pour in the spinach mixture, spreading it evenly over the phyllo. Fold the part of the phyllo that extends out of the pan back over the filling. Lay the remaining phyllo on top, again brushing each sheet with melted butter before adding the next. Now trim off the overlap. Brush additional melted butter on top of the pie and score it into square- or diamond-shapped serving pieces. Bake for 30 to 45 minutes in a preheated 300° oven; let it stand for 30 minutes before serving. Serves 6.

NOTE: This can also be made without precooking the spinach. In that case, squeeze the spinach free of as much water as possible, mix it with the seasonings, and proceed as above, baking it for 1 hour.

INDIVIDUAL SPINACH PIES   ✠   SPANAKOPITTES

Use the same ingredients as in Spinach Pie with Eggs, but increasing the phyllo to 1¾ pounds. Cut the phyllo into long strips about one-third the width of the full sheet. Take the sheets, one at a time (keeping the others covered so they will not dry out), and brush with melted butter; place a heaping tablespoonful of the mixture on one end of the phyllo strip, fold the lower-left-hand corner over to the top of the strip, forming a triangle, then fold the upper-left-hand corner over to form another triangle, continue to fold the triangle over and over until all the phyllo has been wrapped around the spinach, to form individual triangular turnovers. Brush with melted butter; bake in a preheated 300° oven for about 15 to 20 minutes, until golden brown. Makes about 50 appetizer-size pies.

NOTE: These may also be deep fat fried.

LEEKS IN PHYLLO PASTRY   ✠   PRASSOPITTA

3 pounds leeks   salt and pepper to taste
1 cup butter   1 pound phyllo*
7 eggs   butter for brushing the phyllo
1 tablespoon farina
¾ pound feta* cheese, crumbled

Clean the leeks, discarding the green parts and leaves; use only the white part. Cut into quarters, then chop into small pieces; place in a strainer and wash under running water for several minutes. Melt the butter in a pot. Add the leeks, cook until they soften and the water from them has evaporated. Cool.

Beat the eggs in a bowl until light. Put the leeks into another bowl, and add the farina, cheese, salt, and pepper; mix well. Butter a pan the size of the phyllo sheets. Put 4 to 5 sheets of phyllo (reserve 4 for the top) on the bottom of the pan, brushing each with melted butter before adding it. Spread a layer of leeks on the phyllo (see index: About phyllo) and top it with 3 or 4 tablespoons of the beaten egg. Spread 2 sheets of phyllo, again brushing each one with butter. Spread in a second layer of leeks and top with more egg. Continue layering in the leeks and eggs in this manner until all are spread in the pan. Spread the last 4 sheets of phyllo carefully over the top layer, brushing each one with butter. Pour any remaining butter over the top. Score the phyllo with a sharp knife into serving-size pieces. Bake in a preheated 350° oven for about 30 minutes. Serves 6 to 8.

SQUASH PIE ✠ KOLOKITHOPITTA

3 pounds small zucchini squash
¾ pound feta* cheese
1 cup butter
salt and pepper to taste
5 eggs

2 tablespoons chopped parsley
2 tablespoons chopped dill
½ cup toasted bread crumbs
½ cup milk
butter for brushing the phyllo
¾ pound phyllo*

Clean and scrape the squash. Grate it into thick slivers and place in a colander; drain for 1 hour. Cut or crumble the cheese into pieces about the size of peas. Brown half the butter in a large pot. Add the squash and toss a few times (it should not brown), add salt and pepper; remove from the heat. Beat the eggs in a bowl, add the cheese, parsley, dill, bread crumbs, milk, salt, and pepper; mix well. Pour into the pot with the squash, and mix again. Butter a baking pan a little smaller than the phyllo sheets (see index: About Phyllo)—the sheets should extend about 2 inches on all sides. Put half of the sheets, one at a time, each brushed with melted butter, into the pan, then use an additional 2 sheets of those remaining to make the bottom pastry thicker. Pour the squash mixture into the pan, spreading it evenly. Fold the overhanging phyllo up over the squash; brush well with butter. Lay the rest of the phyllo sheets on top, again brushing each sheet with butter. Trim the edges very carefully with a sharp knife; butter the top very well. Place in a preheated 250° oven and bake for about 1 hour. Cool and cut into serving pieces. Serves 6 to 8.

NOTE: It is easier to cut this if you score the pitta before baking.

CHEESE PIE ✠ TYROPITTA ROUMELIOTIKI

2 pounds feta* cheese
10 eggs, lightly beaten

1¼ pounds phyllo*
½ cup (approximately) melted
butter for brushing the
phyllo

Crumble the feta into small particles. Mix the eggs with the cheese. Butter a baking pan the size of the phyllo (see index: About Phyllo) sheets (cut the phyllo to fit, if necessary). Put four sheets of phyllo into the pan, brushing each one with butter. Spoon in some of the cheese mixture; top with 2 phyllo sheets, brushing each with butter before adding it. Add another layer of cheese and another layer of phyllo, again brushing it with butter. Continue in this manner until all the cheese mixture is used. Plan to have 4 sheets of phyllo left for the top layer; add these, first buttering each, then pour the rest of the butter over the top. Score lightly in long strips. Bake in a preheated 300° oven for about 45 minutes. Cut the scored strips into 2-inch pieces and serve hot. Serves 6 to 8.

CHEESE PITTA   ✠   TYROPITTA 1

1½ pounds feta* cheese
5 tablespoons butter
8 tablespoons flour
2 cups milk, scalded but not
   boiled

salt and pepper to taste
7 eggs, lightly beaten
¾ pound (approximately)
   phyllo*
butter for brushing the phyllo

Crumble the cheese into very small pieces. Melt the butter in a small pot. Add the flour, and blend well. Slowly add the scalded milk, stirring constantly to make a smooth béchamel sauce. Add a little salt and pepper. Remove from the heat and stir until cool. Add the crumbled cheese and mix well. Add the eggs and mix again.

Butter a pan about 2 inches smaller than the phyllo sheets (see index: About Phyllo). Use a little more than half of the phyllo sheets to make the bottom layer of the pie. Brush each with melted butter and place it in the pan letting the edges hang over the pan. Pour in the cheese-egg mixture, spreading it evenly. Cover the mixture with the phyllo that extended beyond the pan. This will prevent the mixture from leaking out. Carefully cut the remaining phyllo to fit the pan. Brush each sheet with butter before placing it on the pitta. Brush the top with butter and sprinkle with a little water. Score into strips to make cutting the pie easier after it is baked. Bake in a preheated 300° oven for about 45 minutes. Cut into pieces and serve hot. Serves 6 to 8.

CHEESE TRIANGLES   ✠   TYROPITTA 2

1 cup milk, scalded
3 tablespoons butter
4 tablespoons flour
salt and pepper to taste
¾ pound feta* cheese

4 eggs, lightly beaten
2 teaspoons chopped dill
¾ pound (approximately)
   phyllo*
oil, melted butter, or other
   shortening for brushing the
   phyllo

Melt the 3 tablespoons butter, add the flour, and stir well to blend. Slowly add the hot milk, stirring constantly to make a thick, creamy sauce. Remove from the heat. Add the salt and pepper, and continue to stir the sauce until it is cool. Crumble the cheese into small pieces and add them to the sauce. Add the eggs; stir well, then add the dill, and mix until well blended.

Cut each of the sheets of phyllo (see index: About Phyllo) lengthwise into 3 strips. Take 1 strip at a time (keep the others covered to prevent their drying out). Holding the strip horizontally, brush it with the melted shortening. Put a teaspoonful of the filling in the lower-left corner, then fold the corner over to make a triangle along the strip: Fold the upper-left corner over to close the triangle. Continue to fold the phyllo over and over until the strip has become a small (about 3-inch) triangle of pastry. Brush the top with butter. Continue to prepare all of the pittas like this. Place the triangles on a lightly buttered baking sheet and bake in a preheated 300° oven for 15 to 20 minutes. Serve hot. Serves 6 to 8 people as a main course, or serves about 20 as appetizers.

CHOPPED MEAT PIE ✠ PITTA ME KIMA

2 pounds chopped meat
½ cup butter
2 onions, chopped
1¼ pounds ripe tomatoes,
    peeled and strained, or 1
    tablespoon tomato paste
    diluted with 1 cup water
1 piece of stick cinnamon

1 tablespoon chopped parsley
salt and pepper to taste
2 slices toast
2 cups milk
1 cup grated Parmesan cheese
5 eggs, lightly beaten
¾ pound phyllo*

Brown the meat, half the butter, and the onions in a large pot, stirring with a wooden spoon to break up the meat. Add the tomatoes (or diluted tomato paste), cinnamon, parsley, salt, and pepper. Simmer until all the liquid is absorbed (about 30 minutes.) In the meantime, soak the toast in the milk, then mash it with a fork. Remove the cinnamon stick and add the milk-toast mixture to the meat; remove from the heat. Add the cheese and eggs, and mix well.

Melt the remaining butter; butter a pan about 2 inches smaller than the phyllo (see index: About Phyllo). Put 7 to 8 phyllo sheets, buttering each before adding it, into the pan, letting the phyllo extend on all sides. Pour in the meat mixture and spread it evenly. Fold the overlapping phyllo back onto the meat. Butter these well. Carefully cut the remaining sheets of phyllo to fit the top of the pan. Brush each with butter and lay it on the filling to make the top of the pitta. Pour on any remaining butter and sprinkle the top very lightly with a little water (to keep the phyllo from rising too high). Bake in a preheated 350° oven for 30 to 40 minutes. Cool about 30 minutes and cut into squares to serve. Serves 6 to 8.

NOTE: It is easier to cut this if you score it lightly before baking.

COUNTRY-STYLE MEAT PIE   ✠   KREATOPITTA HORIATIKI

1 medium onion
2 cloves garlic, chopped
2 tablespoons chopped parsley
½ teaspoon chopped fresh mint
2 hard-cooked eggs
3 pounds (approximately) leg
   of lamb
1 cup butter

1 tablespoon tomato paste
   diluted with 1 cup water
salt and pepper to taste
¼–½ pound grated kefalotiri*
   cheese
2 eggs lightly beaten
¾ pound (approximately)
   phyllo*

Chop the onion and rinse it in a strainer under running water; drain. Mix the garlic with the parsley and the mint. Slice the eggs thinly. Cut the lamb from the bone, then cut it into very small pieces (a little coarser than chopped meat). Lightly brown the lamb with the onions in one-third of the butter. Add the tomato paste, salt, pepper, garlic, parsley, and mint, and mix well. Simmer for about 30 minutes. Remove from the heat. Add the cheese and the lightly beaten eggs and mix again. Melt the remaining butter.

Butter a baking pan about 2″ smaller than the phyllo sheets (see index: About Phyllo). Use 9 phyllo sheets for the bottom layer of the pitta—do not trim them—and butter each sheet before laying it in the pan. Pour the meat mixture over the phyllo, spreading it evenly. Place the sliced eggs on top of the meat. Fold the overhanging edges of the phyllo sheets onto the filling. Butter them well. Add the remaining sheets to form the top crust, again buttering each sheet before using it. Score the top lightly with a sharp, pointed knife into serving-size pieces. Pour on any remaining butter. Bake in a preheated 300° oven about 1 hour. Let cool for 30 minutes; cut through, and serve. Serves 8 to 10.

INDIVIDUAL MEAT PIES   ✠   KREATOPITTES

2 cups chopped cooked leftover
   meat (chicken, beef, or lamb)
2 medium onions, chopped
1 cup Thick Béchamel Sauce
   (see index)
½ cup grated Parmesan cheese

salt and pepper to taste
2 eggs, lightly beaten
1¼–1½ pounds phyllo*
½ cup (approximately) melted
   butter for brushing the
   phyllo

Mix meat with the next 5 ingredients. Take one sheet of phyllo (see index: About Phyllo) at a time, brush with melted butter, and fold in half. Put 1 to 2 tablespoonfuls of the meat mixture in the center. Fold over 2 sides to enclose the meat, then fold over the top and bottom edges, and press to seal. Brush the surface with butter. Turn upside on a baking sheet so the edges are on the under side. Brush with butter. Continue in this manner until all the pittes are made. Bake in a preheated 300° oven 20 to 30 minutes and serve hot. Serves 8 to 10.

PHYLLO CHOPPED MEAT ROLL ✠ ROLLO ME KIMA TILIGMENO SE PHYLLO BAKLAVA

1½ pounds chopped veal
1 cup bread
2 eggs
2 tablespoons oil
2 tablespoons chopped onion

½ teaspoon oregano
salt and pepper to taste
4–5 sheets phyllo*
¼ cup melted butter

Soak the bread in water and squeeze out the excess. Mix it together with all the ingredients except the phyllo and butter; knead for a few minutes. Brush the butter on the phyllo sheets (see index: About Phyllo) and place the sheets on top of each other. Put the chopped meat along one edge. Fold the two sides over about 1" to seal the meat in. Roll from the meat edge to completely enclose the meat. Brush butter on the top of the phyllo. Place in a buttered pan. Bake in a preheated 350° oven for about 1 hour. Cool slightly and cut into 6 slices. Serves 6.

CHICKEN PIE 1 ✠ KOTOPITTA 1

1 6-pound stewing chicken
water as needed
1 pound onions, thinly sliced
½ cup milk
1 cup grated Parmesan cheese
5 eggs

salt and pepper to taste
½ teaspoon nutmeg
¾ pound phyllo*
melted butter for brushing the
   phyllo

Clean the chicken and put into a pot with enough water to cover. Bring to a boil; remove the froth as it rises. Add the onions and cook until the chicken is tender (1½ to 2 hours). Remove the chicken from the broth and continue to cook the onions until they become pulpy. When the chicken is cool, remove the skin and the bones, and cut the meat into thin strips. Pass the stock through a strainer to purée the onions and return to the pot. Add the chicken slices and the milk, and cook for about 5 minutes. Remove from the heat. Add the cheese and stir well. Beat the eggs lightly with a little salt and pepper and the nutmeg and add to the pot.

Butter a pan which is smaller than the phyllo sheets (see index: About Phyllo). Line the bottom of the pan with 8 sheets of phyllo, buttering each sheet before you add it; do not trim the phyllo. Pour in the filling and fold the overhanging edge of the phyllo up toward the center, to cover part of the filling; brush well with butter. Cover with the remaining phyllo, first brushing each sheet with butter, and trim the edges wih a sharp knife. Score through the top layers. Pour any remaining butter over the pie, and sprinkle with a little water. Bake in a preheated 350° oven for 1 hour. Cool, cut into portions, and serve. Serves 8.

CHICKEN PIE 2   ✠   KOTOPITTA 2

1 6-pound stewing chicken	3–4 eggs, lightly beaten
3 onions, thinly sliced	2 slices ham, chopped
water as needed	salt and pepper to taste
1½ cups milk	½ teaspoon nutmeg
1 cup butter	¾ pound phyllo*
5 tablespoons flour	phyllo
1 cup grated Parmesan cheese	melted butter for brushing

Clean the chicken and put it into a pot with enough water to cover. Bring to a boil, skimming off the froth as it rises. Add the onions; cook about 1½ hours. Remove the chicken from the stock and let it cool. Cut the meat in thin strips. Strain the stock and the onions; reserve 1 cup. Replace on the heat. Add the milk and keep the stock hot. Melt 5 tablespoons of butter. Add the flour and stir to mix well. Add the hot stock and continue to mix until it thickens (like béchamel sauce), then remove it from the heat. Add the cheese and the eggs and mix well. Add the chicken, ham, salt, pepper, and nutmeg and mix thoroughly.

Butter a pan slightly smaller than the phyllo sheets (see index: About Phyllo). Line the bottom with 9 sheets of phyllo (do not trim them), brushing each first with melted butter. Pour on the filling, spreading it evenly. Fold over the extending sides of the phyllo to partially cover the filling; brush with melted butter. Cover with the remaining phyllo, again brushing each sheet first with butter. Now trim the phyllo to fit the pan. Pour the remaining butter over the pie. Score through the top layers and sprinkle lightly with water. Bake in a preheated 350° oven for 1 hour. Serves 8.

BOUREKIA

BOUREKIA WITH CHOPPED MEAT ✠ BOUREKIA ME KIMA

1½ pounds chopped meat
1 cup butter
1 onion, chopped
1 tablespoon tomato paste
    diluted with 1 cup water

1 tablespoon parsley
salt and pepper to taste
1 piece stick cinnamon
½ cup grated Parmesan cheese
1¼ pounds phyllo*

Put the meat, 4 tablespoons of butter, and the onion into a pot, brown thoroughly, mixing with a wooden spoon to crumble the meat. Add the diluted tomato paste, parsley, salt, pepper, and cinnamon. Simmer until the liquid is absorbed. Remove from the heat and add the cheese. Discard the cinnamon stick. Cut the phyllo sheets (see index: About Phyllo) in half across the width. Take one sheet at a time (keep the others covered so they do not dry out), brush with melted butter, put a little of the filling on one edge. Fold over two sides to enclose the filling; roll up like a cigar. Brush on all sides with melted butter. Place in a pan. Continue until all the filling is used. Bake in a preheated 350° oven for about 15 minutes. Serves 6.

NOTE: These bourekia may be fried in butter or oil instead of being baked.

BOUREKIA WITH BRAINS ✠ BOUREKIA ME MIALA

1 cup chopped boiled lamb's
    brains (see index)
½ cup grated Parmesan cheese
¾ pounds phyllo*
1 cup butter, melted

THE BÉCHAMEL SAUCE

1 cup scalded milk
2 tablespoons butter
3 tablespoons flour
salt and pepper to taste
2 egg yolks, well beaten

Prepare the béchamel, (see index for instructions), using the ingredients indicated above. Prepare the brains, using 1 pair, and chop them. Mix with the béchamel and the cheese. Cut the phyllo (see index: About Phyllo) in half across the width. Take one sheet at a time (keep the others covered), brush it with butter. Place a little of the filling along one edge. Fold over the sides to enclose the filling, and roll it into a cigar-shaped roll. Continue in this manner until all the filling is used. Brush all the rolls with butter. Place in a buttered pan and bake in a preheated 350° oven for about 15 minutes, or until a light brown color. Serve hot. Serves 6 to 10.

NOTE: These can also be fried in butter or oil, if you prefer.

BOUREKIA WITH FRANKFURTERS ✠ BOUREKIA ME LOUKANIKA FRANKFOURTES

¾ pound phyllo*
½ cup (approximately) melted
   butter for brushing the phyllo

THE BÉCHAMEL SAUCE
1 tablespoon butter
4 tablespoons flour
1 cup milk, scalded
1 egg yolk, well beaten
salt and pepper to taste
THE FILLING
4 frankfurters
½ cup grated Parmesan cheese

Prepare the béchamel (see index for method), using the ingredients indicated above. Remove the skin from the frankfurters and cut them into small pieces. Add the franks and the cheese to the béchamel, and mix well.

Cut the phyllo (see index: About Phyllo) into 3 lengthwise strips. Take 1 strip at a time, brush it with butter, and place 1 teaspoonful of the filling at one end. Fold it over and over to make a triangle. Brush the triangles with butter, place in a pan, and bake in a preheated 350° oven for about 20 minutes. Serve hot. Makes about 30 pieces.

BOUREKIA WITH HAM AND SALAMI ✠ BOUREKIA ME ZAMPON* KE SALAMI

1 pound phyllo*
1 cup (approximately) butter,
   melted

THE BÉCHAMEL SAUCE
2 tablespoons butter
3 tablespoons flour
1 cup milk
2 egg yolks, well beaten
3 tablespoons grated Parmesan
   cheese
salt and pepper to taste
THE FILLING
½ cup chopped ham
½ cup chopped salami

Prepare the béchamel (see index for method) using the ingredients indicated above. Mix the ham and the salami into the béchamel. Cut the phyllo (see index: About Phyllo) in half, lengthwise. Take 1 piece at a time, brush it with butter, place a teaspoonful of the filling on the phyllo and fold into triangles. Bake in a buttered pan in a preheated 350° oven for 15 minutes. Makes about 40 pieces.

MEATS

BOILED LAMB ✠ ARNI VRASTO

3 pounds shoulder of lamb
coarse salt
2–3 carrots
2–3 medium onions
4–5 medium potatoes
2–3 stalks of celery
4 tablespoons raw rice
2–3 eggs

1 lemon, juice only
½ cup oil (optional)
⅓ cup vinegar (optional)
1 hard-cooked egg, chopped
  (optional)
salt and pepper (optional)
capers (optional)
parsley (optional)

Wash the lamb and place it in a large pot, add enough water to cover. Add some coarse salt. Bring to a boil, removing the froth as it forms. Add the carrots, onions, potatoes, and celery, and continue to cook until tender (about 20 to 30 minutes). Remove the meat and the vegetables from the broth, arrange on a platter, and set aside to keep warm. Strain the broth. Add water as needed to make enough soup for 6 people. Bring this stock to a boil and add the rice, stirring for the first few minutes to prevent the rice from sticking. Half-cover the pot, and simmer 10 to 15 minutes. Remove from the heat. Beat the eggs in a bowl very well. Beat in the lemon juice. Slowly add some of the hot broth to this mixture, beating constantly, then pour it slowly into the broth, stirring all the while. Serve the hot soup, followed by the meat and the vegetables. Serves 6.

NOTE 1: If you are not planning to serve soup, reserve the broth to use at another time. In this case, do *not* add more water.

NOTE 2: You may serve the meat with an oil-and-vinegar dressing. To make it, beat together the oil and vinegar. Add salt and pepper and the egg. Add some capers and chopped parsley. Pour the dressing over the meat.

LAMB FRICASSEE   ✠   ARNI FRICASE

4–5 pounds leg of lamb	½ cup butter
coarse salt	3 tablespoons flour
1–2 large carrots	salt and pepper to taste
1 stalk celery	2 egg yolks
2–3 onions, peeled	water as needed
2–3 dill stalks	1–2 lemons, juice only

Cut the meat into 1½- or 2-inch cubes; wash well. Place in a pot with 1 cup water and a little coarse salt. Bring to a boil, drain, and discard the water. Return meat to the pot, add 2 cups of fresh hot water, and cook for another 45 minutes or 1 hour. In the meantime, scrape the carrots, clean the celery and the dill. Wash all the vegetables and chop into small pieces.

Add the vegetables and 3 more cups of water to the meat. Cover, and cook until the liquid is reduced to 3 cups (about 30 to 45 minutes longer). Remove from the heat. Strain the liquid and reserve it, keeping it hot. Melt the butter in another pot; add the flour, stirring constantly. Slowly add the hot broth; stir until the sauce thickens. Add a little salt and pepper. Remove from the heat.

Beat the egg yolks in a bowl with 1 tablespoon water. Beat in the lemon juice. Slowly add the sauce to the egg yolks, beating constantly. Pour the sauce into the pot with the meat. Shake the pot gently over low heat until the sauce is well distributed. Serve immediately. Serves 6.

LAMB WITH PEAS   ✠   ARNI ME ARAKA

3 pounds lamb	1 tablespoon chopped dill
½ pound butter or margarine	1 tablespoon chopped parsley
4 scallions, chopped	salt and pepper to taste
1½ pounds ripe tomatoes,	4 pounds peas, shelled and
peeled and strained, or 1	washed
tablespoon tomato paste	water as needed
diluted with 2 cups water	

Cut the meat into 1½- to 2-inch cubes. Wash and drain. Brown the butter in a pot. Add the meat and brown well. Add the scallions, and cook until soft but not dark. Add the tomatoes (or the diluted tomato paste), the dill, parsley, salt, and pepper. Simmer for about 20 minutes. Add the peas and an additional 1 cup of water. Cover, and simmer until all the liquid has been absorbed and only the butter remains as a sauce (about 30 to 45 minutes). Serves 6.

LAMB WITH ARTICHOKES IN AVGOLEMONO SAUCE

✠

ARNI ME ANGINARES AVGOLEMONO

3 pounds boned shoulder of
   lamb
6–8 small artichokes
2 lemons
5 tablespoons butter

2 scallions, chopped
salt and pepper to taste
2 eggs
water as needed

Cut the meat into 1½-inch cubes. Clean the artichokes, cut off the tips of the leaves. Rub the cut parts with lemon juice. Soak in salted water with the juice of half a lemon.

Brown the butter in a large pot. Add the meat and brown it well. Add the scallions and sauté until soft but not brown. Add 2 cups water, salt, and pepper, and cook over medium heat for about 45 minutes. Rinse the artichokes and add them to the meat. Add the juice of half a lemon, and salt and pepper, and cook slowly until the artichokes are tender (30 to 45 minutes). Remove from the heat.

Beat the eggs in a bowl; add the juice of the second lemon, and beat it in well. Add about ¾ cup of the broth, slowly, beating constantly. Pour the sauce over the meat and artichokes, and shake the pot gently over low heat until the sauce thickens. Serve hot. Serves 6.

LAMB WITH FRESH GREEN BEANS

✠

ARNI ME FASOLAKIA FRESKA

3 pounds boned shoulder of
   lamb
3 pounds green beans
¾ cup butter
3 medium onions, chopped

1 pound ripe tomatoes, peeled
   and strained, or 1 tablespoon
   tomato paste diluted with 1
   cup water
2 tablespoons chopped parsley
salt and pepper to taste

Cut the meat into 1½- to 2-inch cubes. Clean the beans and cut them lengthwise. Brown the butter in a large pot. Add the meat and brown well. Add the onions and cook until soft. Add the tomatoes (or diluted tomato paste). Bring to a boil and cook for 3 to 5 minutes, then add the beans, parsley, salt, and pepper. If needed, add ½ cup water. Cook slowly until all the liquid has been absorbed and only the butter remains as a sauce. Serves 6.

LAMB WITH SQUASH AND TOMATOES ✠ ARNI ME KOLOKITHAKIA KE DOMATES

3 pounds breast of lamb
salt and pepper to taste
¾ cup butter
2 medium onions, chopped

1 pound ripe tomatoes, peeled
   and strained, or 1 tablespoon
   tomato paste diluted with 1
   cup water
3 pounds small zucchini squash
water as needed

Cut the meat into 1½- to 2-inch pieces; wash and drain. Season with salt and pepper. Melt half the butter in a large pot; add the meat and brown it. Add the onions and brown them, then add the tomatoes (or diluted tomato paste), and ½ cup water. Cook for 45 minutes to 1 hour.

Meanwhile, clean the squash, and cut each into 2 or 3 pieces. Remove the meat from the heat. Put the remaining butter in a frying pan. Lightly salt and pepper the squash and fry, a few pieces at a time, until they are barely tender (they should be undercooked). Add to the meat and pour in the remaining butter. Place over low heat and cook until all the liquid has been absorbed and only the butter remains as a sauce (about 30 minutes). Serves 6.

NOTE: If you prefer, do not fry the zucchini, but use all the butter in the beginning, and after cooking the meat for 30 minutes, add the remaining ingredients.

POTTED LAMB WITH POTATOES ✠ ARNI TIS KATSAROLAS ME PATATES

3 pounds boned leg of lamb
4 tablespoons butter
2 tablespoons lemon juice
1½ cups (or more) hot water

3 pounds tiny potatoes
butter for frying
salt and pepper to taste

Wash the lamb, wipe dry, and sprinkle with salt and pepper. Put 4 tablespoons butter in a pot, add the lamb; brown on all sides. Add the lemon juice and allow this to boil. Add 1 cup water, and simmer (add more water as needed) 45 minutes to 1 hour or until the meat is tender and 1 cup liquid remains. Remove from the heat. Cool the meat and slice it.

Meanwhile clean the potatoes—small round ones or cut rounds with a melon baller from large ones. Put the potatoes into a frying pan and brown in butter on all sides, then add them to the pot containing the sauce from the meat. Add salt and pepper and ½ cup water; simmer until all the liquid is absorbed and only the butter remains. Before serving, carefully place the meat on the potatoes to heat. Serve hot. Serves 6.

LAMB WITH ASSORTED VEGETABLES ✠ ARNI ME THIAFORA HORTA

3 pounds lamb
salt and pepper to taste
1 pound small potatoes
4–5 medium carrots
1 pound small zucchini squash

4–5 scallions
1 pound peas, shelled
1 cup vegetable oil or butter
2 tablespoons chopped parsley
3–4 small round ripe tomatoes

Cut the lamb into 6 to 8 portions. Wash, wipe dry, and season. Clean the potatoes and cut each into 2 or 3 pieces. Scrape the carrots and cut into 2-or-3-inch lengths. Clean the squash and cut these into round slices. Clean and chop the scallions. Mix the vegetables together and season lightly. (Reserve the tomatoes until the end.)

Brown the meat in a pan, using half the butter. Add the vegetables and brown lightly. Put the meat and vegetables into a roasting pan, sprinkle with the parsley, pour in all the butter from the browning pan, and add to this the remaining butter. Tuck in the tomatoes. Bake in a preheated 250° oven 1½ to 2 hours. Serves 6.

LAMB AND POTATOES RAGOUT ✠ ARNI ME PATATES RAGU

3 pounds leg of lamb
salt and pepper to taste
3–4 tablespoons butter
1 medium onion, chopped
1 carrot, minced

1 tablespoon chopped parsley
1 pound ripe tomatoes, peeled
  and strained
3 pounds potatoes
water as needed

Wash and dry the meat; cut into 1½- to 2-inch chunks; lightly salt and pepper them. Brown the butter in a large pot. Add the meat and brown well on all sides. Remove and place in a deep dish. Add the onion to the pot with the butter and let it brown. Add the carrot and the parsley, and cook until they wilt. Add the tomatoes; bring to a boil. Add the meat and 1 cup of hot water. Partially cook over low heat for about 30 minutes. Meanwhile, peel the potatoes, cut each into 2 or 3 pieces. Add to the pot. Add a little salt and pepper, and cook until the potatoes are tender and most of the liquid has been absorbed (30 to 45 minutes). Serves 6.

**LAMB WITH SQUASH   ✠   ARNI ME KOLOKITHAKIA
IN AVGOLEMONO SAUCE   AVGOLEMONO**

3 pounds breast of lamb   3 pounds small squash
¾ cup butter   2 eggs
salt and pepper to taste   2 lemons, juice only
6 scallions, white part only,   water as needed
   chopped

Cut the meat into 1½- to 2-inch pieces. Wash, and put into a pot with the butter and ½ cup water. Bring to a boil. Add the salt, pepper, and the scallions. As soon as the water has been absorbed and the meat begins to sizzle, add another cup water; cook 30 to 45 minutes longer.

Meanwhile, clean the squash, scrape the skin, and cut each into 2 or 3 pieces. Add to the meat. Again let it simmer until all the liquid has been absorbed and only the butter remains as a sauce.

Beat the eggs in a bowl with 2 tablespoons water. Add the lemon juice, and beat well. Slowly add the butter sauce from the pot, beating constantly, until blended. Pour the sauce over the meat. Shake the pot gently over very low heat until the sauce is evenly distributed and begins to thicken. Serve hot. Serves 6.

TAS KEBAB   ✠   TAS KEBAB

3 pounds lamb or veal   1 tablespoon tomato paste
½ pound butter   diluted with 1 cup water, or
1½ pounds onions, peeled and   1¼ pounds ripe tomatoes,
   sliced   peeled and strained
2 tablespoons chopped parsley   salt and pepper to taste
½ cup white wine

Cut the meat into 1½- to 2-inch pieces. Wash, and put into a pot with the butter into a frying pan, brown it; add the meat, a few pieces at a time, and brown well. Place the browned pieces in a pot. Add the onions to the butter in which you browned the meat, and sauté lightly but do not brown. Pour the onions and butter over the meat. Place over low heat, and as soon as the meat begins to sizzle, add the wine and then the diluted tomato paste (or tomatoes), the parsley, salt, and pepper. Cover the pot; simmer for 1½ hours. Add a little water only if necessary. This recipe calls for the onions to be cooked almost to the melting point so the meat remains in a thick sauce. Serves 6. Serve with rice, potatoes, or squash croquettes (see index).

LAMB AND ESCAROLE   ✠   ARNI ME ANTITHIA
AVGOLEMONO   AVGOLEMONO

4 pounds escarole   salt and pepper to taste
3 pounds breast, shoulder, or   2 lemons, juice only
   neck of lamb   2 eggs
2 medium onions, chopped   1 tablespoon cornstarch
¾–1 cup butter   water as needed

Wash and pick over the escarole. Cut each leaf in half. Add the escarole to a large pot of lightly salted boiling water and cook for a few minutes, until it wilts. Drain and set aside. Cut the meat into 1½- to 2-inch cubes. Put the meat, onions, and butter into a large pot to brown. When the food begins to stick to the pot, add ½ cup water, salt, and pepper. Bring to a boil. Add the escarole; simmer until most of the liquid is absorbed.

Beat the eggs in a bowl and add the lemon juice, beating it in well. Add the cornstarch diluted with 2 tablespoons water. Beat again. Slowly add some of the hot liquid from the pot to this, stirring constantly. Pour the sauce back into the pot and shake the pot gently until the sauce thickens. Serves 6.

LAMB FRICASSEE   ✠   ARNI FRICASE ME KREMMITHAKIA
WITH ONIONS AND LETTUCE   KE MAROULIA

4–5 pounds shoulder or back of   3 heads lettuce
     lamb   2–3 tablespoons chopped dill
¾ cup butter   salt and pepper to taste
10 scallions   2 egg yolks
water as needed   2 lemons, juice only
coarse salt

Cut the lamb into serving-size strips. Place in a pot with the butter. Clean the scallions; chop the white part into small pieces and the greens into larger ones (about 1½- to 2-inches long); add to the meat. Add ½ cup water and a little coarse salt; cook over medium heat for about 1 hour.

Clean the lettuce and cut into 2-inch pieces.

As soon as the meat has absorbed the water it will begin to brown in the butter but do not let the scallions brown. Add the dill, lettuce, salt, and pepper. Cover the pot and simmer over low heat for about 15 minutes. If it is needed, add a little water toward the end of the cooking time (not in the beginning, because then the lettuce will exude water).

Beat the egg yolks with 2 tablespoons of water, add the juice from the lemons, and beat it in well. Add a little of the liquid from the pot, beating constantly. Pour this sauce back into the pot and shake the pot gently to mix the sauce with the food. Serve immediately. Serves 6.

RAGOUT OF LAMB ✠ ARNI ME FRESKES
WITH FRESH TOMATOES DOMATES

3 pounds shoulder of lamb
salt and pepper to taste
flour
¾ cup butter or margarine
½ cup chopped onion

2 teaspoons chopped garlic
½ cup white wine
4 pounds ripe tomatoes, peeled
water as needed
2 teaspoons sugar

Cut the meat into 6 to 8 pieces; wash, and drain. Salt and pepper it and dust very lightly with flour. Place half the butter in a frying pan. Brown it, then add the meat. When that is well browned, put it into a large pot; add the onions to the butter in the pan and sauté them. Add the garlic; cook until it softens but does not brown. Pour the onions, garlic, and butter over the meat, and add the remaining butter and put the pot over medium heat. When the butter browns, add the wine, a little at a time (to form a vapor), and half the tomatoes passed through a strainer. Add ½ cup hot water. Cover the pot. Simmer 1½ hours.

Slice the remaining tomatoes and remove their seeds. Salt and pepper them and sprinkle with 2 teaspoons sugar; set aside to drain. Remove the pot with the meat from the heat. Put the meat on a platter. Arrange the tomatoes on the bottom of the pot and place the meat on top of them. Return to low heat and cook about a half hour. The meat should be in a thick sauce. Serve with pilaf (see index). Place the meat in the center of the platter and surround with the rice. Put the tomatoes on the rice and pour the sauce over the top. The sauce need not be strained as the onions and garlic will have been reduced to a pulp. Serves 6.

LAMB AND PEAS YIOVETSI ✠ ARNI ME ARAKA GIOUVETSI [YIOVETSI]

3 pounds fatty rump or leg of
  lamb
salt and pepper to taste
1–1½ pounds tomatoes, peeled
  and strained

½ cup butter
4½ pounds peas
1 tablespoon chopped dill

Wash and dry the meat. Add salt and pepper, and place in a casserole. Add one-third of the tomatoes and all the butter, and cook in a preheated 325° oven until half done (about 1 hour). Meanwhile, shell, wash, and drain the peas. Add the rest of the tomatoes and 1 to 2 cups of water to the meat. When this begins to simmer, add the peas and the dill. Add a little salt and pepper and cook slowly until the peas are tender (about 1 hour). Serves 6.

ROAST LAMB OREGANO ✠ ARNI LATHORIGAN STO FOURNO

3 pounds breast of lamb
salt and pepper to taste
1 tablespoon oregano

1 cup oil
1–2 lemons, juice only
1 cup (or more) water

Wash the meat, and sprinkle lightly with salt and pepper, and oregano. Put into a roast pan and pour the oil and lemon juice over it. Roast in a preheated 350° oven for about 20 minutes, then add the water. Continue cooking, basting it occasionally with pan drippings, for about 1 hour longer. Add more water if necessary. Serves 6.

POTTED LAMB OREGANO ✠ ARNI LATHORIGANI STIN KATSAROLA

3 pounds breast of lamb, boned
salt and pepper to taste
1 cup oil

2 lemons, juice only
½ cup water
1 tablespoon oregano

Wash the meat and cut into 2- or 3-inch cubes. Sprinkle with salt and pepper, and place in a large pot. Pour in the oil and lemon juice—as much juice as desired. Begin to cook over medium heat. When the meat begins to brown on all sides, add the water and oregano. Cover the pot; let simmer. Add more water as needed. Cook until the meat is tender and only the oil remains (about 1½ hours). Serves 8.

BAKED LAMB AND SPAGHETTI ✠ ARNI ME SPAGETO STO FOURNO

3 pounds leg of lamb
salt and pepper to taste
¼–½ pound butter
1½ pounds ripe tomatoes,
   peeled and strained
   (optional)

4–5 cups water
1½ pounds spaghetti
¼–½ pound kefalotiri* cheese
   grated

Wash the meat and season lightly with salt and pepper. Place in a pan. Dot with the butter and add one-third of the tomatoes. Cook in a preheated 325° oven until done (1¼ to 1½ hours). Remove the meat from the pan; add the rest of the tomatoes and the water. Bring it to a boil. Add the spaghetti, stir for the first few minutes. Cook until the spaghetti is tender (about 9 minutes). Slice the meat. Serve with the spaghetti and pass the cheese. Serves 6.

NOTE: You may omit the tomatoes, if you prefer.

LAMB OR VEAL WITH LASAGNA ✠ ARNI E MOSXHARI ME LAZANIA

Prepare like Baked Lamb and Spaghetti (above), substituting veal for the lamb, and lasagna for the spaghetti.

COUNTRY-STYLE LAMB ✠ ARNI EXOHIKO

3 pounds leg of baby lamb
salt and pepper to taste
1 tablespoon oregano
1 lemon, juice only

¾ cup oil
½ pound kefalotiri* cheese
12 large sheets cooking paper

Have the butcher cut the meat into 6 equal slices. Lightly salt and pepper them and sprinkle with oregano. Put into a shallow pan. Pour the lemon juice over the meat and pour on half the oil; marinate for half an hour. Cut the cheese into 6 slices. Take 6 sheets of the paper, one at a time, and brush each with oil. At one end of each sheet of paper place a slice of cheese, and top with a slice of meat. Fold the paper up over the meat, partially covering it. Roll up the paper, from the meat end, into a cigar-shaped roll; roll the other 6 sheets, unoiled, over these. Place in an oiled pan, with the edge of each roll down so it does not unroll during the cooking. Cook in a preheated 250° oven about 2 hours. Serve with green beans and fried potatoes. Serves 6.

COUNTRY-STYLE LAMB TRIANGLES ✠ ARNI YIA MEZE

3 pounds leg of lamb
salt and pepper to taste
2 tablespoons oregano
½ cup fine-quality oil
½ cup lemon juice

½ cup water
½ pound kefalotiri* cheese
1 pound phyllo* pastry
oil or melted butter for brushing
  the pastry

Have the butcher remove the bones and sinews from the meat and cut it into ½- to ¾-inch cubes. Wash and drain. Add salt and pepper. Place in a small pan with the oregano. Add the oil, lemon juice, and water, and cook in a preheated 325° oven until the liquid has been absorbed (about 45 minutes to 1 hour). Remove from the oven, cool partially. Cut the cheese into small cubes and add to the meat. Mix well.

Cut the phyllo into strips about 2½-inches wide and stack them on top of each other so they do not dry out. Take one strip at a time, brush it with oil (or melted butter). Place a little of the meat in the lower corner and fold it over and over into a triangle (see index: About Phyllo) that will completely enclose the meat. Brush the surface with oil and place it, folded edge down, so it does not open during the baking, on an oiled baking sheet or pan. Bake in a pre-heated 375° oven for 15 minutes. Serve hot. Makes about 36 pieces.

LAMB ON A SPIT ✠ ARNI TIS SOUVLAS

Have the butcher prepare the whole lamb by removing the intestines, entrails, and larynx, leaving only the kidneys, and cutting two holes in the back, level with the kidneys. Salt the lamb inside and out. Secure it on the spit, starting from the tail end and working toward the head; tie the back of the lamb to the spit to keep the meat taut. Sew up the cavity with a thick needle. Bring the rear and front legs up, and tie them to the spit. Rub the entire surface of the lamb with the lemon juice. It is best to use a spit that can be adjusted in height. Start the lamb up high and gradually lower it toward the heat as the cooking progresses. During the cooking, baste the meat with oil or butter and, occasionally, with lemon juice. Keep the heat stronger toward the rear portion of the lamb, as this takes longer to cook. Toward the end of the cooking you may add some oregano to the basting fluids. The lamb is done when the meat separates easily from the bone.

ROAST LAMB ✠ ARNI STO FOURNO

3 pounds (or more) leg of lamb	melted butter as needed
5–8 cloves of garlic	1 cup water
salt and pepper to taste	2 tablespoons butter
1 lemon, juice only	1–2 tablespoons flour

Wash and dry the leg of lamb. Make a few cuts in the surface and stuff a clove of garlic into each cut. Salt and pepper the entire surface of the lamb and pour the lemon juice on it; brush with butter (use 4 to 6 tablespoons for every 3 pounds of lamb); sprinkle with a little flour. Roast in a preheated 350° oven for 1½ to 3 hours (depending on the size of the roast), until it is well browned on all sides. Remove the meat, cool, slice, and place in a warming dish.

Add the hot water to the pan drippings; stir well to break up and absorb all the pieces. Melt the 2 tablespoons butter in a small pot and blend in the flour; stir constantly until it browns lightly. Strain the drippings from the pan and add them to the pot, stirring all the while. Serve the meat hot and pass the gravy. Serves 6 or more.

ROAST STUFFED LAMB   ✠   ARNI YEMISTO STO FOURNO

NOTE: In Greece, the lambs are very small when they are slaughtered. Most of the following recipes are made with baby lambs which were still nursing and not yet eating grass. If older lambs are used, adjust the cooking time.

1 spring lamb, with the intestines	2 tablespoons chopped parsley
3 tablespoons butter	1 tablespoon chopped dill
½ cup chopped scallions (white part only)	1 cup raw rice
	1 cup grated Parmesan cheese
2 cups broth	2 lemons
salt and pepper to taste	2 tablespoons butter, melted
	1–3 tablespoons flour

Have the butcher cut the feet from the lamb. Bring to the boil a large pot of water. Wash the intestines and put them into the boiling water for about 5 minutes (this makes them easier to cut). Remove them with a slotted spoon and reserve 2 cups of the broth. Chop the intestines into small pieces. Brown the butter in another pot; add the scallions and sauté until light golden. Add the chopped intestines and let them brown. Add the 2 cups broth, salt, pepper, parsley, and dill. Cook for 5 minutes. Add the rice and cook until the liquid is absorbed (about 8 minutes). The rice will be only partially cooked at this point. Remove from the heat and stir in the cheese.

Rinse out the lamb, dry it well, salt and pepper the cavity. Fill with the stuffing and sew up the opening well. Rub the outside with lemon, salt, and pepper. Pour the butter over it and sprinkle lightly with flour. Place in a roasting pan and roast in a preheated 350° oven for 2 to 2½ hours, basting occasionally. Remove from the oven, cool slightly; remove the stuffing to the center of a platter. Slice the meat and arrange around the stuffing. Serves 4 to 6.

STUFFED LEG OF LAMB   ✠   BOUTI ARNISIO YEMISTO

3 pounds leg of lamb	1 cup butter
salt and pepper to taste	1 cup white wine
2 tablespoons chopped parsley	2 cups (or more) hot water
4 slices zampon*	3⅔ pounds small, round
¼ pound kefalotiri* cheese	potatoes

Have the butcher bone and flatten the lamb. Wash and dry the meat. Sprinkle with salt, pepper, and the parsley. Put the slices of ham on top of the lamb. Cut the cheese into thin slices and place these on the top of the ham. Carefully roll the lamb into a compact roll and tie. Put the roll into a pan, add the butter, and place in a preheated 300° oven. Cook until brown on all sides (about 30 minutes). Add the wine; baste the roll with the pan sauces. Add the water; cook an additional 30 minutes. Peel the potatoes, wash them, salt and pepper them, and place them in the pan. Lower the heat to about 225° and cook another 1 to 1¼ hours. Add more hot water if necessary during the cooking. Remove from the oven. Cool slightly to make the carving easier, and serve with a fresh green salad. Serves 6.

SHOULDER OF LAMB WITH RICE ✈ SPALA ARNIOU KOKKINISTI ME RIZI

3 pounds shoulder of lamb, boned
salt and pepper to taste
1 pound cherry tomatoes
¾ cup butter
2 medium onions, grated
2 medium carrots, grated
2 cloves garlic, grated

½ cup white wine
1 pound ripe tomatoes, peeled and strained
2 teaspoons chopped parsley
2 cups raw rice
2 teaspoons sugar
water as needed

Wash, dry, and season the lamb. Roll it up and tie with a string. Wash the tomatoes and remove the stems. Put half the butter into a wide pot and brown it, then add the meat and brown it well on all sides. Add the grated onions, carrots, and garlic. Slowly add the wine, then the strained tomatoes, parsley, and 1 cup of water. Cook over low heat for about 1½ hours or until the sauce thickens.

Meanwhile set a large pot of salted water to boil. Add the rice when the water boils, stirring for the first few minutes so the rice does not stick. Cook for 10 minutes; remove from the heat. Pour in 3 cups cold water, then drain it. Brown the rest of the butter and pour over the rice; mix it through. Place in a roast pan. Sprinkle the cherry tomatoes with the sugar and tuck them into the rice. Add the sauce from the pot to the rice and add a cup of hot water. Place in a preheated 350° oven for 15 minutes or until all the liquid has been absorbed.

Remove the string and cut the roast into slices. Remove the rice from the oven and lay the meat on top. Turn off the oven and return the pan with the rice and lamb to it for 10 minutes. Serve the meat on a platter with a tomato on each slice. Surround the meat with a ring of rice and tuck in a few sprigs of parsley. If the food is prepared in an ovenware dish, serve directly from the dish. Serves 6.

ROAST LAMB WITH RICE   ✠   ARNI STO FOURNO ME RIZI GIOUVETSI

3 pounds leg of lamb
salt and pepper to taste
5 tablespoons butter, melted
4 cups hot water

2 cups rice
2 eggs
1 lemon, juice only

Wash the meat and sprinkle lightly with salt and pepper. Place in a pan and pour the butter over it. Cook in a preheated 300° oven to brown on all sides (about 1½ hours). Add the water and the rice, and cook until the rice is tender (20 to 30 minutes). Remove from the oven and keep hot. Prepare an avgolemono: Beat the eggs well, beat in the lemon juice and pour over the rice. Mix well and serve. Serves 6 to 8.

NOTE: This may be served without the avgolemono sauce.

ROLLED STUFFED BREAST OF LAMB   ✠   ARNI STITHOS YEMISTO ROLO

1 lamb breast, boned
salt and pepper to taste
1 cup butter
½ pound chopped veal
½ cup chopped scallions
½ cup white wine

1 pound ripe tomatoes, peeled
    and strained
2 tablespoons chopped parsley
1 tablespoon chopped dill
½ cup toasted bread crumbs
½ cup grated Parmesan cheese
1 lemon

Wash and dry the lamb. Lightly salt and pepper it. Put one-third of the butter into a pot with the chopped veal and scallions, and brown lightly. Add salt, pepper, and the wine, a little at a time, so it steams as it is added. Add the tomatoes, parsley, and dill, and cook over high heat for about 15 minutes or until all the liquid has been absorbed. Remove from the heat and partially cool. Add the bread crumbs and the cheese. Spread the mixture on the lamb breast and roll it up carefully; sew or tie it together. Rub the surface of the lamb with lemon and a little more salt and pepper. Put the remaining butter into a pan, place the rolled meat into it, and roast in a preheated 400° oven for about 20 to 30 minutes, or until brown on all sides, then lower heat to 250° and roast it for about 2 hours longer, or until the meat is tender. Cool slightly to make the carving easier. Serve with beans and sautéed carrots, or other vegetables. Serves 6.

ROAST LAMB AND SQUASH ✠ ARNI ME KOLOKITHAKIA STO FOURNO

3 pounds leg of lamb
salt and pepper to taste
1½ pounds ripe tomatoes,
   peeled

¾ cup butter
3 pounds squash

Wash and dry the lamb; salt and pepper it. Cut the tomatoes into thin slices and spread them in the bottom of a roast pan. Place the meat on the tomatoes. Melt the butter and pour it over the meat. Roast in a preheated 350° oven for 20 to 30 minutes.

Clean and wash the squash and cut each into 2- to 3-inch pieces. Season these with salt and pepper and add them to the meat. Do not add water to this as the squash will exude water in the cooking. Cook until all the liquid is absorbed and only the butter remains as a sauce, and the meat and squash are tender (about 1 hour longer). Serves 6.

ROAST LAMB AND EGGPLANT ✠ ARNI ME MELITZANES STO FOURNO

Prepare like Roast Lamb and Squash, above, but use round, fat eggplants in place of the squash. Cut into round slices, soak them for 15 minutes in salted water, rinse and dry them, and then add to the meat. Complete the cooking as above.

POTTED LAMB OR VEAL ✠ ARNI E MOSXHARI TIS KATSAROLAS

4½ pounds lamb or veal for
   rolling
salt and pepper.

½ pound butter
1 lemon, juice only
water as needed

Roll and tie the meat; lightly salt and pepper it. Put the butter into a large pot and brown it well. Add the meat and brown on all sides. Add the lemon juice, and as soon as the butter darkens, add 2 cups hot water. Cover. Cook over low heat (for about 2½ hours), adding a little water from time to time, until the meat is tender and the liquid is absorbed and only the oil remains. Serves 6 to 8.

VEAL OR LAMB WITH QUINCE ✠ MOSXHARI E ARNI ME KITHONIA

3 pounds veal or lamb
¾ cup butter
1 medium onion, chopped
1 tablespoon tomato paste
 diluted with 1 cup water

3 pounds quince
salt and pepper to taste
water as needed
1 tablespoon sugar (optional)

Cut the meat into cubes and brown it in the butter with the onion. Add the diluted tomato paste, salt, pepper, and 1 to 2 cups water. Bring to a boil, reduce heat, and cook for 30 minutes.

Clean, peel, and seed the quince, and cut each into 6 pieces. Add these to the meat; cook until both are tender (test by piercing with a fork), all the liquid has been absorbed and only the butter remains as a sauce. Serves 6.

NOTE: You may add the sugar before the end of the cooking time, if you so wish.

VEAL OR LAMB WITH OKRA ✠ MOSXHARI E ARNI ME BAMIES

3 pounds (approximately) veal
 or leg of lamb
3 pounds okra
½ cup vinegar
salt and pepper to taste

¾ cup butter
1 medium onion, chopped
1½ pounds tomatoes, peeled
 and strained
water as needed

Put the okra into a bowl of water and wash it well. Cut off the stems carefully so as not to cut the okra. Place in a pan, sprinkle with vinegar, and salt lightly. Cut the meat into 1½- to 2-inch cubes, wash and drain it; salt and pepper lightly. Put into a pot with the butter to brown. While the meat is browning, add the onion and brown this too. Add the tomatoes and 2 cups of water and cook over medium heat for 20 minutes. Drain the okra and add to the meat in neat layers. Cover the pot and simmer until all the liquid has been absorbed and only the butter remains. Serves 6.

NOTE: If you wish, use half of the butter to brown the meat and use the other half to lightly fry the okra. In this case, add only 1 cup water to the meat as the okra will cook more rapidly and less water will be needed.

RAGOUT OF VEAL WITH POTATOES ✠ MOSXHARI ME PATATES RAGU

Prepare like Lamb and Potatoes Ragout (see index), but substitute veal for the lamb.

VEAL IN AVGOLEMONO SAUCE ✠ MOSXHARI BLANKET

3 pounds veal leg, boned and
   cut into 2-inch cubes
water as needed
½ pound onions, chopped
1 tablespoon chopped celery
1 tablespoon chopped parsley
2 bay leaves

4 tablespoons butter
4 tablespoons flour
3 egg yolks
2 lemons, juice only
salt to taste
a few peppercorns

Put the meat into a large pot and cover with water. Add the onions, celery, parsley, and bay leaves, and simmer until tender (about 1 hour). Strain. You should have about 3 cups of stock. Put the meat back into the pot. Melt the butter in another pot, add the flour; blend in well. To this, add the meat stock (add water to make a full 3 cups if necessary), and stir until thick. Remove from the heat.

Beat the egg yolks and add the lemon juice, beating it in well. Slowly add a little of the sauce to this, stirring constantly, and when it is well blended, stir the avgolemono mixture into the sauce. Pour the sauce over the meat, and shake the pot gently to distribute the sauce evenly. Serve hot. Serves 6.

VEAL AND SPINACH ✠ MOSXHARI ME SPANAKI
AVGOLEMONO AVGOLEMONO

3 pounds veal
salt and pepper to taste
¾ cup butter
2 medium onions, chopped

water as needed
3 pounds spinach
2 eggs
2 lemons, juice only

Cut the meat into cubes, wash, and drain well. Add salt and pepper. Brown the butter in a large pot, add the meat and brown lightly; add the onions and cook until they soften but do not brown. Add 1 to 2 cups water, cover the pot; simmer for 1 hour. While the meat is cooking, wash the spinach well, and tear each leaf into 2 or 3 pieces. Boil water in another pot, add salt; add the spinach, and cook just long enough to scald (5 minutes), then remove with a slotted spoon and drain.

Remove the meat from its pot; add the spinach and salt and pepper to the sauce; return the meat to it, and add a little more water if necessary. Cook for 45 minutes to 1 hour longer, or until all the liquid has been absorbed and only the butter remains. Remove from the heat.

Prepare the avgolemono sauce. Beat the eggs, and add the lemon juice, beating it in well. Add some of the hot liquid from the pot to the sauce, beating constantly. Pour back into the pot and shake it gently to distribute and thicken the sauce. Serve hot. Serves 6.

VEAL WITH PEAS ✠ MOSXHARI ME ARAKA

3 pounds peas
3 pounds (approximately) veal
salt and pepper to taste
2 medium onions

½ pound butter
1½ pounds ripe tomatoes
water as needed
2 tablespoons chopped parsley

Shell and wash the peas; set aside to drain. Cut the meat into 1½- to 2-inch cubes; wash and drain. Sprinkle with salt and pepper. Peel and chop the onions; wash in a strainer. Put the butter into a pot to brown, add the onions and the meat, and brown them well. Peel the tomatoes and pass them through a strainer, then add the tomato pulp and juice to the pot with 2 cups of water; cook for about 45 minutes. Add the peas, parsley, salt, and pepper and another ½ to 1 cup water. Cover the pot. Simmer until the peas are tender (about 30 to 45 minutes) and only the oil remains as a sauce. Serves 6.

VEAL WITH PURÉED VEGETABLES ✠ MOSXHARI ME POURE APO THIAFORA HORTA

3 pounds veal steak
¾ cup butter
1½ pounds tomatoes, peeled
  and strained, or 1 tablespoon tomato paste diluted
  with 2 cups of water

2¼ pounds potatoes, peeled
  and washed
1 pound carrots
¾ pound onions
salt and pepper to taste
water as needed

Tie the meat with a white thread, rinse it, and dry it well. Put the butter into a wide pot to brown, and add the meat; brown it carefully on all sides. Add the tomatoes (or the diluted tomato paste), salt, and pepper. Cover the pot; cook for ½ hour. Clean the onions, peel the carrots; cut them into small pieces and add to the meat. Add 1 to 2 cups water, as needed, and cook an additional 45 minutes. Add the potatoes and cook until they are tender. With a slotted spoon, remove the vegetables and put them through a food mill or whirl in the blender. If there is any liquid remaining, cook the meat a little longer until all of the liquid is absorbed and only the butter remains. Remove the meat to a platter, let it cool partially. Remove the string and cut the meat into thin slices. Return the sliced meat to the pot and heat it. Place the puréed vegetables in the center of a platter. Put the meat slices around the edge and serve with the butter poured over the top. Serves 6.

VEAL WITH SPINACH AND TOMATO SAUCE ✠ MOSXHARI ME SPANAKI ME SALTSA DOMATA

Prepare like Veal and Spinach Avgolemono (see index), but substitute 1 tablespoon tomato paste diluted with 2 cups of water for the avgolemono sauce. As soon as the meat is browned, add the diluted tomato paste. Cook for 1 hour, then add the spinach. Cook until all the liquid has been absorbed and only the butter remains (about 1 hour).

VEAL OR BEEF WITH EGGPLANT ✠ MOSXHARI E VOTHINO ME MELITZANES

3 pounds veal or beef
3 pounds long eggplants
2–3 medium onions
½ pound butter

1½ pounds ripe tomatoes
salt and pepper to taste
water as needed

Clean the eggplants and cut each one into 3 or 4 round slices; place in a bowl of salted water to soak for 20 minutes. Cut the meat into serving-size pieces; wash and drain. Clean the onions, chop them and rinse well in a strainer.

Brown half the butter in a pot. Salt and pepper the meat and brown it with the butter; add the onions, and brown them. Pass the tomatoes through a strainer and add to the meat, and bring them to a boil. Add 2 cups of water; simmer about 1 hour for veal, or 1½ hours for beef. The meat should be tender and there should still be a little sauce left.

After the eggplant has soaked for 20 minutes, remove the slices from the bowl, rinse well, wipe with a towel, and fry in the remaining butter, then place carefully on top of the meat; add a little salt and pepper. Cook the meat over medium heat for another 20 minutes, or until all the liquid has been absorbed and only the oil remains. Serves 6.

NOTE: If you wish, cook the meat for 1 hour, then add the eggplant without frying it. Add 1 to 2 cups water and cook another hour, until only the oil remains.

POTTED VEAL WITH POTATOES ✠ MOSXHARI TIS KATSAROLAS ME PATATES

Prepare like Potted Lamb with Potatoes (see index), but substitute veal for the lamb.

VEAL WITH MACARONI ✠ MOSXHARI ME MAKARONAKI KOFTO

3 pounds lean veal
salt and pepper to taste
¾–1 cup butter
2 teaspoons grated onion

2 pounds ripe tomatoes, peeled
    and strained
water as needed
1 pound short macaroni
grated Parmesan cheese

Cut the meat into 6 portions, wash and dry it. Sprinkle lightly with salt and pepper. Put the butter in a wide pot and brown it well; add the meat and brown on all sides. Add the onion and tomatoes. Cover the pot. Cook for 1½ hours, or until the meat is done. Watch the meat during the cooking and add water if necessary. Meantime, cook the macaroni according to the directions on the package.

Remove the meat from the pot, place it on a platter and keep it warm. Measure the sauce, then return it to the heat; bring it to a boil. Place the cooked macaroni in a pan, add the sauce; add hot water, if necessary, to make 6 cups of sauce and place the slices of meat on top of the macaroni. Bake for 15 minutes in a preheated 350° oven. Serve with grated Parmesan cheese. Serves 6.

BAKED VEAL AND SPAGHETTI ✠ MOSXHARI ME SPAGETO STO FOURNO

Prepare like Baked Lamb and Spaghetti but substitute veal for the lamb.

BOILED BEEF OR VEAL ✠ VOTHINO E MOSXHARI VRASTO

3 pounds neck or shoulder of
    beef or veal
2–3 bones, with marrow
coarse salt
1 pound small potatoes
¾ pound small whole squash
2–3 whole carrots

1 pound whole ripe tomatoes
2–3 medium onions
2–3 stalks of celery (tied
    together)
¼–½ pound Orzo or a similar-
    type noodle

Wash the meat and the bones. Place in a large pot and cover with water to about 1 inch above the meat. Add some coarse salt and bring to a boil. Skim the froth as it rises and cook for about 1 hour to an hour and 15 minutes. Add the remaining ingredients and cook for 30 minutes longer. If the vegetables are done before the meat is tender, remove them from the broth with a slotted spoon and keep them warm. Remove the meat to a platter when it is tender and keep it warm. Strain the broth; add enough water to the broth to serve 6. Bring to a boil. Add the noodles and cook until tender (about 7 to 8 minutes). Serve the hot soup followed by the meat and vegetables. Serves 6.

MEAT WITH DRIED BEANS   ✠   KREAS ME FASOLIA XSIRA

1¼–1½ pounds dried beans
3 pounds pork, veal, lamb, or
   beef
½–¾ cup butter (depending on
   the amount of fat in the
   meat)
1 medium onion

1 tablespoon tomato paste
   diluted with 1 cup water, or
   1 2-pound can whole tomatoes
salt and pepper to taste
2 tablespoons chopped parsley
water as needed

Clean the beans and soak them overnight. Drain; boil them partially (for 30 minutes). Meantime, cut the meat into large cubes and place them in a large pot. Add the diluted tomato paste or canned tomatoes (the latter rather than fresh tomatoes are specified because this is a winter dish) passed through a strainer; add the salt, pepper and parsley, and bring to a boil. Add 1 to 2 cups water. Drain the beans and add to the meat. Cook another half hour or until the beans are soft and all the liquid has been absorbed so only the butter remains. Serves 6.

SMYRNA MEATBALLS   ✠   SOUDZOUKAKIA

1½ pounds chopped meat
2–3 slices white bread, trimmed
   of crusts
2–3 cloves garlic, finely chopped
pinch of cumin seed, pounded,
   or ½–1 teaspoon cumin
   powder
flour

butter or oil for frying
1 pound ripe tomatoes, peeled
   and seeded, or 1 tablespoon
   tomato paste, diluted with
   1½ cups water
salt and pepper to taste
1 egg (optional)
¼–½ cup red wine (optional)

Have the meat ground twice. Soak the bread in cold water and squeeze out the excess well. Mix the meat, bread, garlic, and cumin together; form egg-shaped meatballs; roll lightly in the flour. Heat the butter or oil in a deep frying pan. Fry the soudzoukakia until brown on all sides. Remove them from the pan with a slotted spoon and put them into a pot. Pour the tomatoes (or diluted tomato paste) into the pan with the butter or oil and cook together for 3 to 5 minutes. Pour the sauce over the soudzoukakia and cook another 10 to 15 minutes. Serve with rice. Serves 6.

NOTE: If you are using the egg and wine, add both to the meat mixture, and use 1 more slice of bread.

STIFADO ✠ STIFADO

3 pounds lean beef
3 pounds small white onions
  even in size
1 cup oil
½ head garlic, peeled
⅓–½ cup vinegar (to taste)

1 tablespoon tomato paste
  diluted with 1 cup water, or
  1½ pounds ripe tomatoes,
  peeled and strained
2 bay leaves
1 sprig rosemary
salt and pepper to taste
water as needed

This can be made two ways:

1. Wash the meat and cut it into 1½-inch cubes; place in a pot. Add the remaining ingredients and enough water to cover. Bring to a boil, then lower the heat and simmer for 2 to 3 hours. During this time, do not uncover the pot or stir the food; it should absorb all the liquid and only the oil remains.

2. Prepare meat as above, then brown it in oil in a frying pan. Place in a pot, add the tomatoes, and bring to a boil, cook for 5 minutes. Sauté the whole onions in the oil in the frying pan, and add to the meat along with the remaining ingredients. Cover the pot; simmer undisturbed for about 1 to 2 hours until all the liquid is absorbed and only the oil remains. Serves 6.

GRILLED BEEFSTEAK ✠ BRIZOLES VOTHINES STI SKARA

½ pound steak per person
salt and pepper to taste
1–2 teaspoons oregano

oil for basting
lemon juice for basting

Remove all excess fat from the steaks. Season with pepper and oregano. Brush with a little oil and let stand for 1 hour, then season with salt. Grill over high heat to sear the meat and retain the juices. Move from high heat to medium heat, brush with oil and lemon, and cook to taste (rare, medium, or well done).

GRILLED MEAT PATTIES ✠ KEFTAIDES STI SKARA

1½ pounds chopped meat
½ cup bread crumbs
1 medium onion, chopped
2 tablespoons parsley, chopped

2 eggs
salt and pepper to taste
1 teaspoon oil
oil for brushing

Mix together the meat, bread crumbs, onion, parsley, eggs, oil, and seasoning, and shape into patties. Brush the surface of each with a little oil; broil over medium heat. Serves 6 to 8.

FRIED MEATBALLS   ✠   KEFTAIDES TIGANITI

2 pounds chopped meat
1 large onion, chopped
3 tablespoons chopped parsley
1½ cups bread cubes, trimmed
    of crusts and soaked
1 teaspoon chopped, bruised
    mint

2 teaspoons lemon juice
2 eggs
1 teaspoon oregano
salt and pepper to taste
oil for frying
flour

Mix together all the ingredients except the oil and flour; shape into patties or meatballs. Heat the oil in a deep frying pan. Roll the meatballs in flour and shake off any excess. Fry until browned on all sides. Serve hot or cold. Serves 6 to 8.

BAKED MEATBALLS   ✠   KEFTAIDES STO FOURNO

1 recipe Fried Meatballs

4 tablespoons butter, melted
2 lemons, juice only

Prepare the meat as for Fried Meatballs; shape into mounds; place in a buttered pan. Pour on the melted butter and lemon juice. Bake in a preheated 350° oven for about 30 minutes or until brown. Baste with the sauces in the pan. Serves 6.

BREADED MEATBALLS   ✠   KEFTAIDES PANE

1 recipe Fried Meatballs

1 egg
bread crumbs

Prepare the meatballs, binding them with the 3 egg yolks. Beat the egg whites lightly in a bowl. Dip the meatballs into the egg whites, and then roll them in the bread crumbs; fry. Serves 6.

MEATBALLS FRICASSEE ✠ KEFTAIDES FRICASE

THE MEATBALLS

1 cup white bread, trimmed of
   crusts
2 pounds lean chopped meat
3 tablespoons chopped onion
1 tablespoon chopped parsley
1 tablespoon chopped mint
2 eggs, separated
salt and pepper to taste
flour
oil or butter or lard for frying

THE SAUCE

⅓ cup butter
2–3 bunches scallions, white
   parts only, cleaned and
   chopped
½ cup white vinegar
2 cups hot water
½ cup cold milk
1 tablespoon cornstarch

Wet the bread with cold water and squeeze out the excess; mix well with the chopped meat. Add the onion, parsley, mint, egg whites, salt, and pepper. Shape the meatballs, and flour them lightly; fry in the oil (or butter or lard).

To make the sauce, brown the butter in a saucepan; add the scallions; sauté until golden. Add the vinegar and water, and cook for 10 minutes. Add the meatballs, and cook until only half the liquid remains. Beat the egg yolks very thoroughly in a bowl. In another bowl, mix the cornstarch in the milk, add this mixture to the egg yolks, then blend in some liquid from the pot, beating all the while. Pour the egg mixture over the meatballs, shaking the pot gently until the sauce thickens. Serves 6.

MEATBALLS WITH SAUCE ✠ KEFTAIDES ME SALTSA

1 recipe Fried Meatballs (see
   index)
1½ pounds ripe tomatoes,
   peeled and strained, or 1½
   tablespoons tomato paste
   diluted with 2 cups water

1 piece of stick cinnamon
salt and pepper to taste
½ cup white wine

Prepare and fry the meatballs as in Fried Meatballs. Remove them from the pan with a slotted spoon and keep warm. Add the tomatoes, cinnamon, salt, pepper, and wine, and cook in the pan with the oil for 10 minutes. Return the meatballs to the pan and cook for 3 to 5 minutes longer. Serve with spaghetti, rice, or potatoes. Serves 6.

MEATBALLS WITH RICE   ✠   YOVARLAKIA ME RIZI
AND TOMATO SAUCE   KE SALTSA DOMATAS

1 pound ripe tomatoes, peeled   ½ cup raw rice
   and strained, or 1 tablespoon   ½ cup chopped onion
   tomato paste diluted with 2   1 egg
   cups water   ½ cup chopped parsley
½ cup melted butter   salt and pepper to taste
1¾ pounds chopped meat

Put the tomatoes (or the diluted tomato paste) into a large pot with the butter. Mix together the meat, rice, onion, egg, half the parsley, and a little salt and pepper; shape into meatballs and put them into the pot with the sauce. Add the remaining parsley and cook over medium heat for about 45 minutes, or until most of the sauce is absorbed. Serves 6.

MEATBALLS WITH AVGOLEMONO SAUCE ✠ YOVARLAKIA AVGOLEMONO

1¾ pounds chopped meat   2 eggs, separated
½ cup raw rice   salt and pepper to taste
½ cup chopped onion   ½ cup butter
3 tablespoons chopped parsley   1–2 lemons, juice only

Mix together the meat, rice, onion, parsley, egg whites, salt, and pepper; shape into meatballs each about the size of a walnut. Melt the butter in a large pot; place the meatballs in the pot, add enough water to cover; cook over medium heat (about 45 minutes to 1 hour) until only about 1 cup liquid remains.

Beat the egg yolks well; add the lemon juice, beat it in thoroughly. Slowly add some of the hot liquids from the pot, beating all the while. Pour this mixture back into the pot and shake the pot gently over very low heat until the sauce thickens (about 2 to 3 minutes). Serves 6.

PORK WITH LEEKS ✠ HIRINO ME PRASA

3 pounds pork
4½–5 pounds leeks
salt and pepper to taste
2 medium onions, chopped

½ pound butter
1 tablespoon tomato paste
   diluted with 2 cups water

Clean and wash the leeks; cut each into 4 or 5 pieces. Bring a pot of salted water to a boil. Add the leeks and boil them for a few minutes (this removes their sharpness), then drain. Cut the meat into cubes; wash them, and season with salt and pepper. Place the onions in a strainer and run cold water over them; let them drain. Put the butter into a large pot to brown. Add the meat and brown it, then add the onions and brown them. Add the diluted tomato paste to the meat. Add another cup of water. Cover the pot and simmer for 1 hour. Then add the leeks and cook 30 minutes to 1 hour over low heat until all the liquid has been absorbed and only the butter remains. Serves 6.

NOTE: This can be made not only with pork but any meat.

PORK AND CELERY AVGOLEMONO ✠ HIRINO ME SELINO AVGOLEMONO

4½–5 pounds celery (with
   leaves)
salt and pepper to taste
3 pounds pork
½ cup butter
3 medium onions, chopped

water as needed
2 lemons, juice only
2 eggs
1 tablespoon cornstarch

Clean the celery and cut each stalk into 2 or 3 pieces. Fill a large pot with water and bring it to a boil. Add a little salt and parboil the celery for about 15 minutes; drain and set aside. Cut the meat into cubes, wash, and season with salt and pepper. Put the butter into a pot to brown; add the meat and brown it lightly. Add the onions; cook until soft but not browned. Add 2 to 3 cups of water. Cook about 1 hour or until the meat is half cooked. Add the celery and cook until the liquid is reduced to 1 cup and the celery is tender (about 30 minutes longer).

Beat the eggs in a bowl. Dilute the cornstarch in ¼ cup water and add to the eggs. Add the lemon juice, and beat it in well. Slowly add some of the hot liquid from the meat to the egg-and-lemon mixture, beating it in thoroughly. Pour the sauce back over the meat and shake the pot gently until the sauce thickens slightly. Serve hot. Serves 6.

BOILED HAM ✠ HIRINO BOUTI VRASTO

5–7 pounds fresh ham
water as needed
coarse salt
5–8 cloves of garlic

salt and pepper to taste
several peppercorns
2–3 bay leaves

Wash the ham. Pierce it in several places and insert the garlic cloves and peppercorns in these holes. Place the ham in a large pot and cover it with plenty of water. Add some coarse salt and the bay leaves; skim off the froth as it appears. Simmer for 3 to 4 hours, then remove from the heat. Allow the ham to cool thoroughly. Slice and serve as is for cold hors d'oeuvres, or serve it garnished with boiled or fried potatoes and a salad. Serves 6 to 8.

NOTE: If you decide to make a soup from the broth, first remove most of the fat.

VARIETY MEATS

PORK BRAWN PIHTI

1 pig's head
water as needed
coarse salt
5–6 peppercorns
3–4 whole carrots
3–4 stalks celery

2–3 medium onions
5 cloves garlic, peeled
2 bay leaves
3 hard-cooked eggs, sliced
2–3 tablespoons vinegar

Wash the pig's head in warm water to remove all the blood; place in a large pot with enough water to cover. Add a little salt and the peppercorns. Bring to a boil over medium heat, skimming the froth from the surface as it forms. Cook for about 30 minutes, then add the carrots, celery, onions, garlic, and bay leaves. Simmer until the head and vegetables are tender (20 to 30 minutes). If the vegetables are done first, remove them to a platter with a slotted spoon. Remove the head from the broth and let it cool. There should be about 3 cups liquid remaining in the pot; either add enough water to make 3 cups, or let the broth boil rapidly until it cooks down to 3 cups.

Open the head and remove all the meat from it; cut it into small pieces. Slice the carrots into rounds. Strain the broth through cheesecloth; add the vinegar to it. Place the egg and carrot slices in the bottom of a rectangular form; add the meat; pour in the broth. Cool and refrigerate until firm. Unmold onto a platter to serve. Serves 4 to 6.

STUFFED SPLEENS   ✠   SPLINES YEMISTES

12 lamb's spleens
1½ cups oil
1½ cups chopped onion
6–7 cloves garlic, chopped
1¼ pounds ripe tomatoes,
   peeled and strained, or 1
   tablespoon tomato paste
   diluted with 2 cups water

1 cup chopped parsley
salt and pepper to taste
water as needed
½ cup white wine

To make the stuffing, heat half the oil and sauté the onion in it until lightly browned. Add the garlic and tomatoes (or diluted tomato paste); cook for 3 or 4 minutes. Add the parsley, salt, and pepper, and continue to cook until the sauce thickens (about 15 minutes longer).

Meanwhile, wash and drain the spleens. Cut a hole in the top of each, carefully, so as not to tear the surrounding skin, then fill each with the stuffing, being careful not to overstuff them. Sew up each and place it in a pot. Pour the remaining oil over all; add the wine; sprinkle lighty with salt and pepper Cook, uncovered, over medium heat for 30 to 40 minutes, adding a little hot water from time to time. The spleens should be tender and should have absorbed all the liquid except the oil. These are usually served cold. Serves 6.

NOTE: If you prefer, you may prepare the spleens and bake them in a preheated 350° oven. Turn them after 15 or 20 minutes and let them bake on the second side an additional 15 or 20 minutes.

LAMBS' HEADS OREGANO   ✠   KEFALIA ARNISIA RIGANATA

3 lambs' heads, split in half
½ cup lemon juice
½ cup oil

2 teaspoons oregano
1 cup water

Wash the heads and place them in a pan with the brains up. Pour the lemon juice and oil over each head; sprinkle with oregano. Add the water to the pan. Roast in a preheated 350° oven, basting occasionally with the sauce, for 1 to 1½ hours, or until tender. Serves 6.

SKEWERED LAMB'S ENTRAILS ✠ SOUVLAKIA APO ENTOSTHIA

entrails of 1 lamb   2 teaspoons lemon juice
½ cup oil   1 teaspoon oregano
salt and pepper to taste

Cut the liver, kidneys, spleens, and sweetbreads into cubes or small pieces. Wash, and marinate in a little oil for about ½ hour. Season lightly with salt and pepper. Thread on a skewer and broil over low heat. Baste with a mixture of oil, lemon juice, and oregano. Serve with french fried potatoes and a salad. Serves 6.

LAMB'S OR CALF'S FEET ✠ POTHARKIA ARNIOU E MOS-
IN WHITE SAUCE XHARIOU ME LEVKI SALTSA

6–12 lamb's or calf's feet   3 tablespoons flour
    (depending on size)   2 cups stock
water as needed   salt and pepper to taste
coarse salt   2 egg yolks, well beaten
3 medium onions   1 lemon, juice only
several stalks celery   parsley
2–3 carrots   Calamata olives
4 tablespoons butter

Have the butcher split the feet through the nail area. Scorch or sear the feet to remove all the hairs; wash in hot water, and boil, uncovered, in plenty of water with coarse salt added, for about 1 hour (skim any froth from the surface as it forms). Add the onions, celery (with the stalks tied together), and carrots, and continue to cook until the vegetables are tender and the broth is reduced to 2 cups (30 to 45 minutes longer). Remove the feet from the broth; separate the meat from the bones (discarding the latter), and place on a platter; keep hot.

Melt the butter in a small pot; add the flour, blending it in well. Add the 2 cups stock, and cook, stirring constantly, until the sauce thickens. Stir in the salt and pepper. In a bowl, beat the egg yolks and lemon juice until well blended; gradually beat in the hot sauce, and when the whole is well mixed, pour it over the meat. Garnish with the carrots, sprigs of parsley, and olives. Serve hot. Serves 6.

LIVER   ✠   TZIYEROSARMAS

1 lamb's liver   ¾ cup milk
½ cup raw rice   salt and pepper to taste
1 bunch scallions, chopped   5 eggs
2 teaspoons chopped dill   1–2 lamb casings (as for
1 teaspoon chopped fresh mint   sausage)
                                                  4 tablespoons melted butter

For the stuffing, skin the liver and cut it into small pieces with scissors; place
in a bowl. Add the rice, scallions, dill, mint, milk, salt, and pepper; mix well.

Wash the casing and dip it into warm water, to open well. Place the stuffing
in the casing (as you would stuff a sausage). Fold it carefully and place on a
buttered pan with the folded side down. Pour the melted butter over this and
roast in a 325° oven for 45 minutes. Serves 6 to 8.

NOTE: if you wish, the casing may be cut into 6 to 8 portions and stuffed to
make individual servings.

FOIE GRAS EN GELEE   ✠   FOIA GRA AN ZELE

2 tablespoons unflavored gelatin   2 tablespoons retsina*
3–4 hard-cooked eggs   salt and pepper to taste
2 cooked carrots, cooled   sweet butter
10 Calamata olives   parsley
1 8–9-ounce can foie gras   lemon wedges
3 cups water or clear meat broth

Refrigerate the can of foie gras for 3 hours. Soak the gelatin as directed on
the package. Slice the eggs, carrots, and olives; slice the chilled foie gras. Bring
the water (or broth) to a boil and add the wine to it; pour into the gelatin. Strain
through a cheesecloth and place in the refrigerator until partially set (about 1
hour). Season with salt and pepper, and also season the eggs and carrots.

Rinse out a rectangular mold and line the bottom and sides with the slices of
eggs, carrots, and olives. Pour in a layer of gelatin, then place a layer of foie gras
slices on it. Cover that with another layer of gelatin, and then a layer of the
remaining egg and olive slices. Pour on another layer of gelatin; add a final layer
of foie gras; cover with a last layer of gelatin. Place in the refrigerator until set
(2 to 3 hours). Before serving, dip the mold into warm water to loosen, then
turn it out onto a platter. Garnish with lemon wedges, pats of sweet butter, and a
few sprigs of parsley. Serves 6 to 8.

MARINATED LIVER ✠ SIKOTAKIA MARINATA

2–2¼ pounds calf's or lamb
   liver
oil or butter for frying
½ cup excellent-quality oil
2 tablespoons flour plus flour
   for dipping
⅓ cup vinegar

½ tablespoon tomato paste
   diluted with 1 cup water
½ teaspoon sweet rosemary
   (optional)
1 bay leaf
salt and pepper to taste
1–2 cups water

Slice the liver, dip the slices into flour, fry in hot oil (or butter), and place on a platter. Add the ½ cup oil to the oil in which you fried the liver, and when it is hot, slowly add the 2 tablespoons flour, stirring constantly with a wooden spoon until well blended. When the mixture is lightly browned, add the vinegar, tomato paste, and water. Add the rosemary, bay leaf, and salt and pepper. Cook the sauce for 5 to 10 minutes (but do not let it become too thick). Add the liver to the sauce; cook for 2 to 3 minutes longer. Serve hot or cold. Serves 6 to 8.

NOTE: Liver prepared in this fashion will keep for several days, especially during the winter.

LIVER WITH TOMATO SAUCE ✠ SIKOTAKIA ME SALTSA DOMATAS

2–2½ pounds calf's liver
½ cup butter
½ cup white wine
1 tablespoon tomato paste
   diluted with 1 cup water,
   or 1½ pounds ripe tomatoes,
   peeled and strained

½ cup water
2 tablespoons chopped parsley
salt and pepper to taste

Cut the liver into small, narrow strips; wash, and drain well. Brown the butter in a pan, add the liver; sauté well. Add the wine slowly, so it steams; add the tomatoes (or diluted tomato paste), water, parsley, and salt and pepper. Cover the pot; cook until only a little sauce remains. Serve hot. Serves 6 to 8.

BOILED BRAINS ✠ MIALA VRASTO

1 pair lamb or beef brains
coarse salt

water to cover
1—2 tablespoons vinegar

Brains must be parboiled before they can be used. To prepare, first soak them in cold water for about 30 to 45 minutes, so the blood drains and the membranes soften. Remove the membranes with the point of a sharp knife. Add the vinegar to a pot containing the water and salt, and bring to a boil; add the brains. Cook lamb brains for 10 minutes; cook beef brains 15 to 20 minutes. Remove from the liquid and cool. Serve in any of the ways suggested in the recipes below. One pair of brains serves 2.

BOILED BRAINS WITH BUTTER ✠ MIALA VRASTA ME FRESKO VOUTIRO

Prepare the brains as in the recipe above, but do not cool. Serve hot with melted sweet butter.

BRAINS WITH OIL AND VINEGAR ✠ MIALA ME LATHOKSITHO

1 recipe Boiled Brains
½ cup oil
¼ cup vinegar

1 tablespoon dry mustard
1 tablespoon chopped parsley
salt and pepper to taste

Prepare the brains, then cut into slices, and lay on a platter. Beat together the oil and vinegar, and to it add the other ingredients. Pour over the brains and serve.

BRAINS WITH MAYONNAISE ✠ MIALA ME MAYONEZA

1 recipe Boiled Brains
mayonnaise
tomatoes

cucumbers
parsley

Prepare the brains, then cut into slices and lay on a platter. Cover the slices with mayonnaise, surround with slices of tomato and cucumber; garnish with parsley. Serve.

BRAINS WITH BÉCHAMEL SAUCE   ✠   MIALA ME BESAMEL

2 pairs cooked brains
2 tablespoons butter
2 tablespoons flour
1¼ cups scalded milk
1 egg yolk, well beaten
1 tablespoon lemon juice
½ cup grated Parmesan or
  Gruyère cheese

1 teaspoon chopped capers
salt and pepper to taste
4 slices day-old bread
butter for frying the bread
8 olives
parsley

Prepare the brains as in Boiled Brains (see index), and cut them, while they are still hot, into 2 to 4 pieces (depending on the size of the brains). Keep hot.

Melt the 2 tablespoons butter over low heat, add the flour; blend well. Add the milk, a little at a time, stirring constantly so the mixture does not lump, and cook until thickened. Remove from the heat. Slowly add the beaten egg yolk and lemon juice, stirring until well blended, then add half the cheese and the capers.

Cut the slices of bread in half and remove the crusts. Fry lightly in butter until golden. Place the bread on a platter, top each slice with a piece of the brains, and cover with the sauce. Sprinkle the remaining cheese over the top and garnish with finely chopped parsley. Surround with the olives and serve with pieces of parsley tucked between the bread slices. Serves 4.

BRAIN CROQUETTES   ✠   KROKETES APO MIALA

1 recipe Boiled Brains (see
  index)
1 cup Thick Béchamel Sauce
  (see index)
½ cup grated kefalotiri* or
  Parmesan cheese

2 eggs, separated
1 tablespoon chopped parsley
salt and pepper to taste
toasted bread crumbs
oil for frying

Prepare the brains, and cool. Chop. (You should have 2 cups.) Prepare the béchamel sauce. Mix the brains, béchamel, cheese, egg yolks, parsley, and salt and pepper together. Lightly grease your hands and shape the mixture into ovals. Roll in the bread crumbs. Beat the egg whites with 2 tablespoons of water, then dip the croquettes into egg whites, and roll them again in bread crumbs. Fry in very hot oil. Remove carefully and place on absorbent paper to drain. Serve hot. Serves 4 to 6.

SAUTÉED BRAINS ✠ MIALA SOTE

1 recipe Boiled Brains   salt and pepper to taste
butter   chopped parsley

Prepare the brains, and while still hot, cut them into slices. Keep hot. Brown the butter in a pan, and pour over the brains. Add salt and pepper; turn the brains in the butter several times to coat them well. Remove from the heat. Serve hot, garnished with parsley.

BRAINS PANE ✠ MIALA PANE

1 recipe Boiled Brains   bread crumbs
1–2 eggs   butter for frying
flour

Prepare the brains, then cut them into long slices. Beat the eggs together with the seasoning and water. Dust the slices of brains with flour, and dip into the egg mixture; then coat with the bread crumbs. Fry until golden brown; place on several layers of absorbent paper to drain. Serve hot with mashed potatoes.

POULTRY AND GAME

CHICKEN WITH OKRA ✠ KOTTOPOULA ME MPAMIEZ

2 broiler-fryers (about 1½
  pounds each) or 3 pounds
  chicken parts
salt and pepper to taste
3 pounds okra
½ cup vinegar

¾ cup butter
1 medium onion, chopped
1½ pounds ripe tomatoes,
  peeled and strained
2 cups water

Wash the chickens. (If they are whole, cut them into sections). Season lightly with salt and pepper, and set them aside to drain. Wash the okra. Remove the stems carefully, without cutting the okra. Line them up in a large flat pan and sprinkle with the vinegar; place in the sun for 30 minutes to 1 hour.

Brown the butter in a pot, add the chicken, and sauté until brown, then add the onion and let it brown. Add the tomatoes and boil for 3 to 5 minutes. Add the water. Simmer for 30 minutes. Add the okra and continue to simmer, covered, until tender. Watch carefully as this may need a little more water. The okra will have absorbed the liquid and only the oil should remain when the dish is cooked. Serves 6 to 8.

CHICKEN WITH PEAS ✠ KOTTOPOULA ME MPIZELIA

Prepare like Chicken with Okra above, but substitute 3 pounds peas for the okra.

CHICKEN SALAD WITH MAYONNAISE   ✠   KOTTOPOULA MAYONEZA

2 1½-pound broiler-fryers
water as needed
salt to taste
2–3 small onions
4–5 carrots
2 stalks celery

2 recipes mayonnaise (see index)
2–3 hard-cooked eggs
10 Calamata olives
3–4 pickles
1 tablespoon capers
1 bunch parsley

Put the chickens into a pot with enough lightly salted water to cover; bring to a boil. Skim off the froth as it appears. Add the onions, carrots, and celery; simmer until the meat leaves the bone (about 45 minutes). Remove the chickens from the pot and let them cool. (Reserve the broth to serve separately.) Meanwhile, prepare the mayonnaise.

Slice the eggs, pit the olives, slice the pickles. Cut the chicken into chunks, first removing the skin, fat and bones and discarding them. Spread a layer of mayonnaise on a large platter. In a bowl, mix the chicken chunks with 5 tablespoons mayonnaise, then turn out onto the mayonnaise on the platter; spread more mayonnaise over the top. Garnish with the eggs, carrots (cut into slices), olives, pickles, capers, and parsley. Serves 6.

CHICKEN WITH PILAF   ✠   KOTTOPOULA ME PILAFI

3 pounds chicken parts
½ cup butter or other shortening
1 medium onion, chopped
1½ pounds ripe tomatoes,
   peeled and strained, or 1
   tablespoon tomato paste
   diluted with 1 cup water

water as needed
2½–3 cups raw rice
2⅓ cups water for each cup of
   rice used

Wash and wipe the chicken. Brown the butter in a large pot; add the chicken. Brown it on all sides. Add the onion and let it brown. Add the tomatoes (or diluted tomato paste) and the 1 cup water. Cook for about 20 minutes. Add 2⅓ cups water for each cup of rice you will use and continue to cook until the chicken is tender (about 20 to 30 minutes). Remove the chicken parts with a slotted spoon and keep them hot. Add the rice to the sauce in the pot, stirring in the beginning to keep it from sticking. Simmer, covered, until the rice is tender and has absorbed most of the sauce (about 20 minutes). Remove from the heat. Place the chicken on the rice, cover the pot with a clean towel, put the lid back over the towel. Let stand for 10 minutes, then serve. Serves 6.

CHICKEN WITH WALNUT SAUCE ✠ KOTTOPOULA ME SALTSA KARITHIA

3 broiler-fryers (about 1½
   pounds each)
salt and pepper to taste
½ cup butter or oil

1 cup white wine
1 cup hot water
½ cup chopped walnuts

    Thoroughly clean and wash the chickens. Truss them, and allow to drain. Sprinkle lightly with salt and pepper. Melt the butter in a frying pan. Brown the chickens, one at a time, well on all sides, then place them in a wide pot. Pour in the fat remaining in the frying pan, and place this pot over heat. Pour in wine slowly, so it steams, and add the water. Cover. Simmer, adding more water if needed, for about 30 minutes. When the chickens are tender, remove from the heat and cool partially, then cut into quarters. Add walnuts to the sauce, stir, and bring the sauce to a boil, cook for 2 to 3 minutes longer. Add the quartered chickens, and serve hot with fried potatoes and a raw salad. Serves 6.

RABBIT WITH TOMATO SAUCE ✠ KOUNELLI ME SALTSA DOMATAS

1 3- to 6-pound rabbit
vinegar
water as needed
1–2 bay leaves
8 cloves garlic
¼ pound butter

¾ cup oil
½ cup white wine
1½ pounds ripe tomatoes,
   peeled and strained, or 1½
   tablespoons tomato paste
   diluted with 1 cup water

    Clean and wash the rabbit. Put it into a ceramic bowl with enough liquid to cover (half water and half vinegar). Add the bay leaves and half the garlic. Marinate overnight, then remove the rabbit from the marinade and cut it up. Heat the butter and oil in a frying pan, and brown the rabbit, a few pieces at a time, well on all sides. Put the rabbit into a large pot. Sauté the garlic in the oil in the pan, add the wine and the tomatoes (or diluted tomato paste). Cook for 3 to 5 minutes. Add this sauce to the pot with the rabbit, add 1 to 2 cups water. Cover the pot, and simmer over medium heat until the rabbit is tender (1½ to 2½ hours). Add water from time to time, as needed. The rabbit should absorb all the liquid; only the oil will remain when the dish is cooked. Serves 4 to 8.

RABBIT OR HARE STEW ✠ LAGOUS E KOUNELLI STIFADO

1 3-pound rabbit	1 head garlic, cleaned
1 cup vinegar	2–3 bay leaves
2 cups oil	1 sprig rosemary
1½ pounds ripe tomatoes,	salt and pepper to taste
peeled and strained, or 1½	2 cups water
tablespoons tomato paste	3 pounds small white onions,
diluted with 1 cup water	peeled

Wash the rabbit and cut it into serving pieces. Sprinkle with ¼ to ½ cup vinegar, and let it stand for 2 hours. Heat half the oil in a deep frying pan, and brown the rabbit, a few pieces at a time; transfer these to a large pot. To it, add the tomatoes (or diluted tomato paste), the rest of the vinegar, the oil from the frying pan, garlic cloves, bay leaves, rosemary, salt, pepper, and water; cook for 45 minutes.

Put the rest of the oil and the onions into the frying pan and sauté until light brown; add to the pot with the rabbit. Cover, and simmer until tender. (This may take as long as 1½ hours.) All the liquids will be absorbed and only the oil should remain. Serves 4.

NOTE: If you wish, eliminate all the browning. Simply put all the ingredients into a large pot, and simmer until done.

RABBIT WITH LEMON ✠ KOUNELLI ME LEMONI

1 rabbit, cut into pieces	butter for frying
water as needed	oil for frying
vinegar	3 lemons, juice only

Clean and wash the rabbit; place in a ceramic bowl. Add enough liquid (half water and half vinegar) to cover the rabbit, and marinate overnight. Remove the rabbit from the marinade; wash; drain well. Heat equal amounts of butter and oil in a large pot. Brown the rabbit, a few pieces at a time, on all sides, then return the pieces to the pot and pour the lemon juice over them. Steam until the lemon is absorbed. Add 1 to 2 cups water and simmer, covered, until tender. You may have to add a little water from time to time. The rabbit should absorb all the liquid; only the oil remains when the dish is cooked (about 1½ to 2 hours). Serves 4.

ROAST RABBIT ✠ LAGOUS STO FOURNO

1 3- to 6-pound rabbit
½–1 cup lemon juice

½–¾ cup oil
1 tablespoon oregano

Wash the rabbit and marinate it for 2 hours in the lemon juice. Remove, season lightly with salt and pepper, and place in a roast pan. Pour half the lemon juice and the oil over it. Sprinkle with the oregano. Roast in a preheated 350° oven, adding lemon juice and oil as needed, for about 1½ hours. Baste frequently with the sauce. Serves 4 to 6.

RABBIT WITH SKORDALIA* ✠ LAGOUS SKORDALIA

1 3- to 6-pound rabbit
1½ cups vinegar
water as needed

1 cup oil
1 recipe skordalia (see index)

Wash the rabbit and marinate it for 2 hours in 1 cup vinegar and 2 cups water. Remove it from the marinade and put it in a roast pan with the oil and 1 cup water. Roast in a preheated 350° oven for 1 hour, basting often. Remove the rabbit from the pan and cut it into sections. Add ½ cup vinegar and ½ cup water to the pan. Return the rabbit to the pan and roast it for another hour. Prepare the skordalia. Cover the rabbit with the skordalia and roast it for 15 minutes longer. Serve with cooked greens. Serves 4 to 8.

PARTRIDGE SALMI ✠ PERTHIKES SALMI

2–4 partridges
butter for browning
½ cup white wine

1 lemon, juice only
1 cup (or more) hot water

Wash and dry the partridges; save the livers, if possible. Brown the butter in a frying pan, add the birds; brown them well on all sides; transfer to a pot. Cut the livers and brown them. Pour the wine into the pan with the butter; stir to loosen all the particles stuck to the pan. Add the lemon juice and water; mix well. Pour this sauce over the birds. Cover the pot, and simmer, adding a little more water, if needed. Cook about 1½ hours (until the meat separates easily from the bones). Serve with potatoes and a salad.

NOTE: Use this recipe also to prepare snipe and other small game birds.

THRUSH OR PIGEONS
IN TOMATO SAUCE

✠

TSIHLES E PITSOUNIA
ME SALTSA DOMATAS

3–6 birds, plucked, singed, and
    cleaned
butter or oil for browning
salt and pepper to taste

1 cup white wine
1½ pounds ripe tomatoes,
    peeled and strained
1 cup (or more) water

Wash and drain the birds; season lightly with salt and pepper. Heat the
butter (or oil) in a frying pan, and add the birds. Brown them well on all sides;
transfer to a pot. Add the wine and tomatoes to the fat in the pan; cook for
about 5 minutes. Pour the sauce over the birds. Add the water. Cover the pot;
simmer until tender (about 1 hour; the birds are done when the meat separates
easily from the bones). Add a little more water, if needed, during the cooking.
Serve the birds with the sauce, which will thicken during the cooking. Serves 3 to 6.

FISH AND SEAFOOD

MARINATED FISH   ✞   PSARI MARINATA

3 pounds fish (red mullet or
  similar fish)
salt to taste
1 lemon, juice only
flour for dipping the fish
1½ cups oil
3–4 tablespoons flour
½ cup white vinegar

1 teaspoon tomato paste diluted
  with 2 cups water
1 teaspoon sugar
2 cloves garlic, chopped
1 teaspoon rosemary
2 bay leaves
4–5 peppercorns

Clean, wash, and salt the fish; place on a platter. Squeeze the lemon juice over it. Let it stand for a few minutes, then cut it into pieces suitable for frying. Heat the oil, dip the fish in flour, and fry it, a few pieces at a time. Place on a plate to cool. If the oil has become too black from the frying, strain it and wash the frying pan, then return the strained oil to it. Heat. Add 3 to 4 tablespoons flour, and stir until blended. Add the vinegar, diluted tomato paste, garlic, rosemary, sugar, bay leaves, and peppercorns. Bring to a boil. As soon as the sauce begins to thicken, add the fish, and cook for 3 to 5 minutes. Remove the fish to a platter, pour the sauce over. Cool and refrigerate. Serve cold. Serves 6.

FISH SAVORO   ✞   PSARI SAVORO

Prepare like Marinated Fish (above), adding 1½ pounds ripe tomatoes to the sauce. Serve hot instead of cold. Serves 6.

BOILED FISH WITH POTATOES ✠ PSARI VRASTO ME PATATES

3 pounds fatty fish (1 large or
   2–3 small)
1½ pounds small, round
   potatoes
2–3 onions, thickly sliced
2–3 carrots, sliced

3 stalks celery, chopped
1 cup oil
water as needed
salt and pepper to taste
1–2 lemons, juice only

Clean and peel the potatoes; leave them whole. Put the potatoes, onions, carrots, and celery in a wide pot; add the oil and 1 cup water. Simmer over medium heat 30 to 45 minutes.

Clean the fish. Cut it into 6 portions, season with salt and pepper. When the vegetables are almost tender, add the fish to the pot, laying it on the potatoes. Add the lemon juice. Cover the pot and cook for 15 to 20 minutes, or until most of the liquid is absorbed but the oil remains. Serves 6.

BAKED FISH ✠ PSARI PLAKI STO FOURNO

3 pounds fish, whole or cut into
   pieces
salt and pepper to taste
1 lemon
1⅓ cups oil
1½ pounds onions
½ cup chopped parsley

1 head garlic, peeled and
   chopped
½ cup white wine
1½ pounds ripe tomatoes, or
   1 tablespoon tomato paste
   diluted with 2 cups water

Clean and wash the fish; season with salt and pepper, squeeze the juice of the lemon over it, and let it stand for 1 hour. Clean the onions and slice them thinly; rinse with cold water. Pour half of the oil into a pan. Spread the onions in the bottom; sprinkle with half the parsley and half the garlic. Lay the fish on this and sprinkle with the remaining parsley and garlic; pour the remaining oil over it, then the wine and the tomatoes. Bake in a preheated 350° oven for 30 minutes. Serves 6.

NOTE: Using the same ingredients, you can make a potted version of this recipe by following these directions:

Cut the fish into slices if it is large; use whole if it is small. Heat the oil in a wide pot; add the onions, and brown them lightly. Add the wine, then the tomatoes, garlic, and parsley. Season to taste with salt and pepper, and add ½ cup water. Cook the stock for 20 minutes, then add the fish. Cover; simmer for 15 to 25 minutes.

You may also add 1½ pounds potatoes, sliced. In that case, eliminate half the onions, and add the potatoes before the fish. Continue as above. (This may require a little more water.)

BAKED FISH SPETSIOTIKO   ✠   PSARI FOURNO
[ISLAND OF SPETSAI]   SPETSIOTIKO

3 pounds fish (striped bass,
   porgy, red snapper, or similar
   fish)
salt and pepper to taste
1½ pounds ripe tomatoes,
   peeled and strained, or 1½
   tablespoons tomato paste
   diluted with 1 cup water

1 cup oil
½ cup white wine
2–3 cloves garlic, chopped
⅓ cup chopped parsley
½ cup toasted bread crumbs

Clean, wash, and drain the fish, and sprinkle with salt and pepper. Oil a baking pan and place the fish in it.

Place the tomatoes (or diluted tomato paste), oil, wine, garlic, and parsley in a bowl; mix well. Pour some of this sauce on the fish and sprinkle with half of the bread crumbs. Put the rest of the sauce in the pan around the fish. Bake in a preheated 300° oven for 20 to 30 minutes. Baste occasionally with the sauce. When the fish begins to brown, turn it. Baste with the sauce and sprinkle with the remaining bread crumbs. Serves 6.

NOTE: If you have trouble handling a large fish, cut it into serving-size portions, then proceed as above.

BAKED MACKEREL   ✠   KOLIO FOURNO

3 pounds mackerel
salt and pepper to taste
1 lemon
4 teaspoons chopped garlic
4 teaspoons chopped onion
2 tablespoons chopped parsley

2 teaspoons chopped green
   pepper
1 cup oil
1 pound ripe tomatoes, peeled
   and strained
½ cup white wine

Clean and wash the fish; season with salt and pepper. Place in a pan. Squeeze the lemon over the fish, then refrigerate for 30 minutes. Sprinkle the garlic over the fish, then the onion, parsley, and green pepper. Pour the oil over it, then add the tomatoes. Bake in a preheated 250° oven for 15 minutes. Add the wine. Baste the fish with the pan sauce, and bake 30 minutes longer, until most of the liquid is absorbed. Serves 6.

PORGIES WITH CELERY ✠ TSIPOURES ME SELINO
AVGOLEMONO AVGOLEMONO

4½ pounds celery
1 medium onion, chopped
1 cup oil
3 pounds porgies

salt and pepper to taste
2 eggs
2 lemons, juice only

Wash the celery and cut it into 2- to 3-inch pieces. Put into a large pot of boiling water; cook for 3 to 5 minutes; drain and set aside. Put the onions and the oil in the pot and cook until the onions soften but do not brown. Add a cup of water and bring to a boil. Add the celery, and cook until just barely tender (about 20 minutes).

Meanwhile clean, wash, and salt the porgies. Lay them on top of the celery. Add a little salt and pepper, and water, if needed. Cover the pot. Simmer for 20 minutes.

Beat the eggs well; add the lemon juice to them, and beat again. Slowly add some of the hot liquid from the pot, beating constantly, and when well blended, pour the sauce back into the pot. Shake the pot gently over low heat until the sauce thickens. Serve hot. Serves 6.

CODFISH STEW WITH ONIONS, ✠ BAKALIAROS PASTOS ME
CALAMATA STYLE KREMMITHIA, KALAMATIANOS

3 pounds salt cod
water as needed
flour for dipping
1½ cups oil

2 pounds onions, sliced
1½–2 pounds ripe tomatoes,
    peeled and strained
pepper to taste

Cut the cod into small pieces. Skin it, and soak it overnight in enough water to cover, changing it 2 or 3 times. Remove from the water; take out the bones; rinse and dry the fish well. Dip it in flour, shaking off the excess, and fry in hot oil until golden. In the same oil, sauté the onions until they are soft but not brown. Put them in a wide pot, together with the oil from the pan and any of the 1½ cups oil not used in the frying. Add the tomatoes and pepper. Simmer for 30 to 45 minutes, or until the onions dissolve. Add the codfish (and ½ cup hot water if needed), cover the pot, and cook for 10 minutes, until the liquid is absorbed and only the oil remains. Serves 6.

NOTE: This dish is usually made in the summer, when ripe tomatoes are readily available.

BOILED SALT COD WITH ✠ GARLIC SAUCE OR MAYONNAISE

BAKALIAROS PASTOS VRASTOS ME SKORDALIA E MAYONEZA

1 salt cod
water as needed
2 onions

3 carrots
several stalks celery

Cut the cod into fairly large pieces. Remove the skin and soak it overnight in enough water to cover, changing the water 2 or 3 times. To cook it, put the fish in fresh water, add the onions, carrots, and celery. Simmer for 30 to 45 minutes or until tender. Serve with skordalia * (see index).

FRIED SALT COD ✠

BAKALIAROS PASTOS TIGANITES

1 3-pound salted cod
water as needed
3 cups flour

1 teaspoon baking powder
1 egg, beaten
oil for frying

Cut the cod into 5 to 10 pieces, depending on the size of fish; remove the skin. Soak the fish overnight in enough water to cover, changing the water 2 or 3 times. Remove the bones from the fish; rinse, and drain.

Mix the flour with the baking powder, then add enough water to make a thick, pasty batter. Add the egg. This should thin the batter just enough to allow you to dip the fish in it and coat well on all sides. Fry the fish in hot oil in a deep frying pan until golden brown. Serves 6 to 8. Serve with salad and skordalia* (see index).

FISH BOURYETO ✠

PSARI BOURYETO

3 pounds fish (any type)
salt and pepper to taste
2 lemons

1 cup oil
6 cloves garlic, chopped
½ teaspoon oregano

Clean the fish and slice it into serving-size pieces. Sprinkle with salt and pepper, and place in a bowl. Squeeze the juice of the lemons over it.

Put the oil and garlic into a large pot, add the fish and lemon juice; simmer over low heat until the fish is cooked (30 to 45 minutes) and only the oil remains as a sauce. During the last 5 to 10 minutes, add the oregano. Serves 6.

NOTE: Fish will exude some water while cooking but will reabsorb it.

CODFISH STEW WITH POTATOES ✠ BAKALIARO YIAHNI

3 pounds salt cod
1½ cups oil
2 onions, chopped
1½ pounds ripe tomatoes,
    peeled and strained, or
    1 tablespoon tomato paste
    diluted with 1 cup water

4–5 cloves garlic, chopped
½ cup chopped parsley
water as needed
3 pounds potatoes

Clean the cod; remove skin; cut the fish into pieces and soak overnight in enough water to cover, changing it 2 or 3 times. Remove the bones from the fish and rinse. Drain. Sauté the onions in the oil in a wide pot until they are golden. Add the tomatoes (or diluted tomato paste), garlic, parsley, and 1 cup water, and boil for 5 minutes.

Peel the potatoes, cut them into large pieces; add them to the sauce. Cook for 20 to 25 minutes, then lay the codfish on the potatoes, add a little more water if necessary, and salt and pepper to taste. Cover the pot; simmer for 20 to 30 minutes, until all the liquid is absorbed and only the oil remains as a sauce. Serves 6.

LOBSTER WITH OIL AND LEMON SAUCE ✠ ASTAKOS ME LATHOLEMONO

1 lobster
water as needed
coarse salt
½ cup oil

⅓ cup lemon juice
1 teaspoon dried mustard
    (optional)
chopped parsley

In a large pot, bring water to a boil, add coarse salt. Add the live lobster. Cover the pot and cook the lobster 15 to 45 minutes, depending on its size. Remove from the heat; cool. Crack the small legs, remove the meat and save; crack the large claws, remove the meat and save; remove the meat from the tail and cut it into smaller pieces; remove the meat from the body and add to the rest of lobster. Beat together the oil and lemon juice, add the mustard, if desired, and pour the sauce over the lobster. Sprinkle chopped parsley on top.

NOTE: If you prefer, use prepared mustard in the sauce. A combination of lobster, crab, shrimp, and chilled chopped celery is a wonderful appetizer with this oil and lemon sauce, with or without the mustard.

GREEK VERSION OF LOBSTER À L'AMÉRICAINE

✠

ASTAKOS A L'AMERIKIAN

1 3-pound lobster
water as needed
½ cup excellent oil
3 medium onions, chopped
½ cup chopped carrots
1 clove garlic, chopped
2 teaspoons chopped celery
½ cup white wine

1 pound ripe tomatoes, peeled
   and strained
1 bay leaf
salt and pepper to taste
¼ cup cognac
¼ cup butter
2 teaspoons parsley, chopped

Prepare the lobster as in Lobster with Oil and Lemon Sauce (see index). Heat the oil in a pot; sauté the onions in it very lightly. Add the carrots, garlic, and celery, and cook until soft, then add the wine. Boil for about 2 minutes. Add the tomatoes, bay leaf, and salt and pepper to taste. Bring to a boil. Add 1 cup of the water in which the lobster was boiled, and simmer until the sauce thickens to a creamy consistency. Add the lobster pieces and the cognac. Boil for about 2 minutes longer. Place the lobster meat on a platter. Swirl the butter in the sauce, and when it melts, pour the sauce over the lobster. Garnish with the chopped parsley. Serves 4.

NOTE: If you wish, you may strain the sauce first and then pour it over the lobster.

LOBSTER PILAF

✠

ASTAKOS PILAFI

4–6 lobsters
1–1½ cups oil (depending on
   the number of lobsters)

1 onion, chopped
1½ pounds ripe tomatoes,
   peeled and strained

Boil the lobster as in Lobster with Oil and Lemon Sauce (see index); cool. Reserve the liquid. Cut the meat into medium-size pieces. Heat the oil in a saucepan. Brown the onions in it. Add tomatoes, and bring to a boil. Cook for 15 minutes. Add lobster meat and cook about 10 minutes longer.

Using the water in which you cooked the lobster, make the pilaf. Measure 2⅓ cups water for each 1 cup raw rice (allow 1 cup rice for 4 people). Bring the water to a boil. Add the rice. Stir to break it up. Cover; simmer until rice is tender. Remove from the heat. Cover with a clean towel and let stand 5 minutes, until all the liquid is absorbed. Serves 4 to 6.

LOBSTER WITH MAYONNAISE   ✝   ASTAKOS ME MAYONEZA

Prepare the lobster as in Lobster with Oil and Lemon Sauce (see index). Put the lobster meat on a platter, cover with homemade mayonnaise (see index). Garnish with the claws, a few sprigs of parsley, slices of hard-cooked eggs, pickles, and capers.

LOBSTER OR SHRIMP AU GRATIN   ✝   ASTAKOS E GARIDES O GRATEN

2 cups cooked lobster or shrimp
  meat
salt and pepper to taste
1½ cups Thick Béchamel Sauce
  (see index)

¼–½ cup grated Parmesan
  cheese
3 tablespoons bread crumbs
2 tablespoons melted butter

Lightly salt and pepper the lobster or shrimp. Mix with the béchamel. Butter a small pan and spread the lobster mixture in it; sprinkle with the cheese and bread crumbs. Drizzle the melted butter over the top. Bake in a preheated 400° oven about 15 minutes or until golden brown. Serves 4.

SHRIMP IN WINE SAUCE   ✝   GARIDES ME SALTSA

3 pounds cooked, shelled shrimp
1 cup olive oil (finest quality)
¾ cup chopped onions
½ cup white retsina*

¾ pound ripe tomatoes, peeled
  and strained, or 1 tablespoon
  plus 1 teaspoon tomato paste
  diluted with 2 cups water
½ cup chopped parsley
salt and pepper to taste

Heat the oil and sauté the onions in it until golden. Pour in the wine, and stir for a minute. Add the tomatoes (or diluted tomato paste), the parsley, and the salt and pepper. Cook over medium heat until the sauce begins to thicken. Add the cleaned shrimp and simmer for 10 to 15 minutes longer. Serve hot or cold. Serves 6.

SHRIMP CROQUETTES   ✠   GARIDES KROKETES

2 cups cooked, cleaned shrimp
1 cup Thick Béchamel Sauce
   (see index)
2 eggs, separated
1 cup grated kefalotiri* or
   Parmesan cheese

2 teaspoons chopped parsley
salt and pepper to taste
toasted bread crumbs
oil for frying

Cut the shrimp into 3 to 4 pieces. Mix with the béchamel sauce, egg yolks, cheese, parsley, and salt and pepper; blend well. Shape into ovals.

Beat the egg whites with 2 tablespoons of water. Roll the croquettes into the bread crumbs, then dip them in the egg whites; roll again in the bread crumbs. Fry in hot oil over low heat until golden brown. Drain and serve hot. Serves 4.

BOILED OCTOPUS   ✠   XTAPOTHI VRASTO

Boiled octopus is usually served as an appetizer. It must be fresh, and small. Allow 1 or 2 per person.

Wash the octopus. Put it into a large pot with plenty of water and a little coarse salt. Cook until tender (about 30 minutes). Remove from the water and cool. Clean, remove the skin so the octopus has a light color, slice, and serve with oil and lemon.

OCTOPUS WITH WINE   ✠   XTAPOTHI KRASATO

3 pounds octopus
1 cup oil
1 medium onion, chopped
2 cups red wine (preferably very
   dark)

¾ pound ripe tomatoes, peeled
   and strained, or 1 tablespoon
   tomato paste diluted with 1
   cup water
salt and pepper to taste

If the octopus is dried, soak it for 24 hours to soften. Cut into pieces about 3 to 4 inches long. Put into a pot with the oil and onion, and brown. Pour the wine into the pot, very slowly, so it steams as it is added. Add the tomatoes (or the diluted tomato paste), and salt and pepper; cover the pot and simmer until most of the liquid is absorbed (about 30 minutes). If necessary add a little more water during the cooking. Serves 6.

OCTOPUS PILAF ✠ XTAPOTHI PILAFI

3 pounds octopus
1–1½ cups oil
1 medium onion, chopped
3 pounds ripe tomatoes, peeled
and strained, or 1 tablespoon
tomato paste diluted with 2
cups of water from the octopus

salt and pepper to taste
rice as desired

NOTE: Octopus may be fresh, dried, or canned. In Greece, only fresh octopus, which has been tenderized by pounding when it is caught, is used. Canned octopus is ready to use. Dried octopus should be soaked for 24 hours, then drained, and pounded.

Clean the octopus. Boil in ample water with a little coarse salt for about 5 minutes; reserve the broth. Remove the octopus from the broth and cool it. Cut it into small pieces.

Sauté the onions in a saucepan in the oil until they are a light golden color. Add the tomatoes (or the diluted tomato paste) to them. Bring to a boil, add the octopus and cook for 5 minutes. Add 2 cups of broth and ⅓ cup water for each cup of raw rice used (1 cup will serve 2 to 4 people). Stir at first to keep the rice from sticking. Cover the pot and simmer until most of the liquid is absorbed. Remove from the heat. Take off the lid, cover the pot with a towel, and replace the lid. Let stand for 5 minutes, and then serve. Serves 6.

OCTOPUS STIFADO ✠ XTAPOTHI STIFADO

3 pounds octopus
2 pounds small whole onions,
cleaned
1½ cups oil
½ cup red vinegar
1 head garlic, cleaned
3 bay leaves

1 stalk rosemary
salt to taste
peppercorns
1½ pounds ripe tomatoes,
peeled and strained, or 1
tablespoon tomato paste
diluted with 1 cup water

Cut the octopus into 1-to 1½-inch pieces. Put into a pot with the other ingredients. Cover, and simmer about 1 hour until all the liquid has been absorbed and a little oil remains. Serves 6.

FRIED SQUID   ✠   KALAMARAKIA TIGANITA

Wash the squid in plenty of water. Remove the back bones and the ink sac. Discard the head. Remove the skin from the body and slice the skin into thin strips. Cut the squid in half lengthwise and then horizontally. Wash again and drain. Season lightly with salt and pepper. Dip into flour and shake off excess. Heat oil in a frying pan and fry the squid until golden brown. Keep warm, and when all the pieces are fried, return to the pan and pour lemon juice over all. Serve hot.

STUFFED SQUID   ✠   KALAMARAKIA YEMISTA

3 pounds medium-size squid
1½ cups oil
1½ cups chopped onion
1 cup water

1 cup chopped parsley
salt and pepper to taste
¾ cup raw rice
1 lemon, juice only

Wash and clean the squid as in Fried Squid above, but do not cut the squid. Cut off the tentacles and chop them into small pieces, reserving them for the stuffing. Heat two-thirds of the oil, and add the onions and chopped tentacles to it. Brown them, then add the water, parsley, salt, and pepper. Simmer, covered, over low heat for 30 minutes. Add the rice, stir; when the rice begins to boil, cover the pot and simmer for 10 to 15 minutes. Stuff the squid with this mixture but do not overstuff them, as the rice will swell during the cooking but the squid will not stretch. Place the squid upright in a deep pot. Pour in the rest of the oil and the lemon juice, and add an additional cup of water, or more, if necessary. Cover the pot; simmer about 30 minutes until all the liquid has been absorbed and only the oil remains. Serves 6 to 10.

FRIED MUSSELS   ✠   MYTHIA TIGANITA

3 pounds (approximately)
    mussels
salt and pepper to taste
1–2 eggs

4–5 tablespoons milk
⅓ cup flour
1 teaspoon baking powder

Wash and scrub the mussels. Place in a pot with 1 to 2 inches of water. Cover the pot. Cook until the shells open (about 8 minutes). Cool; remove the mussels from the shells, and drain. Season lightly with salt and pepper. Beat together the eggs and milk, add the flour and baking powder; mix well. Dip 2 or 3 mussels at a time into this batter and fry in hot oil until golden. Serves 6 to 8.

TARAMA [CARP ROE] PATTIES ✠ TARAMOKEFTEDES

½ pound tarama*
2 cups white bread (crusts removed), soaked in water and squeezed out
½ cup minced parsley
2 tablespoons chopped dill
2 medium onions, minced

3–4 tablespoons water
2 tablespoons oil
1 tablespoon lemon juice
⅓ cup flour plus flour for frying
1 teaspoon baking powder
oil for frying

If the roe has a skin, soak it for 10 minutes in warm water, then drain. Put a third of the bread into a wooden bowl and mash thoroughly. Add the tarama; mix again. Add the remaining bread and mash again to form a paste. Put this into a small bowl and add parsley and dill.

Boil the onions in the water and when the water is absorbed, add the oil, simmer until golden. Remove from the heat and add to the tarama mixture. Add lemon juice. Sift the ⅓ cup flour and the baking powder together, and add to the mixture. If the consistency is too thick, it may require a few drops of water. Mix well. Shape into patties and flour them lightly. Fry in hot oil until brown on both sides. Serve with hot greens, cauliflower, artichokes, bean salad, or lettuce salad. Serves 6.

NOTE: Tarama is sometimes called botargo.

SAUCES AND DESSERT SAUCES

BÉCHAMEL SAUCE 1 [REGULAR] ✠ SALTSA BESAMEL KANONIKI 1

6 tablespoons butter
7–8 tablespoons flour
4 cups milk, scalded

1–2 egg yolks
salt and pepper to taste

Melt the butter, but do not brown. Add the flour slowly, mixing constantly. Remove from the heat. Slowly mix in the scalded milk. Return to the heat and stir until the sauce thickens. Beat the egg yolks well, and add them with salt and pepper to the mixture, stirring constantly until blended. If you do not serve the sauce immediately, stir it occasionally to prevent a crust from forming.

BÉCHAMEL SAUCE 2 [THICK] ✠ SALTSA BESAMEL PIKTI 2

8 tablespoons butter
10–12 tablespoons flour
4 cups milk, scalded

1–2 egg yolks
salt and pepper to taste

Melt the butter and add the flour slowly to it, blending thoroughly. Remove from the heat and slowly add the milk, mixing constantly. Return to the heat. Stir until the mixture thickens. Beat the egg yolks well; add with the salt and pepper, stirring all the while until well blended. If you do not serve the sauce immediately, stir occasionally to prevent a crust from forming.

143

BÉCHAMEL SAUCE 3 [LIGHT]   ✠   SALTSA BESAMEL AERI 3

3 tablespoons butter
4 tablespoons flour
4 cups milk, scalded

1–2 egg yolks
salt and pepper to taste

Melt the butter, but do not brown it. Add the flour slowly, blending it in thoroughly. Remove from the heat. Add the milk slowly, mixing all the while. Return to the heat and stir until the mixture thickens. Beat the egg yolks well and add with the salt and pepper, mixing constantly until well blended. If you do not serve the sauce immediately, stir occasionally to prevent a crust from forming.

BÉCHAMEL SAUCE 4   ✠   SALTSA BESAMEL SE
[SMALLER RECIPE—THICK]   MIKROTERI ANALOGIA

3 tablespoons butter
4 tablespoons flour
1 cup milk

1–2 egg yolks
salt and pepper to taste

Melt the butter, but do not brown it. Add the flour slowly, blending it in thoroughly. Remove from the heat. Slowly add the milk, mixing constantly. Return to the heat and stir until the sauce thickens. Beat the egg yolks well and add with salt and pepper to the mixture, stirring all the while until well blended. If you do not use immediately, stir occasionally to prevent a crust from forming.

SAUCE VINAIGRETTE   ✠   SALTSA VINEGRETTE

½ cup oil
¼ cup vinegar
2 tablespoons lemon juice
1 hard-cooked egg, minced
2 teaspoons minced parsley

2 teaspoons minced sweet pickle
salt and pepper to taste
1 teaspoon minced capers
1 teaspoon minced onion

Beat the oil, vinegar, and lemon juice together. Add the remaining ingredients. Mix well. Serve over boiled meat, fish, etc.

MAYONNAISE ✠ MAYONEZA

½ teaspoon dried mustard
½ teaspoon sugar
½ teaspoon salt
pinch of white pepper

½ teaspoon white vinegar
2 egg yolks
1⅔ cups best-quality oil
1 lemon, juice only

Mix the mustard, sugar, salt, and pepper together in a glass bowl. Add the vinegar and egg yolks; mix well. Add the oil, drop by drop, and mix in one direction. When the mayonnaise begins to thicken, thin with a little of the lemon juice. Continue to stir, adding lemon juice and oil alternately.

NOTE: If the mixture curdles, it can be repaired by starting over with egg yolks and spices, and then carefully adding the curdled mixture to the new batch when it begins to thicken. Or mix in a blender to prevent curdling.

GREEN SAUCE ✠ SALTSA PRASINI

1 teaspoon parsley juice

2 cups mayonnaise

Dice the leaves of fresh parsley, then put them into a mortar and pound to a pulp. Pass through a strainer. Mix the juice well with the mayonnaise.

YELLOW SAUCE ✠ SALTSA KITRINI

4–5 hard-cooked egg yolks
½ cup white wine

2 cups mayonnaise

Mash the egg yolks in a bowl. Add the wine, a little at a time, and blend well. Add to the mayonnaise and mix well.

SAUCE WITH BRAINS ✠ SALTSA ME MIALA

1 cup Boiled Brains (see index)
salt and pepper to taste

2 cups mayonnaise
2 tablespoons minced parsley

Prepare boiled brains and let them cool, then cut them into small pieces. Add the salt and pepper. Mix with the mayonnaise and garnish with parsley.

TARTAR SAUCE ✠ SALTSA TARTAR

4 teaspoons pickle relish
1 tablespoon capers
1 tablespoon parsley
2 cups mayonnaise

lemon juice (optional)
vinegar (optional)
water (optional)

Chop the first three ingredients fine and add to the mayonnaise. If the sauce is too thick, it may be thinned with a little lemon juice, vinegar, or water.

SAUCE ANTALOUSE ✠ SALTSA ANTALOUS

1½ pounds fresh tomatoes
water
1 tablespoon diced fresh green
   pepper

1 tablespoon diced fresh red
   pepper
2 cups mayonnaise
salt and pepper to taste

Cut the tomatoes into 2 to 3 pieces. Place in a pot with very little water, and salt. Cook until soft, then strain. Put the pulp and juice back into the pot. Cook down until you have about ½ cup paste. Cool. Add with all the other ingredients to the mayonnaise and mix well. Serve cold.

SAUCE WITH WHIPPED CREAM ✠ SALTSA ME CREMA YALAKTOS

3 tablespoons plus 1 teaspoon
   heavy cream

2 cups mayonnaise

Whip the cream and add to the mayonnaise.

HOLLANDAISE SAUCE ✠ SALTSA OLLANDIKI

8 teaspoons vinegar
salt to taste
3–4 peppercorns
4 egg yolks

1½ cups butter, melted
1 tablespoon lemon juice
4 teaspoons milk (optional)

Place the vinegar, salt, and peppercorns in a small enamel pot and bring to a boil; cook until the vinegar is reduced by one half. Remove from the heat; discard the peppercorns; cool. Add the egg yolks, blending in with a fork. Put the mixture into the top of a double boiler, over hot water. Slowly add the butter, stirring constantly. When the sauce begins to thicken, stir in the lemon juice. If the sauce is too thick, thin it with the milk. Serve hot.

GARLIC SAUCE ✠ SKORDALIA*

1 head garlic
¾–1¾ pounds potatoes, boiled
     and peeled
2–3 cups oil

⅓–½ cup vinegar
almonds (optional)
walnuts (optional)

Clean the garlic and mash it completely (put in a blender or food chopper, or pound with a mortar and pestle). Mash in the potatoes, one at a time, until you have a thick paste (the more potatoes you use, the more sauce you will have, but the less potent it will be). Alternately add the oil and vinegar, beating constantly. (A blender is wonderful for this; a mixer is fine, too, but slower.) If the sauce is too thick for your taste, add a little of the broth from the fish. No lumps in this sauce, please!

NOTE: Many people like to add almonds or walnuts to skordalia. These are mashed to a pulp and added to the paste before the potatoes, oil, and vinegar.

GARLIC SAUCE WITH BREAD ✠ SKORDALIA* ME PSOMI

12–18 slices white bread
1 head (about 12 cloves) garlic
2 cups olive oil

⅓ cup vinegar
parsley
Calamata olives

Trim and discard the crusts from the bread; soak in water and squeeze out thoroughly; measure to make 2 cups. Clean the garlic. Pound with a mortar and pestle or whirl in a blender. Add the bread, a little at a time, and mix or blend well with the garlic to a pastelike consistency. Add the oil and vinegar alternately, beating constantly. If the sauce is too thick, add a little fish broth or water to thin it. (But dilute with fish broth only when you plan to serve the sauce on fish; if you will serve it with eggplant, dilute with water.) Garnish with parsley and the olives.

NOTE: This is a thick sauce with a pudding-like consistency. It does not flow off the spoon.

TUNA SAUCE   ✛   SALTSA TUNI

5–6 large pastes sardeles*
  (salt-packed anchovies)
½ cup canned tuna
4 teaspoons chopped parsley
1½ pounds (approximately) ripe
  tomatoes, peeled and
  strained, or 1½ tablespoons
  tomato paste diluted with
  2 cups of water

1 cup oil or ¾ cup butter
2 cloves garlic, cleaned and
  sliced
salt and pepper to taste
1 bay leaf
½ cup grated cheese

Thoroughly clean the anchovies as follows: First, wash these with water, then rinse with vinegar. It is very important that these be thoroughly rinsed and no salt remains. Rub them so the skin and fins are removed. Cut off the tail. Ignore the bones; they are edible, although they may be easily removed. Just peel off the one side of the anchovy, then peel back the bone and tail. Cut into small pieces. Cut the tuna into small pieces. Mix the anchovies, tuna, and parsley together, set aside.

Put the tomatoes to boil with the butter or oil. Add the garlic, salt, pepper, and bay leaf, and cook until thick. Add the fish mixture, and boil 5 to 10 minutes longer. Remove from the heat. Add the cheese, mix well, and serve.

SAUCE WITH GELATIN   ✛   SALTSA ME ZELATINA

2½ teaspoons unflavored
  gelatin

2–3 tablespoons boiling water
2 cups mayonnaise

Soften and dissolve the gelatin in the water; cool. Add to the mayonnaise, a little at a time, mixing constantly. Use before it thickens to cover whole hard-cooked eggs.

SPANISH SAUCE   ✛   SALTSA ISPANIKI

4–5 cups meat broth
2 tablespoons butter
8 teaspoons flour
2 cups Mavrodaphne* wine

½ cup tomato paste (fresh or
  canned), diluted with a little
  water
salt and pepper to taste

Scald—do not boil—the broth. Keep hot. Melt the butter in a small pot. Add the flour slowly, mix in very well. Continue to mix over a low heat for about 10 minutes until the mixture is a light-coffee color, then add the scalded broth. Mixing constantly so it does not form lumps. Add the wine, tomatoes, salt, and pepper. Continue to cook for 15 to 20 minutes longer, stirring constantly, until thick.

TOMATO SAUCE 1 ✠ SALTSA DOMATA 1

2 pounds ripe tomatoes, peeled and strained, or 2 tablespoons tomato paste diluted with 2 cups water

1 medium onion, washed and peeled, chopped
2 pieces cinnamon stick
salt and pepper to taste
4 teaspoons butter

Put the strained tomatoes (or diluted tomato paste) into a large pot with the remaining ingredients. Bring to a boil. Lower the heat and cook until the sauce thickens. Remove the cinnamon. Serve hot over pasta or rice.

TOMATO SAUCE 2 ✠ SALTSA DOMATA 2

2 tablespoons butter
1 onion, chopped
2–3 cloves garlic, chopped
2 pounds ripe tomatoes, peeled and strained, or 2 tablespoons tomato paste diluted with 2 cups of water

3–4 stalks celery
3–4 sprigs of parsley
1 cup broth or water
salt and pepper to taste

Melt the butter and sauté the onions and garlic in it until light in color. Add the tomatoes, the celery and parsley tied in a bunch, and the broth or water. Cook until thickened. Remove the celery and parsley. Cook a few minutes longer. Serve hot over pasta or rice.

TOMATO SAUCE 3   ✠   SALTSA DOMATES 3

1–2 tablespoons tomato paste   1 small onion, peeled and
    diluted with 1–1½ cups   washed
    water; or 1½ pounds ripe   1 piece cinnamon stick
    tomatoes, peeled and   salt and pepper to taste
    strained   2 tablespoons butter

    Put all the ingredients into a pot and bring to a boil. Reduce the heat and
simmer until the sauce has a medium-thick consistency (approximately 45 minutes).
Remove the cinnamon and serve hot over pasta or rice. Makes about 1 cup.

TOMATO SAUCE 4   ✠   SALTSA DOMATES 4

3 pounds ripe tomatoes, peeled   2–3 stalks celery
    and strained   2–3 tablespoons butter
1 medium onion, chopped   1 cup water
2–3 cloves garlic, chopped   salt and pepper to taste
3–4 sprigs parsley

    Tie the parsley and celery together, and place in a pot with the rest of the
ingredients; bring to a boil. Reduce the heat and simmer for about 30 minutes.
Remove the parsley and celery, and continue to cook for another 10 or 15
minutes (until the sauce is thick). Serve hot over pasta or rice. Makes about 2 cups.

GRAVY   ✠   SALTSA PSITOU

butter or fat from the roast pan   2 tablespoons flour
1½–2 cups water   salt and pepper to taste

    When the roast is finished, take 3–4 tablespoons of its fat (or melted butter, if
needed) and place in a pot or frying pan; set it aside. Add the water to the
roast pan and scrape until all the particles stuck to the pan come loose. Heat,
and then strain to make a stock; keep hot. Put the pot containing the fat on to
heat. When it is hot, add the flour; mix well. Stir until it takes on a chestnut color.
Add the stock and mix well. Add salt and pepper. Cook, stirring constantly, until it
thickens. Serve with the meat.

DESSERT SAUCES

SABAYON SAUCE ✠ SALTSA SAMPAYION

4 eggs
1 cup confectioner's sugar

⅛ cup water
½ cup cognac

Put the eggs, sugar, and water into a bowl and beat for 2 minutes. Place the bowl in a pan of boiling water—but not on the stove—and continue to beat. The sauce will slowly begin to froth and swell. Only then put the pan directly over the heat. Continue to beat for about 15 to 20 minutes, at which time the sauce will be thick. Add the cognac and blend well. Remove from the heat and serve hot, in a sauceboat.

APRICOT SAUCE ✠ SALTSA VERIKOKKO

1 cup apricot marmalade
¼ cup boiling water

¼ cup cognac

Blend all the ingredients together and serve hot in a sauceboat.

STRAWBERRY SAUCE ✠ SALTSA FRAOULES

1¼ cups sugar
½ cup water
½ teaspoon lemon juice

1 cup strawberries, washed and
   drained
½ cup orange juice
½ cup cognac

Mix the sugar with the water and lemon juice and boil until it becomes a syrup. Pass the strawberries through a strainer and add to the syrup. Mix well, then bring to a boil. Cook for about 2 minutes, then add the orange juice and cognac. Mix well, and serve hot in a sauceboat.

SPOON SWEETS

Spoon sweets are never missing from the Greek home. The customary welcome to visitors to the house is the offering of a spoonful of seasonal sweets and a glass of iced water, followed by a liqueur. All fruits can be made into sweets by the addition of sugar. Always add a little more sugar, rather than less, so the fruit does not lose its own natural sugar and lump or shrivel, but remains plump and retains its color and shape.

In making spoon sweets, your first concern is the thickening of the syrup. Because these preserves will last almost a year, the syrup is important and must be made so that it will not crystallize or sour. The crystallizing can be prevented by adding lemon juice during the last stages of thickening. Test by dropping from a teaspoon into a glass of cold water. It should make a soft ball. Syrup should boil almost to a bubbling-over stage. Boil at top speed over a high heat to jell quickly and preserve color. *Always boil uncovered.* (Covered sweets are always darker.) Skim all foam from the top, but do not stir the sweets while they are boiling. As soon as they thicken, cool and pack in sterilized jars. If the jellies crystallize, pour back into a pot, add a few drops of water and reboil, or put the jelly in its jar into a pot of boiling water. If the jelly is not thick enough, return it to the pot, add more sugar and reboil as above. If any syrup remains after the fruits are jellied, it can be used for making new preserves, or on toast, pancakes, etc.

EGGPLANT GLYKO ✠ MELITZANAKI

3 pounds very small eggplants
water as needed
blanched almonds

3 pounds sugar
3 sticks cinnamon
4–5 whole cloves
½ teaspoon lemon juice

Select the smallest eggplants (about 2 inches long). Remove the stems. Make a small, lengthwise cut in the side of each eggplant. Put into a ceramic bowl, cover with water, and soak for 24 hours, changing the water 2 or 3 times. Drain well and put 1 or 2 almonds into each cut. (Wrap white thread around each to keep the almonds in during the cooking.) Boil the sugar with 2 cups water, the cinnamon, and cloves for 5 minutes. Add the eggplants and boil 5 minutes longer. Remove from the heat and let stand for 24 hours. Drain the eggplants, saving the syrup, and remove and discard the string, then return them to the syrup and cook over high heat until the syrup thickens (about 10 to 30 minutes). Add the lemon juice; boil 2 or 3 minutes longer. Remove from the heat. Cool and pack in sterilized jars.

MASTIKA GLYKO ☧ MASTIKA GLYKO

3¼ cups sugar	2 teaspoons lemon juice
½ cup water	1 teaspoon mastic powder

Add the sugar to the water and bring to a boil. Stir to dissolve the sugar. Boil to the soft-ball stage. Add the lemon juice, and boil for about 1 minute. Pour into a bowl and cool to lukewarm. Add the mastic powder and stir with a wooden spoon until the mixture thickens and turns white.

VANILLA GLYKO ☧ VANILA GLYKO

Prepare like Mastika Glyko, above, but add 1 teaspoon of vanilla extract.

FRESH TOMATO GLYKO ☧ DOMATAKI FRESKO

3 pounds small seedless tomatoes (plum tomatoes)	1½ teaspoons vanilla
3 pounds sugar (6¾ cups) plus sugar for sprinkling	filberts or hazelnuts, skins removed
1 cup water	2 teaspoons lemon juice

Drop the tomatoes into boiling water for 1 minute. Remove, and peel. Put the tomatoes on a platter and sprinkle with ample sugar. Let stand 24 hours. To the liquid which the tomatoes exude, add a cup of water; mix in the 3 pounds sugar. Bring to a boil, and cook for 15 minutes. Stuff a filbert or hazelnut into each tomato and put these into the syrup. Boil for 3 minutes. Remove from the heat and let stand until the following day. Return to the heat. Add the vanilla and the lemon juice and boil until very thick. Cool, and pack in sterilized jars.

QUINCE GLYKO ✚ KITHONI GLYKO

3 pounds quince
3 pounds sugar
2 cups water
1 teaspoon vanilla

1 teaspoon lemon juice
½ cup chopped blanched
   almonds

Select large, light quince. Wipe off the fuzz and peel them. Thinly slice the quince, and then cut each slice into thin strips like matchsticks. Put these into water as soon as you cut them. Drain, and put into a pot with 2 cups of water. Cook covered, until soft (10 to 15 minutes, but sometimes longer). Add the sugar; boil over very high heat to thicken the syrup quickly. The quince should be a very light color; if cooked too slowly or too long, they will turn red. Add the vanilla and lemon juice as soon as the syrup thickens, and boil for another 2 or 3 minutes. Remove from the heat. Add the almonds, mix well; cool, and place in sterilized jars.

NOTE: Quince Glyko can also be made by grating the quince. If you wish a red color, add a bit more water and cook over medium heat. By the time the syrup thickens, the quince will have turned red.

NOTE: This can also be made with large slices of quince and 2 or 3 rose geranium leaves instead of vanilla.

QUINCE BELTESS AND JELLY BARS ✚ KITHONI BELTESS

THE BELTESS

3 pounds quince
12 cups water
4 cups sugar
1 teaspoon lemon juice
1 teaspoon vanilla
1 cheesecloth bag
1 flannel bag

THE BARS

sugar as needed
1 tablespoon (approximately)
   quince pulp (from the beltess)
blanched almonds
cognac

Wipe the fuzz from the quince; wash them and cut into quarters; peel off the skin and remove the seeds, reserving both. Tie the skins and seeds into the cheesecloth bag. Cut each fruit quarter into 3 or 4 slices and place, with the water, in a large pot; add the bag containing the peel and seeds. Boil until the quince are very tender (about 1 hour, but this depends on the thickness of the fruit). Secure a strainer to a large saucepan (or bowl) and turn the contents of the pot into it, without forcing the quince through, so the liquid strains through. Reserve the fruit; squeeze the cheesecloth bag lightly to remove any liquid, then discard it. Make a bag from a clean piece of flannel and pour the strained liquid into it; allow it to drip through—do not squeeze it through—into a pot or bowl. Boil this strained liquid down to 3 or 3¼ cups. Add the sugar, stir, and boil over high heat until thick (it should fall from the spoon in sheets). Add the vanilla and lemon juice, and boil 2 or 3 minutes longer. Pour immediately into wide-mouthed sterilized jars or glasses. Cool.

With the quince pulp, prepare the Quince Jelly Bars as follows: Pass the pulp through a purée machine or whirl it in a blender (or if you prefer, mash it with your hands). Measure the pulp. Place it in a heavy pot over medium high heat together with ½ cup sugar for each cup of pulp. Cook, stirring constantly, until the mixture thickens and begins to pull away from the sides of the pot. Remove from the heat. Quickly oil a square pan (or a piece of marble, if it is available), and pour the jelly onto it, spreading it with the back of a knife to ½- to 1-inch thickness.

Cool thoroughly, then cut into squares or diamonds. Sprinkle first with a little cognac, then with sugar; press half an almond into each piece. Let the bars stand for 3 or 4 hours, then store them in a box sprinkled with sugar, or wrap each one separately in plastic wrap.

ROSE PETAL GLYKO ✠ TRIANDAFILO GLYKO

1½ pounds rose petals
3 pounds sugar

2 cups water
1 tablespoon lemon juice

Wash the petals well. (The original recipe specifies April roses; we'll use the earliest. If you use insecticide sprays, don't try this recipe. Or else do not spray the roses until after the first blooming. Put the petals into the pot with 1 cup of the sugar and ¾ cup water, and simmer, covered, for 15 minutes. Remove the cover and add the rest of the sugar and water. Raise the heat and boil until the syrup thickens; skim off any froth with a slotted spoon. Add the lemon juice, and boil for an additional 2 or 3 minutes. Remove from the heat. Cool; store in sterilized jars.

NOTE: There is more lemon juice in this recipe because it crystallizes easily.

PEACH GLYKO ✠ ROTHAKINO GLYKO

3 pounds peaches
2 tablespoons quick lime
3 pounds sugar
water as needed

1½ teaspoons vanilla
1 teaspoon lemon juice

Select large peaches, not too ripe. Peel and cut each into 6 pieces, discard the pits. Dilute the quick lime in 8 cups of water, add the peaches, and soak for 1 hour. Rinse well in ample water and drain. Boil the sugar and 2 cups of water to make a thick syrup. Remove from the heat and cool. Add the peaches, bring to a boil, and cook until the syrup thickens again. Add the vanilla and lemon juice. Boil another minute. Remove from the heat. Cool and store in sterilized jars.

CHERRY GLYKO   ✠   VISSINO GLYKO

3 pounds sour cherries
6½ cups sugar

1 cup water
1 tablespoon lemon juice

Wash the cherries in ample water; remove the stems; remove the pits carefully so as not to mash the cherries. (The Greeks use a hairpin for this.) Place the cherries alternately with the sugar in layers in a large pot and let stand for 3 or 4 hours. Add the water and bring to a boil over high heat. Remove all froth with a slotted spoon as it rises, and when the syrup thickens, add the lemon juice. Boil 2 to 3 minutes longer. Remove from the heat, cool, and put into sterilized jars.

NOTE: If at the same time you want to make more syrup to use for Vissinada,* the classic Greek iced drink, use 6 pounds of sugar. It will make extra syrup.

STRAWBERRY GLYKO   ✠   FRAOULES GLYKO

3 pounds strawberries
4 lemons, juice only

3 pounds sugar
1 cup water
1 teaspoon lemon juice

Select large firm berries. Clean them carefully, wash well. Place on a platter or in a shallow bowl and pour the juice from the 4 lemons over them. Let stand for 3 or 4 hours; drain. Boil the sugar with the water until it thickens to a syrup. Add the berries, and cook over medium heat for about 8 minutes. Remove from the heat and carefully remove the berries with a slotted spoon. Return the syrup to high heat; cook until it is well thickened. Add the strawberries again, and remove any froth that rises with a slotted spoon. Add the teaspoon lemon juice; boil for about 2 minutes. Remove from the heat, cool, and place in sterilized jars.

BITTER ORANGE GLYKO   ✠   NERANTZAKI GLYKO

3 pounds bitter oranges
water as needed

7 cups sugar
1 teaspoon lemon juice

Select small, dark-green bitter oranges. (Unripe and small, they resemble pingpong balls). Scrape the skins with a sharp knife to remove the outer, very bitter layer. Using a very thin pointed knife, cut a small hole through each orange to remove the pips; do not cut it open. Wash the oranges well and put into a large pot with ample water. Bring to a boil and cook until they are soft (about 1½ hours; test often by piercing with a needle; if they fall off the needle, they are cooked enough). Do not overcook or they will harden in the syrup. Remove from the heat, pour off the water, and replace it with cold water. Soak the oranges for

48 hours, changing the water 3 or 4 times. Boil the sugar with 2 cups water for 5 minutes. Drain the oranges well and add to the syrup. Boil for 5 minutes. Remove from the heat and let stand overnight. Again, bring to a boil, add the lemon juice, and cook until the syrup thickens. Cool and put into sterilized jars.

APRICOT GLYKO ✠ VERIKOKKO GLYKO

3 pounds apricots
2 tablespoons quick lime
3 pounds sugar
1 cup water

blanched almonds
1 teaspoon lemon juice
1 teaspoon vanilla

Select firm apricots that are not too ripe. Wash them, trim with a sharp knife, carefully peel off the skin. Hold the apricot firmly in your palm and poke the pit out with a nail. (This way the apricot does not have to be split.) Put the lime into 10 cups of water in a ceramic or glass bowl; mix well. The lime solution will turn milky white. Stand the apricots in this solution for 1 to 2 hours, then rinse in ample water several times and put on a towel to dry.

In the meantime, boil the sugar and water to a thick syrup; cool. When the apricots are dry, put a blanched almond in each one in place of the pit, and place them in the syrup; turn the heat very high to quickly rethicken. Add the vanilla and lemon juice, and boil for about 2 minutes. Remove from the heat. Let stand overnight. If the apricots have exuded water, so the syrup is thin, reboil to thicken. Let cool, and put into sterilized jars.

ORANGE GLYKO ✠ PORTOCALI GLYKO

4 thick-skinned oranges
3 pounds sugar

1 teaspoon lemon juice
1½ teaspoons vanilla

Lightly grate the skins, then put the whole oranges into a pot with plenty of water. Bring to the boil and cook for about two hours, so the oranges soften completely. Remove from the heat and plunge them into cold water; let stand for 8 hours, changing the water every 2 hours. Carefully cut each orange into 4 slices, and then cut each slice in half. With a sharp knife or small scissors, cut off the skin and place the orange pieces on a deep platter in rows, with the fleshy part up. Sprinkle with a little sugar, and let stand overnight. Put the sugar and the liquid exuded by the oranges during the night in a large pot. Stir to mix well, and bring to a boil. Cook until it becomes a thick syrup. Remove from the heat, cool, and add the oranges. Return to high heat and boil rapidly to rethicken. Add the lemon juice and vanilla, and boil for another 1 or 2 minutes. Remove from the heat and cool. This process may have to be repeated the next day, as the oranges exude a great deal of water. Simply boil over high heat as quickly as possible until the syrup thickens.

MARMALADES AND COMPOTES

ORANGE MARMALADE 1   ✠   MARMELADA PORTOCALI 1

6–8 thick-skinned oranges
water as needed

3 cups (approximately) sugar

Grate the oranges lightly to remove the outer color from the rind. Cut them into 5 or 6 lengthwise slices, and remove the skins, reserving them. Put the pieces of orange into a pot with very little water, and cook them until soft (test by piercing with a fork). Pass them through a strainer. Measure the puréed pulp, and put it into a pot with an equal amount of sugar; boil until thick.

In the meantime, cut a third of the peel into very thin slices (like matchsticks), and cook with a little water in another pot until tender. Drain, then add the peel to the marmalade; boil it another 2 or 3 minutes. Remove from the heat and cool. Pack into sterilized jars and seal.

ORANGE MARMALADE 2   ✠   MARMELADA PORTOCALI 2

Prepare the oranges as for Orange Marmalade 1, above. Cut a third of the peel into narrow, matchlike strips, and boil in ample water. Drain, and rinse 2 or 3 times in cold water. Remove the pits and skins from the oranges, and using only the fleshy part, measure the quantity. Measure out an equal amount of sugar, and put this into a saucepan with just enough water to dissolve it completely (about ⅓ cup water for 1 cup sugar). Boil until you get a very thick syrup. Add the oranges, and stir them into the syrup; cook until the marmalade thickens. Add the precooked skins, and cook for 2 or 3 minutes longer. Cool, pack into sterilized jars and seal.

ORANGE MARMALADE 3   ✠   MARMELADA PORTOCALI 3

Use thin-skinned oranges for this. Grate them lightly to remove the outer color from the rind; pierce with a needle in several places, then put them into a pot; add water. Boil for about 40 minutes, or until the skin can be pierced easily with a fork. Transfer them to another pot with enough cold water to cover, and soak for 24 hours, changing the water 3 or 4 times. Drain; cut into thick slices; remove the pits, any hard membranes, and the skin. Put the oranges through a meat grinder, or cut them with a knife into small pieces. Measure this pulp, and add it to a pot, and for every 2 cups of pulp, add 3 cups sugar and 1 cup water. Bring the whole to a boil over high heat; stir constantly until the mixture becomes a thick marmalade. Cool. Pack into sterilized jars, and seal.

NOTE: You can make this recipe with bitter oranges, also. Soak them for 48 hours (instead of 24), and increase the amount of sugar by ½ cup. Or combine regular oranges and bitter oranges for an excellent marmalade, then proceed as above.

PEAR MARMALADE   ✠   MARMELADA AXLADIA

3 pounds ripe pears   lemon juice
water as needed   4½ cups sugar

Remove the stems from the pears and cut each into 4 to 6 pieces. Remove the pits. Put the pears into a bowl of water with a little lemon juice to prevent discoloring. Drain, then rinse. Cook them in 2 cups water until they become pulpy. Pass them through a strainer. Put the purée with the sugar into a wide pot, stir with a wooden spoon, and cook over high heat until marmalade thickens. Add the 1 teaspoon lemon juice, and cook for another 2 or 3 minutes. Remove from the heat, cool, and serve, or store in glass or ceramic jars.

APPLE MARMALADE   ✠   MARMELADA MILO

Make like Pear Marmalade, above, but peel the apples first.

PEACH MARMALADE   ✠   MARMELADA ROTHAKINO

Make like Apple Marmalade, above.

QUINCE MARMALADE ✠ MARMELADA KITHONI

Make like Apple Marmalade, above.

STRAWBERRY MARMALADE ✠ MARMELADA FRAOULES

3 pounds strawberries   1 teaspoon lemon juice
3 pounds sugar

Use ripe, solid strawberries for this. Wash them very well and remove the stems. Put the berries into a bowl and crush them. Place the pulp and juice into a wide pot, add the sugar, and mix well. Cook over medium heat until the mixture falls from a wooden spoon in wide, thick sheets. Add the lemon juice, cook for another 3 or 4 minutes. Remove from the heat and pack in glass or ceramic jars.

FIG MARMALADE ✠ MARMELADA SIKO

3 pounds ripe figs   1 teaspoon lemon juice
3 cups sugar

Peel the figs and proceed as for Strawberry Marmalade, above.

APRICOT MARMALADE ✠ MARMELADA VERIKOKKO

3 pounds apricots   1 cup water
3 pounds sugar   1 teaspoon lemon juice

Select ripe but firm apricots. Wash them, remove the pits, and boil with the water. When the fruit is soft, pass it through a strainer. Put the purée and the sugar into a wide pot. Cook over high heat, stirring with a wooden spoon so it does not scorch. When the mixture falls from the spoon in wide sheets, add the lemon juice; cook another 2 minutes. Remove from the heat, cool, and pack in glass or ceramic jars.

PLUM MARMALADE ✠ MARMELADA KOROMILA

Make like Apricot Marmalade, above, but use ½ cup water. Proceed as directed.

MIXED FRUIT COMPOTE ✠ KOMPOSTA ANAMIKTI

¾ pound pears
¾ pound apples
¾ pound peaches
¾ pound apricots
lemon juice

1½ pounds sugar
2 pieces of stick cinnamon
3 cups water
3–5 cloves
1 lemon rind

Peel the pears and the apples; cut into quarters, remove the seeds and the hard core. Put them into a bowl of water with a little lemon juice. Wash the peaches and apricots and remove the pits; slice the peaches, and cut the apricots in half. Rinse the pears and apples, and put them into a pot with the remaining ingredients except the peaches and apricots. Bring to a boil; cook for 5 minutes. Add the peaches and cook for another 5 minutes, then add the apricots and cook 3 minutes longer. Remove the fruits to a compote dish with a slotted spoon and continue to boil the syrup until it thickens. Remove the cinnamon, cloves, and lemon rind, and discard them. Cool the syrup and pour it over the fruit.

APPLE COMPOTE ✠ KOMPOSTA MILA

1½ pounds cooking apples
lemon juice
1 cup sugar

water as needed
1 piece of stick cinnamon
1 lemon peel

Clean the apples and cut them into 2 to 4 pieces. Remove the seeds and the hard section near the core and place in a bowl of cold water with a little lemon juice. Rinse the apples, then put them in a wide pot with the sugar and 2 cups water; bring to a boil. Add the cinnamon stick and lemon peel. As soon as the apples are soft, remove them carefully with a slotted spoon and place in a compote dish. Cook the syrup a few minutes longer to thicken it slightly. Remove the cinnamon and lemon peel, and pour the syrup over the apples.

PLUM COMPOTE ✠ KOMPOSTA KOROMILA

1½ pounds plums
1½ pounds sugar

⅓ cup water
1 piece of stick cinnamon

Remove the stems from the plums, wash them, drain, and put in a pot. Cover with the sugar. Add the water (they will exude more) and cook over low heat until the sugar dissolves. Then add the cinnamon, raise the heat, and cook quickly so the plums do not collapse. As soon as the syrup thickens slightly, remove from the heat; discard the cinnamon. Cool and serve.

PEAR COMPOTE   ✠   KOMPOSTA AXLADIA

2 pounds pears   1 cup sugar
water as needed   1 lemon rind
lemon juice   ½ teaspoon vanilla

Remove the stems from the pears. Cut them into 3 or 4 pieces, remove the seeds and the hard parts of the core. Put into a bowl with water and a little lemon juice, to prevent their discoloring. Rinse; drain well, then put them in a pot with the sugar, and 1½ cups water, and cook over medium-high heat until the pears are soft, adding the lemon rind after the first 5 minutes. Remove from the heat, add the vanilla; cool, and serve in a compote dish.

PEACH COMPOTE   ✠   KOMPOSTA ROTHAKINO

1½ pounds peaches   1 cup sugar
water as needed   1 lemon rind
lemon juice   2 tablespoons cherry liqueur

Select peaches that are not too ripe. Wash and cut them into 3 or 4 pieces and put in a bowl of water with a little lemon juice. Boil 1 cup water, sugar and lemon peel in a saucepan for 2 minutes. Drain the peaches and add to the syrup; remove them with a slotted spoon and place them into a compote dish or bowl as soon as they are soft. Continue to boil the syrup until it thickens slightly. Remove from the heat, add the cherry liqueur, and pour over the peaches.

APRICOT COMPOTE   ✠   KOMPOSTA VERIKOKKO

1½ pounds apricots   1 cup water
1 cup sugar   ¼ cup cherry liqueur

Select large, firm apricots. Wash them and remove the pits. Boil the sugar and water together in a saucepan for about 5 minutes, then add the apricots. Cook about 5 minutes (watch them because they soften very quickly); then remove with a slotted spoon and place in a compote dish. Continue to boil the syrup until it thickens slightly. Remove from the heat. Add the liqueur, and pour over the apricots.

NOTE: Since the skin of the apricot loosens during cooking, you may remove it with a sharp knife, if you like, before pouring the syrup over the fruit.

CHESTNUT COMPOTE ✠ KOMPOSTA KASTANA

1½ pounds chestnuts
water as needed
1½ cups sugar

1 lemon rind
1 teaspoon vanilla

Remove the shells from the chestnuts. Put them into a pot of cold water and boil until tender but whole (about 25 minutes). Strain, and remove the skins. In another pot, boil together the sugar, lemon rind, and 1½ cups water until the syrup thickens slightly. Add the chestnuts; simmer for about 8 minutes. Remove the chestnuts to a compote dish with a slotted spoon. Add the vanilla to the syrup and boil a few minutes longer to thicken further. Cool the syrup, and pour over the chestnuts.

STRAWBERRY COMPOTE ✠ KOMPOSTA FRAOULA

1½ pounds strawberries
1 cup sugar
½ cup water

½–1 cup sweet dark-red Samos
wine (to taste)

Remove the leaves and stems from the berries and wash and drain them thoroughly. Boil the sugar and water together until the syrup thickens (as for jellies), then add the strawberries; cook for 3 to 5 minutes. Remove them with a slotted spoon and place in compote dish. Continue to boil the syrup until quite thick. Add the wine. Remove from the heat, cool, and pour over the strawberries.

CHERRY COMPOTE ✠ KOMPOSTA KERASI

1½ pounds cherries
1 cup sugar
1 piece of stick cinnamon

½ cup water
¼ cup cherry liqueur

Remove the stems from the cherries, wash them and, with a hairpin, pull out the pits. Boil together the sugar, cinnamon, and water for 8 to 10 minutes, then add the cherries. Continue to cook until done. (They must be tasted to determine when they are cooked.) Add the liqueur, boil for another 2 to 3 minutes. Remove from the heat and cool. Serve in a compote dish.

QUINCE COMPOTE ✠ KOMPOSTA KITHONI

1½ pounds quince, cleaned	1½ cups sugar
water as needed	1 lemon rind
lemon juice	

Wipe the quince and cut into quarters, then cut each quarter into thin slices. Remove the skin, pits, and hard core. Put the quince into a bowl of water with a little lemon juice added to prevent discoloring. Rinse; drain well; place in a pot and cover with the sugar. Add 2 cups water and the lemon rind, and bring to a boil. Cook for 15 to 20 minutes, or until the quince are soft and turn color. Remove from the heat, cool, and serve in a compotè dish.

NOTE: If you prefer a thicker syrup, remove the quince with a slotted spoon and continue to boil the syrup a little longer. Pour over the quince and serve.

FRIED PASTRIES

| LOUKOUMADES | ✠ | LOUKOUMADES |

THE BATTER

5 cups flour
1 teaspoon salt
1 package granular yeast
water as needed
5 cups oil for frying

THE SYRUP

2 cups sugar
1 cup honey
1 cup water

cinnamon

Sift the flour and salt together into a ceramic bowl; make a well in the middle. Dissolve the yeast in 1 cup water; pour into the flour. Mix lightly. Add water as needed to make a sticky batter, not too thin but not too thick (the batter will be just right when you can pull some of it up between your fingers and it will hold together without breaking off). Beat for 2 minutes; cover with a towel. Place in a warm place until it doubles in bulk (the batter is ready to use when it bubbles and blisters).

Pour the oil into a pot and heat it. Wet your hand (keep a bowl of water handy with which to keep wetting down your hand), place a spoonful of batter in your palm; squeeze gently so the batter oozes up out of the top of your closed fist into a bubble. Break off this bubble of batter (using a spoon, if you prefer), and drop it into the hot oil (the oil should be hot enough so the batter rises to the top immediately but does not immediately brown the puff), turn it at once, and keep turning it with a slotted spoon until it is golden; it will then be thoroughly cooked. Remove from the oil and drain on absorbent paper. You can probably fry 8 to 10 of these puffs at one time. Serve immediately. Makes at least 6 dozen loukoumades.

While the puffs are cooking, place the sugar, honey, and water for the syrup in a saucepan; bring to a boil. Cook until it is syrupy. Serve the loukoumades hot with the syrup; sprinkle with cinnamon.

SVINGI WITH SYRUP   ✠   SVINGI ME SIROPI

THE SVINGI	THE SYRUP
3 cups water	1½ cups sugar
1 cup butter	½ cup honey
1 teaspoon salt	1 cup water
1 lemon rind	2–3 cloves
3 cups flour	1 piece of stick cinnamon
8 eggs	½ cup cognac
oil for frying	

To make the svingi, put the water, butter, salt, and lemon rind into a pot and bring to a boil. Boil for 2 minutes, then discard the lemon rind. Remove the pot from the heat. Add the flour, all at once, mixing it in with a wooden spoon until well blended. Return the mass to the fire, and cook until it becomes sticky and pulls away from the sides of the pot. Again remove it from the heat; cool. Add the eggs, 1 at a time, beating them in well so the batter is very smooth. Heat the oil in a heavy pan; drop in the batter, a teaspoonful at a time (keep the amount small because the svingi puff up greatly during the frying). Fry 3 to 5 at a time, for about 5 minutes or until golden brown. Remove with a slotted spoon and drain on paper towels. Place on a platter. Makes about 60 svingi.

To make the syrup, place the sugar, honey, water, cloves, and stick cinnamon in a saucepan and boil for 5 minutes. Discard the cloves and cinnamon, and add the cognac. Pour into a sauceboat or pitcher, and serve with the svingi.

CUSTARD-FILLED SVINGI   ✠   SVINGI ME KREMA

1 recipe Svingi (above)	1½ pounds confectioner's sugar
1 recipe Crème Pâtissière	2 tablespoons cinnamon
(see index)	

Prepare the svingi, making them a little larger than usual. Prepare the custard, and insert it in a pastry bag fitted with a small round tip. Push the tip into each of the svingi and fill them with the custard. Place the filled svingi on a platter, and sprinkle with the confectioner's sugar and cinnamon. Makes about 40 svingi.

NOTE: If you like a thinner custard, modify the Crème Pâtissièri recipe by beating 2 egg whites until stiff, and adding to them 2 tablespoons confectioner's sugar and ½ teaspoon vanilla; fold into the prepared custard, and then fill the svingi as directed above.

FRIED TOAST   ✠   FRIYANES

THE TOAST

2 cups milk
3 eggs, lightly beaten
1 teaspoon vanilla
about 12 slices day-old white
   bread
butter or oil for frying

THE SYRUP

2½ cups sugar
2 cups water
1 lemon rind

confectioner's sugar (optional)
cherries (optional)

Put the milk and the eggs into a bowl and beat lightly; add the vanilla and mix well. Dip the bread, a slice at a time, into this mixture, and place on a platter. If any batter remains, spoon it carefully onto each slice. Fry the bread in hot butter or oil until golden brown on both sides. Place on a platter to cool.

Prepare the syrup; Put the sugar, water, and lemon rind into a pot. Bring to a boil, and cook for about 5 minutes. Remove the lemon. Pour syrup over the toast slices. Serves 6.

NOTE: You may also serve these with confectioner's sugar and a sweet cherry on each slice.

PUFFS WITH MILK AND EGGS   ✠   TIGANITES ME YALA KE AVGA

THE PUFFS

2 cups flour
4 teaspoons baking powder
½ teaspoon salt
1 cup milk
4 eggs
½ cup sugar
1½ teaspoons vanilla
oil or other shortening for frying

THE SYRUP

2½ cups sugar
2 cups water
1 lemon rind

confectioner's sugar (optional)
cinnamon (optional)

Sift the flour into a bowl together with the baking powder and salt. Stir in the milk. In another bowl, beat the eggs with the sugar until thick; add to the flour mixture. Add the vanilla. Beat well with a wire whisk to make a thick batter. Heat the oil (or other shortening) in a deep pot; drop the batter by spoonfuls into it. When the puffs are golden on one side, turn them, being careful not to pierce them, and let them fry on the other side. Remove to a platter.

While the puffs are frying, prepare the syrup: Put the sugar, water, and lemon peel into a pot, and boil for 5 to 8 minutes. Cool slightly and pour over the puffs. Makes about 36 large or 48 small puffs.

NOTE: If you wish, omit the vanilla and the syrup, and serve the puffs covered with confectioner's sugar and cinnamon.

THIPLES WITH FLOUR ✠ THIPLES ME ALEVRI

2½–3 cups flour
1 teaspoon baking powder
3 eggs
2 tablespoons sugar
½ cup cherry liqueur
  (maraschino) or Mastiha*

1–2 cups confectioner's sugar
1–2 teaspoons cinnamon
oil for frying
honey (optional)
chopped shelled walnuts
  (optional)

Sift 2½ cups of flour together with the baking powder into a bowl. Make a well in the middle. In another bowl, beat the eggs with the sugar until thick. Add the liqueur slowly to the egg-sugar mixture, then add that to the flour. Knead well to make a stiff dough. Add the rest of the flour only if needed to make a stiff dough (how much of the rest you may need depends on how large the eggs are). Let the dough rest for 30 minutes, then knead again. Pinch off small pieces and roll each into a thin sheet. Cut each sheet into strips about 2 inches wide, and tie these carefully into bowknots or loop them into circles. Heat the oil in a deep pot and drop the thiples in, one at a time. As soon as one side cooks to a light-golden color, turn it, using a slotted spoon so as not to pierce it, and cook until golden on the second side. Watch these very carefully because they cook quickly. Drain on paper towels, and serve sprinkled with confectioner's sugar and cinnamon. Makes 20 to 30 thiples.

NOTE: Thiples may also be served with honey and walnuts poured over them.

MARMALADE PANCAKES ✠ KREP ME MARMELADA

1 cup flour
2 eggs
1 tablespoon sugar
1 teaspoon vanilla
2 cups milk

butter for the pan
marmalade
confectioner's sugar
cinnamon

Sift the flour. In a bowl, beat the eggs with the sugar until very thick and light in color. Add the vanilla; mix well. Slowly add the milk to the eggs, and beat in well with a wire whisk. Add the flour and beat to make a smooth batter. No lumps, please.

Melt the butter in a small frying pan. Drop in a tablespoonful of batter and tilt the pan to spread the batter evenly. Cook on one side and turn with a spatula, or flip, and cook on the other side. Place on a platter. Continue to cook the crêpes, adding butter to the pan before making each. Spread marmalade on each crêpe and roll it up to resemble a cigar. Sprinkle with confectioner's sugar and cinnamon. Serve immediately. Makes about 24 pancakes.

SWEET PIROSKI

1 recipe Piroski pastry (see
  index)
3 tablespoons sugar

GLYKA PIROSKI

½—1 cup marmalade
chopped glazed fruits
confectioner's sugar

Prepare the pastry, adding the sugar when you add the salt. Fill with the marmalade and glazed fruits. Serve lightly dusted with confectioner's sugar.

DOUGHNUTS ✠

2½ tablespoons butter or other
  shortening
1 cup sugar
3 eggs
1 cup milk
9 cups (approximately) flour
4 teaspoons baking powder

KOULOURAKIA DONATS

½ teaspoon cinnamon
¼ teaspoon nutmeg
¼ teaspoon salt
butter or oil for frying
2 cups (approximately)
  confectioner's sugar
1 tablespoon cinnamon

Beat the butter with half of the sugar until very light. In another bowl, beat the eggs with the other half until thick. Combine the two mixtures and blend well; add the milk. Sift 8 cups of the flour (reserve 1 cup) with the baking powder, cinnamon, nutmeg, and salt. Slowly add the dry ingredients to the batter; knead to make a medium dough. Add the reserved flour, if needed. Pinch off pieces of the dough and roll each into a ¼- or ½-inch-thick sheet. Using a doughnut cutter or a glass, cut out the doughnuts. Heat the butter or oil in a deep frying pan and fry the doughnuts, a few at a time. They will puff up immediately. When golden brown on one side, turn them, being careful not to pierce them, and cook on the other side. Drain on paper towels. Serve sprinkled with confectioner's sugar and cinnamon. Makes about 80 doughnuts.

COOKIES

LENTEN SKALTSOUNIA   ✠   SKALTSOUNIA

THE TURNOVERS
3 cups flour
1 teaspoon baking powder
1 cup tahini (sesame-seed oil)
   or regular cooking oil or
   other shortening
2 tablespoons honey
½ cup warm water

THE FILLING
½ cup chopped walnuts
½ cup chopped almonds
1 cup chopped glazed fruit
   (optional)
½ cup orange marmalade
2 tablespoons honey
½ cup white raisins

rose or orange water
1½ cups confectioner's sugar

To make the skaltsounia, sift the flour and baking powder together into a bowl; add the tahini (or other shortening); blend well with the fingers. Make a small well in the center, and to it add the honey diluted with water. Knead well to make a stiff dough. Roll into a sheet about a third of an inch thick (roll a small amount of dough at a time, if you prefer).

For the filling, mix together in another bowl the walnuts, almonds, marmalade, honey, and raisins. Cut 3- to 4-inch rounds from the dough (depending on how large you want the turnovers to be); place a small amount of filling in the center of each, and fold the dough over to make half circles. Seal the edges by dampening the bottom half of the pastry and pinching the edges closed. Place the turnovers on an ungreased baking sheet and bake in a preheated 350° oven for 20 to 30 minutes. Remove from the oven and sprinkle with the flower water. Sift a thick layer of confectioner's sugar onto a platter, lay the skaltsounia on it, and sift additional confectioner's sugar over them.

NOTE: You may substitute the chopped glazed fruit for the nuts, in the filling, if you prefer.

CINNAMON ZWIEBACK ✠ PAXIMATHAKIA KANELLAS

10—12 cups flour
1 tablespoon baking powder
2 cups water
1 tablespoon cinnamon
2—3 pieces stick cinnamon

5—6 cloves
1 cup oil
3 eggs
1 cup sugar

Sift 10 cups of the flour into a bowl with the baking powder and the powdered cinnamon, scoop out a well in the center. Put the water, stick cinnamon, and cloves into a pot and bring to a boil, then remove the cinnamon and cloves from the liquid and let it cool to lukewarm. In another pot, heat the oil until it begins to smoke, and pour it immediately into the flour. Let the mixture cool for a few minutes (until you can handle it), then rub the flour and oil between your hands until well blended. In another bowl, beat the eggs with the sugar until thick, then add the flour; mix well. Add the lukewarm liquid. Knead well. The dough should not stick to the fingers, nor should it be too soft to hold its shape in the baking; use additional flour, if necessary, to reach the right consistency, but avoid adding too much flour or the dough will be too dry. Shape into small loaves, each about 1 to 1½ inches high and 8 inches long. Place on a buttered baking sheet and bake in a preheated oven at 350° for about 30 minutes. Cool, slice in half-inch- to inch-thick slices; lay these on an ungreased baking sheet and return to the oven to brown lightly on both sides. Makes about 12 dozen zwieback.

EASTER COOKIES ✠ KOULOURAKIA PASHALINA

11—12 cups flour
1 tablespoon baking powder
¾ cup butter
8 eggs, separated

1½ cups sugar
1½ teaspoons vanilla
¼ cup warm milk
1 egg, beaten

Sift 11 cups of flour with the baking powder into a ceramic or glass bowl; scoop out a well in it. Brown the butter and pour into the flour. Let stand until cool enough to handle. Rub the flour and butter between the palms of your hands until well blended. Make another well in the middle of the mixture. Beat the 8 egg yolks with the sugar and vanilla until thick and light; beat the egg whites in another bowl until stiff. Add the yolks, whites, and warm milk to the flour, and knead to make a fairly soft dough. Add additional flour if needed. The dough should not stick to your hands. Taking a little dough at a time, roll out to quarter-inch thickness. Cut into shapes with a cookie cutter. Place on a buttered baking sheet, allowing enough space between the cookies for them to expand. Brush the tops with beaten egg. Bake in a preheated 350° oven for about 20 minutes. Makes about 10 to 11 dozen cookies.

VANILLA COOKIES ✠ VANILIAS KOULOURAKIA

6 eggs
1⅔ cups sugar
2 teaspoons vanilla
1½ cups butter

1 cup warm milk
11—12 cups flour
1 tablespoon baking powder
1 egg, beaten

Beat the eggs, sugar, and vanilla together in a bowl until thick and light in color. Cream the butter in another bowl until very light. Add the egg mixture and warm milk to the butter, and beat in well. Sift 11 cups of flour with the baking powder, and slowly add to the batter. Knead well to make a soft dough, adding a little more flour if necessary (the dough should not stick to the fingers, but add as little flour as possible to achieve this state). Break off small portions of the dough with your hands, flatten to about quarter-inch thickness, and cut into various shapes with cookie cutters. Place on buttered baking sheets. Brush the tops with beaten egg. Bake in a preheated 350° oven for 15 to 20 minutes. Makes about 10 dozen cookies.

BUTTER COOKIES WITH CONFECTIONER'S SUGAR ✠ KOURAMBIEDES

4–5 cups sifted flour
1 teaspoon baking powder
2 cups butter
½ cup sugar
2 egg yolks

½ cup Mastiha* liqueur
1 teaspoon vanilla
1½ pounds confectioner's sugar
flower or rose water (if available)

Set aside 1 cup of the flour; mix the baking powder into the rest. Cream the butter in a bowl until very light, then add to it the sugar and the eggs, beating continuously until thoroughly blended. Add the Mastiha and vanilla, mixing them in well. Slowly add 2 to 3 cups of the dry ingredients, and knead in well, then knead in the rest, a little at a time. Inasmuch as the size of the eggs—even the weather—can affect the consistency of the dough, check it as follows to be sure it is right for handling: Using the palms of your hands, roll a small piece of dough into a fat cord about as thick as a finger; shape it into an S. If the curves of the S show little cracks, the dough has enough flour; if not, or if the dough is too soft to handle, add a little more flour (from the reserve cup), kneading it in well. After you have made these cookies a few times, you will have acquired the "feel" of the dough. When the dough has the proper texture, pinch off pieces and roll them as above and shape into the traditional S's, circles, crescents, etc., or put through a cookie press (for the latter, press out a few test cookies, first). Place on a buttered baking sheet and bake in a preheated 300° oven for 15 to 20 minutes.

As soon as you remove them from the oven, sprinkle them with the flower water and dust thickly with confectioner's sugar. Makes about 5 dozen cookies.

NOTE: Serve in individual paper cups, like cupcakes, for easier handling.

SMYRNA TWISTS 1 ✠ TSOUREKAKIA SMYRNEIKA 1

1½ cups butter
4 egg yolks
2 cups sugar
¼ cup lukewarm milk
6 cups flour
2 teaspoons baking powder

1 teaspoon salt
2 tablespoons grated lemon peel
3 ounces blanched almonds, chopped
1 egg white, lightly beaten
sugar for sprinkling

Cream the butter until very light in color. Beat the egg yolks and sugar together in another bowl, and add to the butter; mix in the warm milk. Sift together the flour, baking powder, and salt; add the lemon peel. Slowly add the dry ingredients to the egg-butter mixture; blend to a soft dough. Roll pieces of the dough between your palms into 3-inch ropes about ½ inch thick, and place them side by side on a buttered baking sheet; pinch the ropes of dough together at either end. Brush with the egg white and sprinkle with a little sugar. Bake in a preheated 350° for 20 minutes.

SMYRNA TWISTS 2 (EGGLESS) ✠ TSOUREKAKIA SMYRNEIKA 2 (XORIS AVGA)

6 cups flour
4 teaspoons baking powder
½ teaspoon salt
4 teaspoons grated lemon peel
1½ cups butter

1½ cups sugar
1 cup warm milk
1 egg yolk, beaten
sugar for sprinkling

Sift the flour into a bowl together with the baking powder and salt; mix in the grated lemon peel. In another bowl, cream the butter with the sugar until thick and light in color; add the milk to this, alternately with the dry ingredients, then knead to make a smooth dough. If the dough sticks to your fingers, add a little more flour to it. Shape as in Tsourekakia Smyrneika 1, above, and place on a buttered baking sheet. Brush with the egg yolk and sprinkle with sugar. Bake in a preheated 350° oven for 20 minutes.

MELOMACARONIA WITH FARINA ✠ MELOMAKARONIA ME SMIGDALI [FENIKIA]

THE COOKIES	THE SYRUP
1 cup oil	¾ cup water
¼ cup sugar	½ cup sugar
¼ cup cognac	1 cup honey
¼ cup orange juice	
1 teaspoon baking soda	1 cup chopped walnuts
2 tablespoons grated orange rind	½ cup sugar
½ cup flour	1 teaspoon cinnamon
2½ cups farina	

Beat the oil with the sugar for about half an hour; add the cognac. Add the baking soda dissolved in the orange juice; add the orange rind; mix well. Add the flour and the farina, and knead very well to blend all the ingredients into a medium-soft dough. Shape the melomacaronia into mounded ovals, flat on the bottom, scrape the top lightly with a fork to make shallow grooves. Place on a buttered cookie sheet and bake in a preheated 250° oven for 20 to 30 minutes. Remove from the oven; cool.

While the cookies are cooling, boil the water, sugar, and honey together in a saucepan, removing the froth as it rises. Boil about 3 minutes. Dip the cold cookies into the warm syrup, using a slotted spoon. Remove carefully and drain. Place on a clean platter and sprinkle with the walnuts. Mix together the cinnamon and sugar, and sprinkle on top. Makes about 3 dozen cookies.

VANILLA-ALMOND BISCUITS ✠ BISCOTA VANILIAS ME AMIGDALA

3 cups flour	1 cup finely chopped blanched almonds
3 teaspoons baking powder	
½ cup butter	½ cup warm milk
3 eggs	2 teaspoons vanilla
1 cup sugar	

Sift the flour with the baking powder. Cream the butter in a bowl until very light. In a separate bowl, beat the eggs with the sugar until thick and light, and add to the butter. Add the almonds and the flour, and mix well. Blend in the milk and vanilla, and knead to make a fairly stiff dough. Pinch off small pieces of the dough and shape them between the palms of your hands into flat rounds. Place on a buttered sheet and bake in a preheated 300° oven for about 15 minutes. Cool and serve. Makes about 6 dozen cookies.

ALMOND COOKIES ✠ AMIGDALOTA

1¼–1½ pounds almonds,
  blanched and chopped
1¾ cups sugar
2–3 egg whites
2–3 tablespoons farina or
  toasted bread crumbs

2 teaspoons vanilla
¾ pound confectioner's sugar
candied cherries
rosewater or flower water
  (optional)

If you blanch your own almonds, place them in the oven for a few minutes to dry, then chop them finely. Place in a deep bowl. Add the sugar. Beat egg whites lightly in another bowl, and add to the almonds. Add the farina or bread crumbs and the vanilla, and knead well. Pinch off small pieces and roll each into a ball. Press half a cherry on top of each. Place on a well-buttered baking sheet and bake in a preheated 250° oven for about 20 minutes. Place the cookies on a plate, sift confectioner's sugar on them, and transfer them to a platter to serve.

NOTE: If you have access to rose- or flower water, sprinkle some on the cookies as soon as they come out of the oven.

ALMOND PRALINE ✠ AMIGDALA PRALINE

1 cup almonds
1 tablespoon butter

3–4 tablespoons sugar
drop of lemon juice

Blanch the almonds. Put the butter, sugar, and almonds in a frying pan and brown the almonds to a light-coffee color, stirring constantly with a wooden spoon. Add a drop of lemon juice to keep the sugar from crystallizing. Pour onto a buttered marble slab, a buttered platter, or a buttered baking sheet. Spread out evenly and let cool. Break into pieces, or crumble to use on tarts or ice cream.

ERGOLAVI ✠ ERGOLAVI

6 cups almonds
3 cups sugar

3 egg whites
2 teaspoons vanilla

Blanch the almonds. Dry them in the oven, mash them with a mortar and pestle, or pulverize in a blender or grinder. Place the sugar, egg whites, and vanilla in a bowl; add the almonds. Blend, using your fingers, into a thick dough or mass. Shape into narrow "fingers," and place on a buttered baking sheet. Bake in a preheated 300° oven for about 20 minutes.

RAISIN COOKIES ✠ BISCOTA ME STAFIDES

4 cups flour	3 eggs, separated
2 teaspoons baking powder	2 tablespoons grated orange
1 cup butter	rind
2 cups sugar	1 cup white or black raisins

Sift the flour with the baking powder. Cream the butter in a bowl until very light. Add the sugar, egg yolks, and orange rind, beating them in thoroughly. Add half the flour; and the raisins. Beat the whites in another bowl, until stiff but not dry. Fold into the mixture. Add the remaining flour and knead to make a stiff dough. Pinch off small pieces and shape into cookies. Place on a buttered pan and bake in a preheated 375° oven for about 15 minutes. Makes about 6 dozen cookies.

SAVAYAR ✠ SAVAYAR

2 cups flour	1 teaspoon vanilla
2¼ cups sugar	sugar for sprinkling
6 eggs, separated	

Sift the flour. Beat the egg yolks in a bowl with the sugar and vanilla until thick and light. In another bowl, beat the whites until they are stiff but not dry. Add the whites alternately with the flour to the yolk mixture, folding in gently.

Cover a baking sheet with a piece of waxed paper. Using a cookie press with a wide, flat opening, squeeze the dough onto the waxed paper in the shape of fat macaroni—each cookie should be about a half inch thick and 2½ inches long. Sprinkle the cookies with a little sugar (brush the excess from the waxed paper or it will burn during the baking), and bake in a preheated 350° oven for about 15 minutes. Cool *slightly*, then peel off the paper. Makes about 6 dozen cookies.

NOTE: Watch these carefully, as they bake quickly and the edges may burn.

BUTTER COOKIES BISCOTA VOUTIROU

4 cups flour	6 eggs
2 teaspoons baking powder	1 teaspoon vanilla
¾ cup butter	½ cup chopped blanched
1¾ cups sugar	almonds

Sift the flour and the baking powder together. Cream the butter in a bowl until it is very light, add the sugar, and continue to beat until the mixture is thoroughly creamed. Beat 5 of the eggs in another bowl until light; add the vanilla, then add this mixture to the butter and sugar. Beat the batter for another 2 or 3 minutes. Add the flour slowly; knead well until a soft dough is formed. Cover with waxed paper and set it aside for 30 minutes. Knead again, and divide the dough into 4 parts.

Roll out each piece of dough a half inch thick, and cut it into 2- or 3-inch rounds. (Use the rim of a water glass for this, if you like.) Place the rounds on a buttered baking sheet. Beat the remaining egg, and brush it on the cookies; sprinkle them with the almonds. Bake in a preheated 300° oven for 15 to 20 minutes—watch them carefully so they do not get too brown. Makes about 4 dozen cookies.

MERINGUES 1 ✠ MERINGUE 1

4 egg whites
1 teaspoon lemon juice

2 cups confectioner's sugar
1 teaspoon vanilla

Beat the whites with the lemon juice until stiff, then gently blend in the sugar and vanilla. Butter a piece of waxed paper and dust it with flour, shaking off the excess, and place on a baking sheet. Drop the meringue by the spoonful onto the paper or force it through a cookie press. Bake in a preheated 350° oven for 20 to 25 minutes.

MERINGUES 2 ✠ MERINGUE 2

1 cup confectioner's sugar
3 egg whites

1 teaspoon lemon juice

Put all ingredients into a bowl and beat until stiff. Drop by the teaspoon onto a baking sheet covered with waxed paper. Bake immediately in a preheated 350° oven for 20 to 25 minutes. Makes about 3 dozen cookies.

MERINGUE WITH ALMONDS MERINGUE ME AMIGDALA

Prepare like Meringues 2, above, but just before baking, sprinkle the meringues with chopped blanched almonds.

PEZEDES   ✠   PEZEDES

2 cups sugar
½ cup water
1 teaspoon lemon juice

4 egg whites
1 teaspoon vanilla
1 cup confectioner's sugar

Boil the sugar, water, and lemon juice together to make a thick syrup, but do not let it carmelize. Remove from the heat and keep hot. Beat the egg whites until stiff, and add the hot syrup slowly to them, beating constantly. Fold in the confectioner's sugar and vanilla, blending well. Butter and lightly flour a piece of waxed paper and place it on a baking sheet. Drop the batter by teaspoonfuls or force through a cookie press onto the sheet and bake in a preheated 350° oven for 20 to 25 minutes. Remove from the oven, cool, and place on a platter.

NOTE: These may be made into sandwich cookies by putting marmalade or butter between 2 cookies, then storing in the refrigerator until you serve them.

"CATS' TONGUES"   ✠   LAGK-TE-SA

½ cup sweet butter
½ cup sugar
1 teaspoon vanilla

2 egg whites
¾ cup flour, sifted

Cream the butter with the sugar. Add the vanilla and egg whites, and beat well. Add the flour, and mix it in well. Put the dough into a cookie press and press through a wide round opening to make pencil-shaped cookies. Place them, far apart, on a cold, buttered cookie sheet. Bake in a preheated 400° oven for 7 to 8 minutes. Watch carefully to prevent their burning.

SANDWICH COOKIES WITH MARMALADE   ✠   BISCOTA THIPLA ME MARMELADA

3 cups flour
3 teaspoons baking powder
4 eggs, separated
1 cup sugar
1 teaspoon vanilla

½ cup butter, melted
1 cup milk
½ cup blanched almonds
2 cups apricot marmalade

Sift the flour with the baking powder into a bowl; make a well in the middle of it. In another bowl, beat the egg yolks with the sugar and the vanilla, then pour it into the flour. Add the melted butter. Knead the mixture into a soft dough, slowly adding the milk as you knead. Let the dough rest for 10 minutes.

Separate the dough into 4 parts and roll each out a quarter inch thick; cut into rounds, and place them carefully on a buttered cookie sheet. Beat the egg whites lightly, brush over the cookies; press half an almond into the center of each. Bake in a preheated 300° oven for about 15 minutes. Remove from the oven and cool. Spoon some marmalade onto half the cookies and top them with the others. Serve immediately.

SESAME COOKIES ✠ KOULOURAKIA ME SOUSAME

10–12 cups flour	4 eggs
2 teaspoons baking powder	⅔ cup sugar
¾ cup butter	1 teaspoon vanilla
1⅓ cups warm milk	12 ounces sesame seeds

Sift 10 cups of the flour into a bowl together with the baking powder; make a well in it. Brown the butter until it smokes, and add it to the flour. Cool slightly. Rub the flour and butter between the palms of your hands until well blended. Again make a well in the flour mixture and add the warm milk; mix in. Beat the eggs and the sugar in another bowl until thick; add to the flour mixture. Add the vanilla. Knead well to make a soft dough. Roll (or pat) out, shape the cookies as desired, and roll in the sesame seeds. Bake on a buttered baking sheet in a preheated 350° oven for about 20 minutes. Makes about 10 dozen koulourakia.

CAKES

ALMOND SPONGE CAKE ✠ PANTESPANI ME AMIGDALA

1 cup almonds, shelled but not
  blanched
2 cups flour
1 teaspoon baking powder

4 teaspoons sweet butter
8 eggs, separated
1½ cups sugar
1 teaspoon vanilla

    Chop the almonds. Sift the flour; mix it with the baking powder. Cream the butter, and to it add the egg yolks and sugar; beat until light. Add the vanilla. In another bowl, beat the egg whites until stiff but not dry. Alternately fold into the batter the dry ingredients, egg whites, and almonds. Pour into a well-buttered pan and bake in a preheated 325° oven for 20 minutes.

    NOTE: This may also be made using walnuts in place of the almonds. The cake has a rather heavy texture.

SWEET-BUTTER CAKE ✠ KEIK ME FRESKO VOUTIRO

2½ cups flour
2 teaspoons baking powder
¾ cup sweet butter
4 eggs, separated
1¼ cups sugar

1 teaspoon vanilla
5 ounces baking chocolate
½ cup almonds, blanched and
  chopped

    Sift the flour; mix it with the baking powder. Cream the butter very well. In another bowl, beat the egg yolks with the sugar and vanilla, then add to the butter and beat it thoroughly. Beat the egg whites until stiff but not dry, and add them alternately with the flour to the batter, folding in gently. Pour into a buttered pan. Slice the chocolate and push the pieces into the center of the batter. Sprinkle the almonds on top and bake in a preheated 350° oven for 45 minutes.

YOGURT CAKE   ✠   KEIK ME YIAOURTI

3 cups flour
1½ teaspoons baking powder
2 tablespoons grated lemon peel
1 cup butter
1½ cups sugar

½ pint yogurt
5 eggs, separated
sweet butter for the top
confectioner's sugar

Sift the flour and mix it with the baking powder and lemon peel. Cream the butter with the sugar until very light; add the yogurt, mixing well. Beat the egg yolks well, and blend into the batter. Beat the egg whites in another bowl until stiff but not dry, and add them alternately with the flour mixture to the batter, folding in lightly with a wooden spoon. Pour into a buttered pan and bake in a preheated 325–350° oven for 1 hour or longer. Remove from the oven. Brush with sweet butter and dust with confectioner's sugar.

ALMOND YOGURT CAKE   ✠   KEIK ME YIAOURTI KE AMIGDALA

Prepare like Yogurt Cake, above, but use only 2½ cups flour and add ¾ cup chopped blanched almonds.

SPONGE CAKE   ✠   PANTESPANI

3 cups flour
1 teaspoon baking powder
1½ cups sugar

8 eggs, separated
1½ teaspoons vanilla
4 teaspoons sweet butter, melted

Sift the flour together with the baking powder. Beat the sugar with the egg yolks and vanilla until very light. In another bowl, beat the egg whites until stiff but not dry. Add the dry ingredients alternately with the egg whites to the yolk mixture, folding in lightly, then add the melted butter; fold gently until well blended. Bake in a well-buttered pan in a preheated oven at 350° for about 30 minutes. The cake may be split into several layers after baking. Or it may be baked in 2, 3, or 4 layers.

NOTE: Although this is a sponge cake, it is much heavier in texture than the sponge cake with which most Americans are familiar. It may be served plain, or it may be the basis for many other Greek desserts. For instance, when it is used as the base for a pie (frequently having a custard filling), it should be prepared the day before, as this makes cutting it easier.

ALMOND CAKE ✠ KEIK ME AMIGDALA

3 cups flour
1 teaspoon baking powder
1 cup butter
1½ cups sugar
5 eggs, separated

1 teaspoon baking soda
½ cup warm milk
1 teaspoon vanilla
1 cup blanched almonds,
   coarsely chopped

Sift the flour together with the baking powder. Cream the butter, add the sugar; beat until fluffy. Add the egg yolks one at a time, beating thoroughly after each addition. Dissolve the baking powder in the warm milk, and add to the batter. Beat the egg whites in another bowl until stiff but not dry. Alternately fold the egg whites, almonds, and flour into the batter. Gently mix in the vanilla. Bake in a buttered pan in a preheated 300° oven for 45 minutes.

ORANGE CAKE ✠ KEIK ME PORTOCALI

3½ cups flour
2 teaspoons baking powder
¾ cup butter
1½ cups sugar

4 eggs, separated
1 teaspoon baking soda
1½ cups orange juice
4 teaspoons grated orange peel

Sift the flour together with the baking powder. Cream the butter with the sugar until very light, then add the egg yolks, one at a time, beating well after each addition. Dissolve the baking soda in the orange juice and add to the batter. Beat the egg whites in another bowl until stiff but not dry, and fold them into the batter alternately with the dry ingredients, using a wooden spoon. Lightly fold in the orange peel. Pour into a well-buttered pan and bake in a preheated 300° oven for 45 minutes.

If you prefer, you may substitute tangerines for the oranges.

PLAIN CAKE ✠ KEIK APLO

1 cup butter
1¼ cups sugar
4 eggs, separated
1 teaspoon vanilla

½ cup warm milk
3 cups flour
2 teaspoons baking powder

Cream the butter, then add the sugar and egg yolks to it, beating them in thoroughly. Beat the egg whites in another bowl until stiff but not dry. Blend the vanilla and milk into the batter; fold in the egg whites. Sift the flour with the baking powder and add to the batter, mixing lightly. Pour into a buttered pan and bake in a preheated 300° oven for 45 minutes.

APPLE CAKE ✠ KEIK ME MILA

2 cups peeled, seeded and
  thickly sliced apples
water as needed
a little lemon juice
2½ cups flour
2 teaspoons baking powder

¾ cup butter
1½ cups sugar
4 eggs, separated
1 teaspoon cinnamon
2 teaspoons sugar for sprinkling

Put the apples into water with the lemon juice. Sift the flour and baking powder together. Cream the butter and sugar until very light, and add the egg yolks to them, one at a time, beating well after each addition. In another bowl, beat the egg whites until stiff but not dry. Lightly fold the flour and egg whites alternately into the batter with a wooden spoon. Butter a pan heavily, and dust it with flour and sugar. Drain the apples and dry them well; spread the apples evenly in the pan and sprinkle with the cinnamon and sugar. Pour the batter over the apples. Bake in a preheated 300° oven for 45 minutes. Cool completely before removing the cake from the pan.

LENTEN CAKE ✠ KEIK NISTSIMO

3½ cups flour
1 teaspoon baking powder
¾ cup oil
½ cup white raisins
1¼ cups sugar
½ cup chopped walnuts
2 teaspoons grated orange peel

½ cup cognac
1 teaspoon baking soda
1½ cups orange juice
2 teaspoons cinnamon plus
  enough for sprinkling the top
confectioner's sugar

Sift the flour into a ceramic bowl and mix in the baking powder; scoop out a well in the center. Heat the oil in a frying pan and pour it into the flour. Add the raisins, sugar, nuts, orange peel, cognac, baking soda dissolved in the orange juice, and cinnamon. Mix to make a stiff dough. Put into a buttered tube pan or baking pan and bake in a preheated 300° oven for about 1 hour. As soon as you remove it from the oven, sprinkle with the cinnamon and confectioner's sugar.

WALNUT-RAISIN CAKE ✠ KEIK ME KARIDIA KE STAFIDES

3 cups flour
3 teaspoons baking powder
1 cup butter
1½ cups sugar
4 eggs, separated

1 teaspoon vanilla
½ cup warm milk
½ cup white raisins
½ cup chopped walnuts

Sift the flour together with the baking powder. Cream the butter, and add the sugar, egg yolks, and vanilla to it, beating them in thoroughly. Beat the egg whites in another bowl until stiff. Add the milk, the flour, and egg whites alternately to the batter; mix in the raisins and walnuts. Bake in a preheated 300° oven for 45 minutes to 1 hour.

CINNAMON CAKE ✠ KEIK KANELLAS

3½ cups flour
3 teaspoons baking powder
2 teaspoons cinnamon
½ cup warm milk

2 teaspoons cognac
1 cup butter
4 eggs, separated
1½ cups sugar

Sift the flour together with the baking powder and cinnamon. Mix the milk with the cognac. Cream the butter until very light. In another bowl, beat the egg yolks and the sugar until very thick. Add to the butter and blend in thoroughly. Add the milk. Beat the egg whites until stiff but not dry, and add them alternately with the dry ingredients to the batter, folding in lightly with a wooden spoon. Pour into a buttered pan and bake in a preheated 300° oven for 45 minutes.

FRUIT CAKE ✠ KEIK FRUTON

3 cups flour
1 teaspoon baking powder
½ cup glazed fruits, diced
½ cup white raisins
½ cup chopped walnuts
1 cup butter

5 eggs, separated
1¼ cup sugar
1 teaspoon vanilla
1 teaspoon baking soda
½ cup warm milk

Sift the flour together with the baking powder; mix in the fruits, the raisins, and the walnuts. Cream the butter. Beat the egg yolks with the sugar until very light, then add to the butter, beating in thoroughly. Add the vanilla. Dissolve the baking soda in the warm milk and add to the batter. In another bowl, beat the egg whites until stiff but not dry, and fold them, alternately with the flour mixture, into the batter, using a wooden spoon. Pour into a buttered loaf pan and bake in a preheated 350° oven for 1 hour or longer.

PIES (PITTES), TARTS (TARTA), AND GREEK TORTES (TARTOLETES)

PITTES AND TARTA

OPEN-FACE APPLE PIE ✠ TARTA MILOU

THE PASTRY
2 cups flour
2 tablespoons sugar
½ teaspoon baking powder
¾ cup shortening
1 tablespoon rum
1 egg yolk

THE FILLING
1½ pounds apples, peeled and
    sliced

½ cup sugar
½ cup water
4 cups milk
½ cup cornstarch
10 tablespoons sugar
2 eggs, separated
½ teaspoon vanilla
4 ounces chopped blanched
    almonds
½ tablespoon cinnamon
2 tablespoons sugar

To prepare the pastry, sift the flour into a bowl with the sugar and baking powder. Add the shortening, rum, and egg yolk. Knead to a soft dough. Cover with a cloth while you prepare the filling.

Cook the apples with the ½ cup sugar and water until soft. Drain well, and pass through a strainer or mash with a fork.

Butter a pan, spread the dough on the bottom and around the sides; pierce in several places with a fork. Bake in a preheated 350° oven for about 15 minutes (until half done).

Meanwhile, prepare the Crème Piatou (see index), using the milk, cornstarch, 10 tablespoons sugar, the 2 egg yolks, and vanilla. Spread the apples in the half-baked pie shell, sprinkle with the cinnamon; pour the custard over all.

Beat the egg whites in a bowl with the 2 tablespoons sugar until they are stiff, then spread over the custard. Sprinkle the whole with the almonds. Return to the oven, bake for about 20 minutes longer at 250°. Serves 6 to 8.

OPEN-FACE STRAWBERRY PIE   ✠   TARTA ME FRAOULES

½ recipe Pasta Flora dough
   (see index)
about 1¼—1½ cups strawberry
   marmalade

2¼ pounds strawberries,
   cleaned, washed, and
   drained
about 1½ cups whipped cream

Prepare the pastry as for Pasta Flora, and roll it out to fit the bottom and sides of a deep pie plate or a square or rectangular pan. Smooth the dough with the fingers and palms to make an even, thick crust. Cover with a sheet of waxed paper and pour some dried beans (any kind) onto it. (These will act as a weight and keep the crust down during the baking.) Bake in a preheated 350° oven for about 15 minutes; remove from the oven. Discard the waxed paper and the beans. Put the crust back into the oven and bake until golden. Remove from the oven and cool thoroughly.

Carefully spread the marmalade on the crust. Place the whole strawberries in a neat circular pattern on the marmalade. (Start with one in the center and work them round and round.) Top with whipped cream and serve immediately.

OPEN-FACE APRICOT PIE   ✠   TARTA ME VERIKOKKO

1 recipe pastry (see Apple Pie
   [Milopitta] 2)
2¼ pounds (approximately)
   apricots
1 pound apricot marmalade

½ cup sugar
2 tablespoons melted butter
½ cup hot water
½ cup cognac

Prepare the pastry. Spread the dough in a rectangular baking pan, covering the bottom and sides of the pan; pierce the bottom several times with a fork. Partially bake in a preheated 350° oven for about 15 minutes.

Wash the apricots. Cut them in half and remove the stones. Drain. Spread a third of the marmalade in a thin layer over on the half-baked crust; add the apricots and sprinkle them with the sugar. Drizzle on the butter. Return the pie to the oven and bake for 15 to 20 minutes longer.

Dissolve the rest of the marmalade in the hot water; add the cognac. As soon as you remove the pie from the oven, pour on the marmalade-cognac mixture. Cool so the marmalade can set. Cut into squares and serve.

OPEN-FACE CHERRY PIE   ✠   TARTA ME KERASIA

½ recipe Pasta Flora dough
   (see index)
1½ pounds cherries
½ cup sugar
1¼–1½ cups apple preserves

½ cup rum
¼ cup hot water
3 ounces chopped blanched
   almonds

Prepare the pastry as for Pasta Flora, roll out to a thin sheet; line the bottoms and sides of the baking pan with it. Pierce the bottom with a fork in several places to prevent the dough from puffing. Bake in a preheated 350° oven for about 15 minutes. Wash the cherries, and remove the pits (the Greeks use a hairpin for this). Remove the partially baked pastry from the oven and spread the cherries in it. Sprinkle them with the sugar. Return the pie to the oven and bake in a 400° oven about 30 minutes longer. In the meantime, dilute the marmalade in the rum and the water. As soon as the pie is baked pour on the marmalade, sprinkle the almonds over it, and let cool. Serve, cut into squares.

ALMOND CREAM PIE   ✠   TARTA ME KREMA KE AMIGDALA

1 recipe pastry for Open-Face
   Apple Pie (see index)

THE FILLING
4 cups milk
8 tablespoons cornstarch
½ teaspoon vanilla

¾ cup sugar
2 eggs, separated
2 tablespoons fresh butter
1 cup apricot marmalade
1 cup chopped blanched, roasted
   almonds
2 tablespoons sugar

Prepare the pastry according to the directions and roll it into a thickish crust. Fit this into a deep pie plate or baking pan, covering the sides as well as the bottom. Smooth the dough in the pan with your fingers to an even thickness. Cover the pastry with waxed paper and pour some dried beans (any kind) on it (to serve as a weight during the baking). Bake in a preheated 350° oven for about 15 minutes. Remove from the oven; discard the paper and beans. Return the crust to the oven and bake it about 5 minutes longer, or until golden.

Prepare the custard (see index for Crème Piatou, and follow those instructions), using only the yolks of the eggs. Add the butter to the custard, and mix half the almonds into it.

Spread the marmalade over the baked crust and pour the custard over it. In a bowl, beat the 3 egg whites (1 is leftover from the pastry recipe; 2 are from the custard ingredients) with the 2 tablespoons sugar until stiff; spread over the custard. Sprinkle with the remaining almonds. Bake in a preheated 300° oven until the meringue is a light-golden color. Cool, and serve.

PASTA FLORA ☩ PASTA FLORA

3 cups flour	⅓ cup sugar
1 teaspoon baking powder	½ cup cognac
1 cup butter, melted	2 teaspoons grated lemon peel
1 egg yolk	1–1½ cups apricot marmalade

Sift the flour into a bowl, and mix in the baking powder. Add the butter, egg yolk, sugar, cognac, and lemon peel; and knead to make a fairly soft dough. Separate into 2 parts. Roll one out into a fairly thick crust; place in a square pan. Break off a piece of dough from the remaining half and roll between your palms into a coil to fit around the crust. Wet the edge of the crust with a little water and gently press the coil around the edges, so it adheres to the crust, and against the sides of the pan; shape with the fingers to form the side crust. Spread the marmalade over the bottom crust. Shape additional coils, each about as thick as your little finger, from the rest of the dough, and lay them on the marmalade in a crisscross latticework pattern. Join to the crust (as above) with a little water. Bake in a preheated 300° oven for 30 to 40 minutes. Cool and cut into squares.

STRAWBERRY TARTS 1 ☩ TARTELETES ME FRAOULES 1

Prepare like Open-Face Strawberry Pie (see index), but bake in individual tart pans. Add the strawberry marmalade to the baked crusts, lay the whole strawberries on top, and top with Whipped Cream Chantilly (see index).

STRAWBERRY TARTS 2 ☩ TARTELETES ME FRAOULES 2

Prepare like Strawberry Open-Faced Pie, but bake in individual tart pans. Fill the baked crusts with strawberries, and pour over them the following sauce:

THE SAUCE	¾ cup sugar
2 tablespoons cornstarch	1–2 drops red food coloring
1 cup water	½ teaspoon vanilla

Dissolve the cornstarch in half the water. Bring the second half cup of water to a boil and add the cornstarch mixture to it, stirring constantly. When it is well blended, add the sugar. Continue to stir until the solution has the consistency of light cream. Stir in the coloring and vanilla, then remove from the heat and pour over the tarts.

STRAWBERRY TARTS 3   ✠   TARTELETES ME FRAOULES 3

Prepare like Open-Face Strawberry Pie, but bake as small, individual tarts. Fill the baked crusts with Crème Piatou (see index), then add the strawberries. Dilute the marmalade with a little water and pour it over the tarts.

CHERRY TARTS   ✠   TARTALETES ME KERASI

Prepare like the Open Face Cherry Pie (see index), but bake individually in small tart pans.

ALMOND TARTS   ✠   TARTALETES ME AMIGDALA

⅔ recipe Pasta Flora dough (see index)
1. cup apricot marmalade
2 cups chopped blanched almonds
½ cup toasted bread crumbs

½ teaspoon cinnamon
2 tablespoons cognac
1 cup sugar
4 egg whites

Divide the dough into 10 or 12 pieces. Roll into half-inch-thick circles, and place each in a tart pan. Spread some of the marmalade in each. Mix the almonds, bread crumbs, cinnamon, and cognac together in a bowl. In another bowl, beat the sugar with the egg whites until stiff, then fold them into the almond mixture. Fill the tarts with this, and bake in a preheated 250° oven for about 30 minutes. Cool and serve.

APPLE PIE 1   ✠   MILOPITTA 1

THE CRUST
2 cups flour
2 tablespoons sugar
1 teaspoon baking powder
¾ cup shortening
1 egg yolk
1 teaspoon cognac

THE FILLING
2 pounds apples
½ cup sugar
1 tablespoon cinnamon
1 tablespoon sweet butter
1 egg white

To make the pastry, sift the flour together with the sugar and baking powder. Add the egg yolk, shortening, and cognac, and knead to a soft dough. Roll out to ⅛-inch thickness, then spread in a buttered baking dish. Stretch the dough to fit the sides of the dish, if necessary. Pierce with a fork in several places to prevent warping during the baking. Bake in a preheated 350° oven for 15 minutes.

To prepare the filling, peel the apples and cut them into slices; mix with the sugar and the cinnamon. Beat the egg white in another bowl until it holds a peak, and add to the apples. Spread the pie crust with the apple mixture; melt the butter and pour it over the top. Return to the oven and bake at 350° for 20 to 30 minutes longer.

NOTE: This can be served with whipped cream.

APPLE PIE 2   ☩   MILOPITTA 2

Prepare like Apple Pie (Milopitta 1) but roll the dough into two thinner crusts. Partially bake one in a buttered pie plate. Meanwhile, prepare the filling, eliminating the egg white, and spread the filling in the half-baked pie crust. Cover with the second crust; seal the edges carefully with a little egg white; Pierce the top crust with a fork in several places. Bake in a preheated 350° oven for 30 minutes.

APRICOT PIE   ☩   PITTA ME VERIKOKKO

THE DOUGH	THE FILLING
2 cups flour	1¼–1½ pounds apricots
2 tablespoons sugar	¾ pound apricot marmalade
½ teaspoon baking powder	½ cup sugar
1 egg yolk	1 teaspoon sweet butter, melted
½ teaspoon vanilla	1 egg white, beaten
1 tablespoon cognac	
¾ cup shortening	

Sift the flour into a bowl with the sugar and baking powder. Add the egg yolk, vanilla, cognac, and shortening, and knead to make a soft dough. Divide into 2 unequal parts. Wash and split the apricots, and remove the pits. Roll out the larger portion of dough. Place it in a buttered pie pan and pierce with a fork in several places. Partially bake in a preheated 350° oven for about 7 minutes. Remove from the oven. Spread the marmalade on the crust; place the apricots on the marmalade, and sprinkle with the sugar. Pour the butter over the top. Roll out the rest of the dough and cover the apricots. Brush the dough with the egg white and seal the edges. Pierce the top in several places. Bake in a preheated 350° oven for 30 minutes.

HONEY PIE   ✠   MELOPITTA SIFNOU

THE DOUGH
2 cups flour
2 tablespoons sugar
½ teaspoon salt
½ teaspoon baking powder
½ cup butter or other shortening
water as needed

THE FILLING
3 cups mizithra (unsalted cottage
   cheese)
½ cup sugar
2 teaspoons cinnamon
1½ cups honey
5 eggs
4 tablespoons flour
cinnamon for sprinkling

Sift the flour into a bowl, and mix in the sugar, salt, and baking powder. Rub in the butter or shortening, and add water, a few drops at a time, to make a stiff dough. Knead well.

Pass the cheese through a strainer. Add the sugar and the cinnamon and mix well. Add the honey, beat the eggs with the flour; add to the cheese and mix in well.

Roll the dough into a circle large enough to line a pie plate and extend up the sides. Pour in the filling. Bake in a preheated 325° oven for about 1 hour. Remove from the oven. Sprinkle with cinnamon. Cool and serve. Serves 6 to 8.

PUMPKIN PIE   ✠   KOLOKITHOPITTA

THE PIE
4 cups grated pumpkin
1½ cups excellent oil
½ cup honey
½ cup sugar
½ cup toasted bread crumbs
2 cups chopped walnuts
2 tablespoons cinnamon

¾ pound phyllo (see index:
   About Phyllo)
oil for brushing the phyllo
THE SYRUP
½ cup sugar
½ cup honey
1 cup water

Select a ripe pumpkin. Remove the pumpkin from the shell and remove the seeds. Grate the pumpkin. Place in a pot with a little water and bring to a boil. Put it into a strainer and let drain overnight. Put it into a pot.

Heat half of the oil in a pan and pour it into the cooked pumpkin. Cook for about 10 minutes, stirring so it does not stick to the pot. Remove from the heat. Add the honey, sugar, bread crumbs, walnuts, and cinnamon, and mix well. Select a baking pan a little smaller than the phyllo; brush oil over the surface. Line the bottom with 9 sheets of phyllo, brushing each one with oil and letting the phyllo extend over the sides of the pan (do not trim). (see index: About Phyllo). Pour in the pumpkin. Fold the phyllo over the filling and brush again with oil. Place the rest of the phyllo sheets on top, brushing each with oil; cut off the excess with a sharp knife. Score through the top layers into squares or diamonds. Bake in a preheated 350° oven for 45 minutes.

In the meantime, boil the sugar, honey, and water together for the syrup. Cook for about 5 minutes. When the pitta is baked, remove from the oven, and let it cool; reheat the syrup and pour over the pie.

NOTE: This is not a pie as we know it.

CUSTARD PIE ✠ YALLATOPITTA

THE PIE
5 cups milk
1½ cups rice flour
⅔ cup flour
6 eggs
1½ cups plus 4 tablespoons
   sugar
2 teaspoons vanilla
6 tablespoons chopped roasted
   almonds

4 tablespoons sweet butter
8 sheets phyllo (see index:
   About Phyllo)
butter for brushing the phyllo

THE SYRUP
3 cups sugar
2 cups water
1 lemon rind
1 teaspoon lemon juice

Scald half of the milk. Put the rest of the cold milk into a bowl and mix with the two kinds of flour. Beat 4 of the eggs with the 1½ cups sugar and the vanilla until very thick, then add to the milk-and-flour mixture. Blend well, and slowly add the hot milk, stirring constantly. Pour the custard into a pot and place over low heat; cook until thickened. Remove from the heat and add the almonds and butter. Stir well, and let cool.

Butter a pan a little smaller than the phyllo. Spread the phyllo on the bottom of the pan, buttering each sheet well before adding the next. Pour the custard onto the phyllo. Trim any excess phyllo.

Beat the remaining 2 eggs with 4 tablespoons of sugar until thick; spread it over the custard. Bake in a preheated 350° oven for 30 to 40 minutes.

Prepare the syrup: Boil the sugar with the water, lemon rind, and cinnamon for 8 minutes. Remove the pie from the oven, and pour on the hot syrup. See that it goes into the sides and saturates the phyllo crust. Serves 6 to 8.

WALNUT PIE 1   ✠   KARITHOPITTA 1

⅔ recipe Pasta Flora dough   1 tablespoon cinnamon
   (see index)   2 cups sugar
10 ounces (approximately)   ½ cup water
   apricot marmalade   6 egg whites
4 cups walnut meats

Prepare the dough and spread it in a pie plate, bringing it up to cover the sides. Pierce the bottom of the crust with a fork in several places (to prevent the dough from puffing during the baking). Bake in a preheated 350° oven for about 10 minutes. Remove from the oven.

Spread the marmalade on the partially baked crust. Mix together the walnuts and the cinnamon. Bring the sugar and water to a boil in a suacepan, and cook until you have a very thick syrup. Meantime, beat the egg whites in a bowl until stiff. Pour the hot syrup slowly over them, beating constantly; fold in the walnuts. Spread the mixture over the marmalade, and return to the oven to bake for 20 minutes. Cool thoroughly, then serve. Serves 6-8 exceptionally hungry people—this is very rich.

TORTES

NOTE: Although the recipes in this section are called "pies" in English (to conform to the Greek *pittes*), they are, in reality, more like cakes or tortes.

LENTEN WALNUT PIE   ✠   KARITHOPITTA NISTISMI

4 cups flour   1½ cups sugar
1 tablespoon powdered cloves   2 cups water
3 teaspoons baking powder   1 teaspoon baking soda
½ cup white raisins   ½ cup cognac
½ cup black raisins   1 tablespoon grated lemon peel
1 cup oil   1½ cups walnut meats, chopped
                                           confectioner's sugar
                                           cinnamon

Sift the flour into a ceramic bowl with the cloves and the baking powder. Sprinkle a little of this over the raisins. Add the oil to the flour and rub between the palms of your hands until well blended. Make a well in the center of the flour-oil mixture. Add the sugar, water, and baking soda dissolved in the cognac. Mix lightly. Add the lemon peel, raisins, and nuts. Mix well. Grease a baking pan and pour in the batter. Bake in a preheated 350° oven for about 1 hour. Remove and sprinkle with confectioner's sugar and cinnamon. Cut into squares and serve cold.

ALMOND PIE ✠ AMIGDALOPITTA

2 cups toasted bread crumbs
1 teaspoon baking powder
3 cups almonds (not blanched)
1 tablespoon cinnamon

8 eggs, separated
1½ cups sugar
½ cup cognac

Mix together the bread crumbs and baking powder, and set them side. Chop the almonds, and mix them with the cinnamon. Beat the egg yolks in a bowl until very thick; add the sugar, beating it in thoroughly. Add the almonds and the cognac, and mix lightly. In another bowl, beat the egg whites until very stiff. Add them alternately with the bread crumbs to the batter, folding in gently. Pour the batter into a buttered baking mold and bake in a preheated oven at 325° for 25 to 45 minutes. Serves 6 to 8.

NOTE: If you prefer, you may substitute walnuts for the almonds.

ALMOND PIE WITH SYRUP ✠ AMIGDALOPITTA ME SIROPI

Prepare like Almond Pie, above, but use 1 cup less of sugar: bake as directed. While it is baking, prepare the syrup.

2½ cups sugar

2 cups water
1 piece of stick cinnamon

Place the ingredients in a saucepan and bring to a boil; boil for 5 minutes; remove the cinnamon. As soon as the amigdalopitta is removed from the oven, pour the hot syrup over it.

NOTE: You may blanch the almonds before chopping them to give you a lighter-colored pie.

WALNUT PIE 2 ✠ KARITHOPITTA 2

2 cups flour
1 tablespoon cinnamon
2 teaspoons baking powder
3 cups walnut meats
1⅓ cups sugar
3 ounces baking chocolate

6 eggs, separated
confectioner's sugar

Sift the flour with the cinnamon and baking powder, and set aside. Chop the walnuts; mix them with a third of the sugar. Grate the chocolate and add it to the walnuts. Beat the egg yolks with the remaining sugar until very thick and light. Beat the egg whites in another bowl until stiff. Combine the walnut-chocolate mixture with the well-beaten yolks. Fold the flour and egg whites alternately and gently into the batter. Butter a baking mold generously; sprinkle it with sugar and a little flour. Pour in the batter, and bake in a preheated 350° oven for about 1 hour. Remove from the oven and sprinkle with confectioner's sugar. Serves 6 to 8.

WALNUT PIE WITH SYRUP ✠ KARITHOPITTA ME SIROPI

THE PIE
½ cup butter
4 eggs, separated
¾ cup sugar
½ cup cognac
3 cups walnut meats

1½ cups toasted bread crumbs
1½ teaspoons baking powder
1 tablespoon cinnamon
THE SYRUP
2 cups water
2 cups sugar
1 lemon rind
1 piece of stick cinnamon

Cream the butter until light in color. In a separate bowl, beat the egg yolks until thick, then add the sugar to them, beating it in thoroughly. Add this mixture to the butter, and continue to beat until well blended. Mix in the cognac, then add the walnuts, mixing them well into the batter.

Mix the bread crumbs with the baking powder and cinnamon. Beat the egg whites until stiff. Fold the bread crumbs and egg whites alternately into the batter; stir gently; pour into a buttered baking pan or mold. Bake in a preheated 350° oven for about 1 hour. Remove from the oven and cool partially, then turn out of the mold (or pan) onto a platter.

Meantime, prepare the syrup. Put the water, sugar, lemon rind, and cinnamon stick into a saucepan and bring it to a boil. Boil for 5 minutes; remove the rind and cinnamon, and pour hot over the karithopitta. Serves 6 to 8.

YOGURT PIE WITHOUT BUTTER OR EGGS ✛ YIAOURTOPITTA XORIS VOUTIRO KE AVGA

2 cups yogurt
3½ cups farina
1 teaspoon baking soda
2 teaspoons baking powder
2¼ cups sugar
¼ pound blanched almonds,
   coarsely chopped

2 tablespoons grated orange
   peel

THE SYRUP
3½ cups sugar
3 cups water
1 lemon, grated peel only

Put the yogurt into a bowl and beat it lightly with a fork. In another bowl, mix the farina with the soda and baking powder; add to the yogurt. Add the sugar, almonds, and orange peel, and mix well for 2 or 3 minutes. Pour the batter into a well-buttered baking pan and bake for 30 to 40 minutes in a moderate oven.

While the pie is baking make the syrup: Place the water and sugar in a saucepan and bring to a boil. Add the lemon peel. As soon as the pie is baked—while it is hot—pour the syrup over the top. Allow it to cool; serve.

PHYLLO DESSERTS

ABOUT PHYLLO (also spelled fillo, phylo, filo)

Phyllo is a special dough, rolled as thin as tissue paper, and used to make pastries, or coverings for many meat and cheese dishes. Phyllo is very difficult to make at home, but—fortunately—it is available, prepared commercially, wherever Greek food products are sold. It is packed and sold in 1-pound packages, and the average package contains about 20 to 24 12- x 18-inch sheets. Phyllo must be kept well wrapped and refrigerated to keep it from drying out. It can be stored about a month.

Using phyllo: It is important to use just one sheet of phyllo at a time, and keep the rest carefully covered with a piece of paper and a damp towel. Phyllo can be cut as desired. However, if it tears, use the torn sheet between whole sheets; do not attempt to patch it with water, for it will only become pasty and sticky.

The secret to using phyllo is *butter.* Melt the butter and brush it on each sheet as you use it. Do not skimp on the amount of butter you use, or skip spreading it on some of the sheets, or your pastry will emerge thick and heavy, instead of flaky and crisp.

Use from 4 to 9 sheets of phyllo for the bottom layer of any recipe requiring it—even more, if the filling is very moist. If you are preparing a large "pie," or *pitta,* as these dishes are called, select a pan smaller than the phyllo sheets so that about 2 inches of phyllo extends over the pan on all sides. *Do not cut the phyllo to fit the pan.* Pour in your filling and fold the overhanging phyllo back over the filling to partially enclose it. Brush each sheet with butter as you turn it toward the middle of the pitta. Finally, cover the filling with more layers of phyllo, trimming these to fit the pan so that they completely seal the filling. Some recipes tell you to sprinkle the top of the pitta with a little water. The best way to do this is to wet your hands and shake them over the surface of the pitta. The amount of water that falls from them will be just right.

Score the surface of the pitta with a sharp knife just before baking. This will allow you to cut through the baked pitta cleanly when serving it.

To make triangles, or "turnovers," as we call them, the phyllo is cut into long strips 2 to 4 inches wide. The narrower strips are just right for making hors d'oeuvres and appetizers; the wider ones are suitable for main-course individual portions. Use this technique to prepare the turnover: Place the strip horizontally on the table, with the wide part parallel to you and the narrow ends to your left and right. Put a little filling in the middle of the left corner. Lift the lower left corner carefully, and bring it up to the top edge to form a small triangle. Continue to turn the triangle over and over until you reach the end of the strip. The filling will be completely enclosed in a triangular strudel-like pastry. Place the turnover, open edge down (to prevent it from opening during the baking), on a baking sheet. Make all the turnovers the same way.

ABOUT KATAIFE

Kataife is similar to phyllo but comes shredded. It must be used in thicker layers than phyllo to make sure that the filling in the pitta is enclosed. Brush the kataife generously with butter, as it is very absorbent.

Kataife can be purchased in Greek bakeries or pastry shops.

BAKLAVA KIMIS   ☩   BAKLAVA KIMIS

This is an excellent version of Almond Baklava (see index). However, it is made with home-made phyllo (even though store-bought phyllo is easier to use).

To make the phyllo, knead about 4 cups flour with enough water to form medium-stiff dough. (Inasmuch as the consistency of the dough depends entirely on feel, no specific instructions for the amount of water can be given.) Add a pinch of salt, and continue to knead the dough, adding water, a few drops at a time, or adding more flour as necessary. Roll the dough into thin sheets. You will never be able to roll these as thin as commercially prepared phyllo, but try to come close. Since the home-made sheets will be heavier, use only 2 or 3 for the bottom layer of the baklava and reserve 3 for the top layer. Brush each sheet with plenty of butter—do not skimp. Proceed to fill the pan as in Almond Baklava. Cover with the remaining 3 sheets of phyllo, again brushing very heavily with butter. Bake in a preheated oven at 250° for about 1 hour.

While the baklava is baking prepare the syrup:

6 cups sugar	1 piece of stick cinnamon
4 cups water	5–6 cloves

Put all ingredients into a large pot; bring to a boil. Continue to boil until a thick syrup is formed. Keep the syrup hot and pour it *hot* over the *hot* baklava. IMPORTANT: This is an exception to the basic rule of generally pouring hot on cold.

ALMOND BAKLAVA ✠ BAKLAVA ME AMIGDALA

THE BAKLAVA	THE SYRUP
4 cups chopped, blanched almonds	4 cups sugar
½ cup sugar	3 cups water
1 tablespoon cinnamon	½ cup honey
1¼ cups butter, melted	1 piece of stick cinnamon
1½ pounds phyllo* (see index: About Phyllo)	5–6 cloves

Mix together the almonds, sugar, and cinnamon. Select a pan the size of the phyllo sheets; brush well with melted butter. Use 4 sheets of phyllo for the bottom layer, brushing each one with butter before adding it. Top with a sheet of unbuttered phyllo, and sprinkle a handful of the almonds on it. Cover with a sheet of buttered phyllo and then again with an unbuttered one, and sprinkle a handful of almonds on this last one. Continue in this manner until all the ingredients are used, reserving 5 phyllo sheets for the top layer. Brush each of these top sheets with ample butter; pour any remaining butter over the top baklava. Trim the edges if necessary. Score the baklava into the traditional diamond-shaped pieces without cutting through the bottom layers. Wet your fingers and shake them over the baklava to sprinkle the top with water. Bake in a preheated 250° oven for about 1 hour. Remove from the oven and cool.

To prepare the syrup, put the sugar and water into a large pot and bring it to a boil; boil for 5 minutes. Add the honey, cinnamon, and cloves, and boil for 5 minutes longer. Pour the hot syrup onto the cold baklava. Cool, then cut through the bottom layers, and serve following the score marks.

NOTE: You must always pour hot over cold—never hot on hot. This procedure will not affect the taste of the baklava but will turn it into a soggy, unappetizing mass. This pastry should always be crisp, and moist at the same time.

ROLLED WALNUT BAKLAVA ✠ BAKLAVA ME KARITHIA, ROLLO

THE PASTRY	THE SYRUP
1¼ pounds chopped walnuts	4 cups sugar
½ cup sugar	3 cups water
2 tablespoons cinnamon	1 piece of stick cinnamon
1½ pounds phyllo*	1 teaspoon lemon juice
1 cup (approximately) melted butter	

To prepare the pastry, mix the walnuts with the sugar and cinnamon. Take 2 sheets of phyllo (see index: About Phyllo) at a time; place on a marble surface or a sheet of waxed paper. Brush each sheet with butter, then place one sheet on top of the other, and sprinkle it with a handful of the nut mixture. Top with 2 more sheets of phyllo, brushing each, as before, with butter, and sprinkling nuts over the top one. Repeat twice more (until the baklava is 8 sheets thick). Roll the phyllo up tightly, then cut the roll into half-inch-thick slices, placing the pieces on a buttered baking sheet. Continue to form and slice the rolls until all the ingredients are used. Pour melted butter over the baklava slices, and bake in a preheated 350° oven for about 20 minutes. Remove from the oven and cool.

Prepare the syrup. Put the sugar, water, stick cinnamon, and lemon juice into a saucepan and bring to a boil. Boil for 8 minutes. Pour the hot syrup over the cold baklava, and serve.

WALNUT BAKLAVA ✠ BAKLAVA ME KARITHIA

Prepare like Almond Baklava, above, but substitute walnuts for the almonds, and for the syrup, increase the sugar to 3½ cups and the honey to 1½ cups.

NOTE: An excellent baklava can be made with a combination of almonds and walnuts.

SARAILI ✠ SARAILI

THE PASTRY
1 pound chopped walnuts
6 tablespoons sugar
2 tablespoons cinnamon
2 pounds phyllo*
1½ cups melted butter

THE SYRUP
4 cups sugar
3 cups water
1 piece of stick cinnamon
1 teaspoon lemon juice

To prepare the pastry, mix the walnuts with the sugar and cinnamon. Count the sheets of phyllo (see index: About Phyllo). Divide the walnut mix, allowing 1 portion for each 2 phyllo sheets (i.e., 20 portions nuts for 40 sheets). Take 1 sheet of phyllo, brush it with melted butter, and top it with a second phyllo sheet; sprinkle 1 portion of the walnuts on this sheet. Carefully roll the phyllo up, tightly, into a long, cigar-like shape, pushing it on both ends to ruffle it slightly. Repeat the process until all the phyllo sheets and nut mixtures are used up. Place each saraili on a buttered baking pan as soon as it is completed, laying all as close together as possible. Pour melted butter over the top, and bake in a preheated oven at 350° for 20 minutes, or until the saraili are golden brown. Remove from the oven and cool slightly.

Prepare the syrup: Boil the sugar, water, stick cinnamon, and lemon juice together in a saucepan for 8 minutes. Pour the hot syrup over the cold saraili.

WALNUT OR ALMOND FLOYERES ✠ FLOYERES ME KARITHIA E AMIGDALA

THE PASTRY	1 cup (approximately) melted
2½ cups chopped walnuts or almonds	butter
½ cup toasted bread crumbs	THE SYRUP
2 eggs	3½ cups sugar
¾ cup sugar	2½ cups water
1 teaspoon cinnamon	1 piece of stick cinnamon
1½ pounds phyllo*	1 lemon rind
	1 teaspoon lemon juice

To prepare the pastry, mix the nuts and bread crumbs together. In a separate bowl, beat the eggs with the sugar and cinnamon; mix in the nuts. Cut the phyllo sheets (see index: About Phyllo) across the width into 3 strips each. Working with 1 strip at a time, brush it with melted butter, then place a little filling along one side, extending it only to within a half inch of either end. Fold these ends over the filling, then roll the floyera up over the filling into a long, flutelike shape. Brush with butter, and lay it in a buttered baking pan. Prepare all the floyeres the same way, placing them next to each other in the pan. Drizzle any leftover butter over the pastry. Dip your hands into cold water and shake the excess over the floyeres. Bake in a preheated 350° oven for about 15 minutes. Remove from the oven, and cool partially.

Prepare the syrup: Boil all the ingredients together in a saucepan for 8 minutes. Pierce the partially cooled floyeres with a fork in 2 or 3 places, and, using a slotted spoon, dip them, one at a time, into the hot syrup, then place them on a platter. After this process is completed, bring the syrup to a boil again and let it cook to thicken. Pour the thickened syrup over the floyeres.

FLOYERES WITH CUSTARD ✠ FLOYERES ME KREMA

1 recipe custard from	THE SYRUP
Yalatoboureko (see index)	2 cups sugar
1½ pounds phyllo*	1 cup water
1 cup butter, melted	1 lemon rind
	½ teaspoon vanilla

Prepare the custard; allow it to cool and thicken. Cut the phyllo sheets (see index: About Phyllo) across the width into 3 strips each. Working with 1 strip at a time, brush it with melted butter, and spread 1 tablespoonful of the custard along the long side, to within a half-inch of either side. Fold the ends over the filling to cover and seal it, then roll the pastry over and over into a long, flutelike shape. Brush the phyllo with butter and place the floyera on a buttered baking pan. Repeat this process until all the floyeres are shaped. Pour any remaining butter over them, and bake in a preheated oven at 350° for about 15 minutes. Remove from the oven, and cool partially.

Prepare the syrup: Put all the ingredients into a saucepan and bring to a boil; boil for 5 minutes. Pierce the floyeres in 2 or 3 places with a fork, and, using a slotted spoon, dip them into the hot syrup, then place them on a platter. Bring the syrup to a boil again and let it cook for 5 minutes longer to thicken, then pour it, hot, over the floyeres.

NOTE: If you prefer, you may shape these into triangles (see the procedure in About Phyllo) instead of rolling them up.

KATAIFE* WITH CUSTARD 1   ✠   KATAIFE ME KREMA 1

3 pounds kataife
1 recipe custard for
 Yalatoboureko (see index)
1½ cups butter

THE SYRUP
4 cups sugar
3 cups water
½ cup glucose (optional)

Prepare the kataife (see index). Prepare the custard, then put some of it along one side of the pastry, then fold the kataife pastry over the filling on 2 sides, and roll up tightly into cigar-like shapes. Prepare the syrup by boiling the ingredients together in a saucepan for 10 minutes, and pour the hot thickened syrup over the hot kataife.

KATAIFE* WITH CUSTARD 2   ✠   KATAIFE ME KREMA 2

2¼ (approximately) pounds
 kataife
1 recipe custard for
 Yalatoboureko (see index)
1 cup butter, melted

THE SYRUP
4 cups sugar
3 cups water
1 teaspoon vanilla
½ cup glucose (optional)

Divide the kataife dough (see index: About Kataife) into 2 parts, and spread out gently with your fingers. Butter a small pan. Spread half the kataife in it; pour ample butter over it. Prepare the custard and spread that evenly over the kataife; top it with the remaining kataife, and pour the rest of the butter over all. Bake in a preheated 350° oven for about 30 minutes.

In the meantime, prepare the syrup: Boil together all the ingredients in a saucepan for about 10 minutes or until the syrup begins to thicken. Remove the kataife from the oven as soon as it is baked, and immediately pour the hot syrup over it. Let it cool, then cut into diamond-shaped pieces. Serves about 15.

ALMOND KATAIFE*   ✠   KATAIFE ME AMIGDALA

THE PASTRY
4 cups chopped blanched
   almonds
¼ cup sugar
½ teaspoon cinnamon
2 eggs
3 pounds kataife pastry

1½ cups butter, melted
THE SYRUP
3½ cups sugar
5 cups water
1 lemon rind
1 teaspoon lemon juice

To make the pastry, mix the almonds, sugar, and cinnamon together. Beat the eggs in a separate bowl and add them to the nut mixture. Pull a handful of kataife (see index: About Kataife) at a time, and place it on a marble surface or piece of waxed paper. Put a little of the filling on one edge, and roll the kataife up into a cylinder, rolling tightly at the start so the filling is completely sealed in, and rolling the outside a little more loosely. Place the kataife in a buttered pan. Repeat this process until all the kataife are made, then carefully spoon melted butter over the tops. Bake in a preheated 350° oven for about 30 minutes.

In the meantime, prepare the syrup: Boil the sugar, water, and lemon rind together in a saucepan for 10 minutes, then add the lemon juice, and boil a few minutes longer, until the syrup beings to thicken. When the kataife are done, remove them from the oven and, while they are still hot, pour the hot syrup over them. Cover with a clean towel and let them stand until cool. They will absorb the syrup.

NOTE: Be sure not to place the kataife rolls too closely together in the pan or they will not bake properly, and will become sticky when the syrup is poured over them.

KATAIFE* YIANNIOTIKO   ✠   KATAIFE YIANNIOTIKO

THE PASTRY
3 cups chopped blanched
   almonds
3 tablespoons sugar
1 teaspoon cinnamon
¾ pound phyllo*

1 pound kataife
1 cup butter, melted

THE SYRUP
4 cups sugar
¾ cup glucose (optional)
3 cups water

To make the pastry, mix the almonds together with the cinnamon and sugar. Butter a pan 2 inches smaller than the phyllo sheets (see index: About Phyllo), and spread 6 or 7 of the sheets in it, one at a time, brushing each with melted butter before adding the next. Do not trim off the overhanging phyllo. Divide the kataife (see index: About Kataife) into 2 parts, using your fingers, and gently spread half on the phyllo. Sprinkle with butter, and spread with the almond mixture. Top the almonds with the rest of the kataife, again spreading it on gently, and sprinkle with more butter. Fold the edges of the phyllo back over the filling, buttering each piece again; top with the remaining phyllo, repeating the process of buttering each sheet as you add it. Trim any excess phyllo from these top sheets so they fit the pan, and score the pastry into diamond-shaped pieces. Sprinkle the remaining butter over the top. Wet your hands, and shake the excess water from them onto the pastry. Bake in a preheated oven at 350° for 45 minutes to 1 hour.

Prepare the syrup: Boil all the ingredients together in a saucepan for about 10 minutes. Pour the hot syrup over the hot kataife.

WALNUT KATAIFE* ✝ KATAIFE ME KARITHIA

Prepare like Almond Kataife (see index), but substitute walnuts for the almonds, and (in the syrup), 2 pieces of cinnamon stick for the lemon rind.

BOUGATSA ✝ BOUGATSA

4 cups milk	½ cup (approximately) butter,
1 lemon rind	melted
1 cup farina	¾ pounds phyllo*
4 eggs	1 tablespoon cinnamon
1 cup sugar	1 cup (approximately)
1 teaspoon vanilla	confectioner's sugar

Scald the milk with the lemon rind, then lower the heat and add the farina to it, mixing constantly with a wooden spoon until thick. Beat the eggs well in a bowl with the sugar and vanilla. Add to the farina, and stir over very low heat until the mixture thickens again. Remove from the heat and discard the lemon rind. Stir occasionally to prevent a crust from forming.

Select a pan about 2 inches smaller than the phyllo (see index: About Phyllo). Lay about 8 sheets of phyllo in it for the bottom layer, brushing each sheet with melted butter before adding it. Do not trim the overhanging phyllo. Pour in the filling. Fold the overhanging phyllo back over the filling to seal it; brush with butter. Butter each of the remaining phyllo sheets and place them on top of the filling. Trim the excess so the phyllo fits the pan. Score into desired serving-size pieces. Pour any remaining butter over the top. Bake at 350° for 30 to 40 minutes.

Mix together the cinnamon and confectioner's sugar and sift it over the hot cake. Serve immediately, hot.

COPENHAGEN*   ✠   KOPEHAGI

| THE PASTRY | ¾ pound phyllo* |
| THE PASTRY | 1 cup (approximately) melted |

THE PASTRY

1 cup toasted bread crumbs
1 teaspoon baking powder
1 teaspoon cinnamon
6 eggs, separated
1 cup sugar
½ cup cognac
3 cups shelled almonds, coarsely
      chopped

¾ pound phyllo*
1 cup (approximately) melted
      butter

THE SYRUP

3½ cups sugar
2½ cups water
1 piece of stick cinnamon
1 teaspoon lemon juice

Mix the bread crumbs together with the baking powder and cinnamon. Beat the egg yolks in a separate bowl until very thick, then add the sugar, and beat again until well blended. Add the cognac, then add the almonds. Beat the egg whites in another bowl until very stiff, and add them alternately with the bread-crumb mixture to the batter, folding in gently.

Line the bottom of a buttered pan about 2 inches smaller than the phyllo sheets (see index: About Phyllo) with 8 sheets of the phyllo, brushing each well with butter before adding the next. Do not trim the overhanging phyllo. Pour the filling into the pan, and fold the overhanging phyllo back over it to partially cover the filling; this will seal the pastry. Top with the remaining phyllo, again brushing each sheet with butter, but do trim these sheets to fit the pan. Score the pastry into diamonds; bake in a preheated oven at 350° for about 25 minutes.

In the meantime, prepare the syrup: In a saucepan, boil together the sugar, water, and stick cinnamon for 5 minutes. Add the lemon juice, and boil 2 minutes longer. Pour the hot syrup over the hot pastry as soon as you remove it from the oven.

COPENHAGEN PASTA FLORA   ✠   KOPEHAGI ME PASTA FLORA

THE PASTRY

½ recipe Pasta Flora dough
      (see index)
½ cup apricot marmalade
1 cup sugar
½ cup toasted bread crumbs
3½ cups chopped almonds
6 eggs, separated
½ cup cognac
1 teaspoon cinnamon

1 teaspoon baking powder
8 sheets phyllo*
½ cup (approximately) melted
      butter

THE SYRUP

3½ cups sugar
2½ cups water
1 piece of stick cinnamon
1 teaspoon lemon juice

Prepare the Pasta Flora dough and, using your palms and fingers, spread it evenly in a buttered pan, pressing it in. Bake in a preheated oven at 350° for about 10 minutes. Remove the partially baked crust from the oven; spread the marmalade on it. Following the instructions given for Copenhagen (see index) use the rest of the remaining pastry ingredients to prepare the rest of filling; pour it over the marmalade. Cover the pastry with the phyllo sheets (see index: About Phyllo) buttering each before you lay it over the filling; trim the excess with a sharp knife. Score the phyllo into diamonds. Bake in a preheated 350° oven for about 20 minutes.

In the meantime, prepare the syrup, also according to the instructions for Copenhagen. Pour the hot syrup over the hot pastry. Cool, and serve.

YALATOBOUREKO ✠ YALATOBOUREKO

THE CUSTARD		1⅓ pounds phyllo*
4 cups milk, scalded		½ cup melted butter
1 cup farina		
5 eggs		THE SYRUP
1½ cups sugar		2½ cups water
1 teaspoon vanilla		3½ cups sugar
3 tablespoons sweet butter		1 lemon rind
		1 teaspoon lemon juice

Add the farina to the scalded milk, stirring constantly with a wooden spoon; cook until the mixture thickens. This becomes the custard base. Beat the eggs in a bowl, and add the sugar and vanilla to them, beating in well. Remove the farina mixture from the heat, and add the eggs very slowly to it, beating constantly. Add the butter, mixing it in well. Let the custard cool, stirring occasionally to prevent a crust from forming.

Butter a pan about 2 inches smaller than the sheets of phyllo (see index: About Phyllo). Lay half the phyllo in it, brushing each sheet with melted butter before adding it. Do not trim the overhanging phyllo. Pour in the custard filling. Fold the extending leaves of phyllo back over the filling to partially cover it (this will seal the pastry); brush the ends with butter. Top with the remaining phyllo, again brushing each sheet well with butter before adding it, and trimming the phyllo to fit the pan. Score the pastry into diamonds, and pour the remaining butter over it. Dip your hands into cold water and shake the excess from them over the phyllo. Bake in a preheated 350° oven for 30 minutes.

In the meantime, prepare the syrup: Put the water, sugar, and lemon rind into a saucepan and bring to a boil. Boil for 5 minutes, then add the lemon juice, and boil for 3 minutes longer. Discard the lemon rind.

As soon as you remove the pastry from the oven, pour the hot syrup over it.

CUSTARDS, CREAMS, PUDDINGS

CRÈME PIATOU ✠ KREMA PIATOU

2¾ cups milk
1 lemon rind
5 tablespoons cornstarch
8–10 tablespoons sugar

2 eggs (yolks only, or whole
    eggs)
cinnamon
a few drops vanilla (optional)

Heat 1 cup of the milk with the lemon rind to the scalding point, but do not boil. Dissolve the cornstarch in the remaining milk; add the sugar, and mix well. Very slowly add about 2 tablespoons of the hot milk to the milk-cornstarch mixture, stirring constantly, then pour the whole cool mixture into the hot, stirring constantly with a wooden spoon until well blended. Place over very low heat and continue to stir until it thickens into a smooth custard. Remove from the heat; discard the lemon rind.

Beat the egg yolks or eggs in a bowl until very thick, and slowly blend them into the custard, again stirring constantly. (If you are using whole eggs, you may prefer to beat the whites and yolks separately before adding them.) Return the custard to very low heat and cook for 2 or 3 minutes, until thickened. (If you use the whites, the cream must be eaten the same day.) Pour into a bowl or individual custard cups and sprinkle with cinnamon. If you like a vanilla flavor, add the flavoring when you add the eggs.

NOTE: If the custard thickens suddenly and becomes lumpy, remove it from the heat and beat with a wire whisk or a wooden spoon until the lumps disappear. Serves 5 to 6.

BANANA CRÈME PIATOU ✠ KREMA PIATOU ME BANANAS

Prepare like Crème Piatou; flavor with a few drops vanilla. Slice as many bananas as desired. Put a layer of banana slices in the bottom of the custard cups and pour a layer of the custard over it. Add another layer of banana slices; top with a thicker layer of the custard. Cool and refrigerate.

APPLE CRÈME PIATOU ✠ KREMA PIATOU ME MILA

1 recipe Crème Piatou
Apple Compote (see index) as
    desired

Prepare the custard. Put some Apple Compote in each cup; top it with the custard. Refrigerate. Serve with syrup from the compote poured over the top.

BUTTER CREAM 1 ✠ KREMA VOUTIROU 1

2 cups sweet butter
2 cups confectioner's sugar

4 egg yolks (or 3 whole eggs)
1 teaspoon vanilla

Cream the butter until very light. Slowly add the sugar, beating it in thoroughly. Add the egg yolks (or whole eggs) and vanilla, and beat until smooth and thick. Use as a filling for tarts, pies, and the like. Store in the refrigerator.

BUTTER CREAM 2 ✠ KREMA VOUTIROU 2

Prepare like Butter Cream 1, above, but use whole eggs. Beat the whites separately in another bowl until stiff, then beat thoroughly into them 2 tablespoons confectioner's sugar. Add to the basic recipe, beating in very well. It will add to the bulk of the cream. IMPORTANT: this must be used the same day it is made.

BASIC CHOCOLATE CREAM ✠ KREMA VOUTIROU SOKOLATA

2 cups sweet butter
1 cup confectioner's sugar
3 egg yolks

¼ cup maraschino liqueur
1 cup semisweet cocoa

Cream the butter. Slowly add the sugar to it, beating all the while. In another bowl, beat the eggs with the maraschino liqueur; add to the butter-sugar mixture; beat a few minutes longer. Add the cocoa, blending it in well with the other ingredients. Store in the refrigerator to thicken. Use as a filling or frosting.

SAVAYAR CUSTARD ✠ KREMA SAVAYIAR

1 recipe Crème Piatou
2 Savayar cookies (see index)
liqueur (any kind)

1–2 tablespoons chopped
   almonds

Prepare the custard. Put the cookies into a bowl; sprinkle a little liqueur over them; pour the hot custard over all. Sprinkle with the almonds. Cool; chill in the refrigerator.

WHIPPED CREAM CHANTILLY ✠ KREMA SANITILLY

This is whipped cream with sugar beaten into it. It may also have a specific flavor added to it—vanilla, for instance.

CRÈME PÂTISSIÈRE [CUSTARD] 1 ✠ KREMA PATISSERI 1

4 cups milk
½ cup flour
⅓ cup cornstarch
5 eggs

1 cup sugar
1½ teaspoons vanilla
1 lemon rind
2 tablespoons sweet butter

Stir the flour and cornstarch into 1 cup of the milk. Beat the eggs in another bowl with the sugar and vanilla until very thick and light. Blend into the flour-milk mixture. Scald the remaining milk with the lemon rind; remove and discard the rind. Add the hot milk very slowly to the egg mixture. Pour the whole into a clean pot and place over low heat; stir constantly until thick and smooth. Remove from the heat, add the butter, stir until blended. Cool, stirring occasionally so a crust does not form. This is a basic custard that can be used as a dessert custard, or filling for many kinds of baked desserts.

CRÈME PÂTISSIÈRE [CUSTARD] 2 ✠ KREMA PATISSERI 2

5 cups milk
6 eggs
1 scant cup sugar
2 teaspoons vanilla

¾ cup rice flour
¾ cup flour
4 tablespoons sweet butter

Scald half of the milk. Beat the eggs in a bowl with the sugar and vanilla until very thick and smooth. Stir the rice flour and flour into the cold milk, very carefully, so it does not lump. Add this to the eggs, mixing in well. Slowly add the hot milk, stirring constantly. Pour the whole into a clean pot and place over a low heat. Stir until it becomes a thick, smooth custard, then add the butter, stirring while it melts. Remove from the heat and cool, stirring occasionally so a crust does not form. Use in the same way as Crème Pâtissière 1.

CRÈME PÂTISSIÈRE 3   ✠   KREMA PATISSERI 3

1 quart milk
10 tablespoons cornstarch
6 egg yolks

1 scant cup sugar
2 teaspoons vanilla
2 tablespoons sweet butter

Scald half of the milk. Thoroughly dissolve the cornstarch in the cold milk. Beat the egg yolks in a bowl with the sugar and vanilla until very thick and light. To the yolks add the cold milk with the cornstarch, stirring constantly, then slowly add the hot milk, stirring all the while. Pour into a clean pot and place over low heat. Stir until the custard thickens and is very smooth. Remove from the heat. Add the butter. Cool, stirring occasionally so a crust does not form.

LEMON BUTTER CREAM   ✠   KREMA VOUTIROU ME LEMONI

2 cups sweet butter
2½ cups confectioner's sugar
4 egg yolks

1 lemon rind, grated
2 tablespoons lemon juice

Cream the butter. Slowly add the sugar to it, beating it in thoroughly. Add the lemon rind and the egg yolks, beating very well. Add the lemon juice, and beat until smooth. Use as a frosting or filling.

ORANGE BUTTER CREAM   ✠   KREMA VOUTIROU ME PORTOCALI

1 recipe Butter Cream 1
 (see index)
½ cup orange juice

3 tablespoons grated orange
 rind

Prepare the butter cream. Add the orange juice and orange rind, and beat in well. Use as a frosting or filling.

CHESTNUT CREAM ✠ KREMA KASTANO

2 pounds chestnuts
water as needed
1 pound sugar

1½ cups milk
¾ cup fresh butter
1½ teaspoons vanilla

Shell the nuts and boil them in ample water until they soften. Drain, remove the skins, and purée in a blender. Put the purée into a pot with ½ cup of the sugar. Place over low heat. Slowly add the milk, stirring constantly so the mixture does not become lumpy. Turn off the heat; add the butter and vanilla; mix very well. Put the remaining sugar into another pot with 1 cup water and boil to make a thick syrup. Cool, and slowly add to the chestnuts, stirring constantly. This should be a light cream, similar in texture to butter cream. Use like butter cream.

MAHALEMPI CUSTARD ✠ KREMA MAHALEMPI
WITH VISSINO GLYKO ME VISSINO GLYKO

4 cups milk
¾ cup cornstarch
10 tablespoons sugar

1½ teaspoons vanilla
1 cup Vissino Glyko (see index)

Pour 2 cups of the milk into a bowl and dissolve the cornstarch and sugar in it. Put the other 2 cups milk into a pot; heat to scalding. Lower the heat, and slowly add the milk-cornstarch-sugar mixture, stirring constantly. Cook over very low heat until it becomes a thick, smooth custard. Butter individual cups and pour in the custard. Cool and chill in the refrigerator. To serve, turn out onto small plates. Top with a tablespoonful of Vissino Glyko and pour some Vissino syrup over all. Serves about 8.

CUSTARD IN CHAMPAGNE GLASSES ✠ KREMA SE POTIRIA SAMPANIAS

THE CREAM
2¾ cups milk
7 tablespoons sugar
4 tablespoons cornstarch
5 egg yolks

THE TOPPING
6 tablespoons sugar
2 tablespoons water
1 teaspoon lemon juice
5 egg whites
1½ teaspoons vanilla
½ cup chopped roasted almonds
½ cup Vissino Glyko (see index)
cherry or vissino syrup

Reserve 1 cup of the milk; put the rest into a pot; heat—do not boil. Dissolve the sugar and cornstarch in the cold milk. Beat the egg yolks in a bowl until very thick; add to the cold milk. Slowly add about 2 tablespoons of the hot milk to the cold milk, stirring constantly, then pour the cool mixture into the pot with the rest of the hot milk. Lower the heat and stir to make a thick custard. Cool slightly. Fill the champagne glasses two-thirds full.

Bring to a boil in a saucepan the 6 tablespoons sugar, the water, and lemon juice and make a thick sauce, yellowish in color. Beat the egg whites in a separate bowl until very stiff. Add the vanilla. Slowly add the hot syrup, beating constantly until all the syrup is used. Fold in the almonds. Fill the rest of the champagne glasses with this mixture. Top with 2 or 3 cherries. Pour a bit of Vissino syrup or cherry syrup over the top. Serves 8 to 10.

FARINA PUDDING   ✠   POUTIGKA ME SIMIGDALI
WITH PRUNE SAUCE   KE SALTSA DAMASKINO

THE PUDDING	¼ cup white raisins
2 cups milk	THE SAUCE
½ cup farina	3 cups prunes, soaked overnight
6 eggs, separated	in cold water
1 cup sugar	1 cup sugar
1½ teaspoons vanilla	1 cup water
4 teaspoons sweet butter	

Bring the milk to a boil and immediately add the farina, a little at a time, stirring constantly with a wooden spoon. Let it cook until it thickens. Meantime, beat the egg yolks in a bowl with the sugar and vanilla. Remove the farina from the heat and add the egg mixture to it. Stir well. Blend in the sweet butter. Cool. Beat the egg whites in another bowl until stiff, then gently fold into the pudding. Fold the raisins in gently. Pour the pudding into a well buttered, lightly sugared and floured tube pan, place this in a pan with water (bain-marie), and bake in a preheated 350° oven for 45 minutes to 1 hour. Remove from the heat, cool, and turn onto a platter.

To make the sauce, cook the prunes with the sugar and water to make a compote (see any compote in index). Remove a third of the prunes from the sauce, drain, and remove the pits. Set these pitted prunes aside. Pass the rest of the prunes through a strainer, and mix with the syrup to a sauce. Unmold the pudding and garnish with the whole prunes. Pour the prune sauce into the center.

RICE PUDDING
WITH APRICOT SAUCE

✠

POUTIGKA ME RIZI
KE SALTSA VERIKOKKO

THE PUDDING
1 cup raw rice
2 cups water
1 lemon rind
4 cups hot milk
1½ cups sugar
4 eggs, separated

2 tablespoons cornstarch
1 cup white raisins

THE SAUCE
1 cup Apricot Marmalade (see index)
¼ cup hot water
¼ cup cognac

Cook the rice in 1½ cups of the water, with the lemon rind added. Stir gently to separate the grains. As soon as the rice has absorbed the water, add the hot milk; stir well. Cook until the rice is almost tender (about 7 minutes longer). Add the sugar; stir in well. Beat the egg yolks in a bowl and add the cornstarch dissolved in the remaining half-cup water. Add this mixture, a little at a time, to the rice, and stir over low heat until the mixture thickens. Remove the rice from the heat and discard the lemon rind. Cool. Stir in the raisins.

Beat the egg whites in another bowl until stiff and fold them gently into the cooled pudding. Butter a baking dish and lightly sprinkle it with sugar and flour. Turn the rice pudding into this. Place in a pan of water, and bake in a preheated oven at 350° for 30 to 45 minutes. Remove from the oven and cool.

Prepare the sauce: Dilute the marmalade with the water. Mix in the cognac. Serve with the pudding. Serves 6 to 8.

RICE PUDDING

✠

RIZOGALO

1 cup raw rice
2 cups plus 2 tablespoons water
4 cups milk
1½ cups sugar

2 egg yolks
1 teaspoon vanilla
2 tablespoons cornstarch

Boil the rice in the 2 cups water for about 6 to 8 minutes, then add the milk; stir well. Continue to cook over low heat until tender (about 8 minutes longer). Add the sugar to the rice. Beat the egg yolks in a bowl with the vanilla; to this, add the cornstarch dissolved in the 2 tablespoons water, and mix well. Add the egg mixture to the rice and stir it in well; cook until the pudding thickens slightly. Remove from the heat and pour into a bowl or individual dishes. Cool and serve.

NOTE: Be careful not to cook this until it is very thick; the pudding will thicken as it cools.

RAISIN PUDDING ✠ POUTIGKA ME STAFIDES

3 ounces (about ½ cup) white
    raisins
3 ounces (about ½ cup) black
    raisins
7–8 slices white bread, crusts
    removed
2 cups scalded milk

6 ounces (about 1 cup) chopped
    walnut meats
5 eggs
1 cup sugar
1 tablespoon grated lemon peel
1 recipe Apricot Sauce (see
    index)

Wash and dry the raisins; dust witn a little flour. Cut the bread into small cubes. Butter a 2-quart mold and sprinkle with flour and sugar. Scald—do not boil—the milk. Spread one layer of bread cubes in the mold, top with a layer of the white raisins, then one of walnuts, then one of black raisins. Repeat this process, making as many layers as possible. Beat the eggs well in a bowl with the sugar, then beat in the lemon peel and the milk, a little at a time. Pour this mixture into the mold, by the spoonful, so the bread absorbs it. Place the mold in a pan of water and bake in a preheated 350° oven, until it expands and puffs. Test for doneness by inserting a toothpick; if the toothpick comes out clean, the pudding is done. Remove from the oven and cool thoroughly. Serve with Apricot Sauce. Serves 6 to 8.

BREAD-CRUMB PUDDING ✠ POUTIGKA ME FRIGANIA

3 cups toasted bread crumbs
2 teaspoons baking powder
6 eggs, separated
1 cup sugar

⅓ cup maraschino liqueur
1½ cups blanched chopped
    almonds

Mix the toasted crumbs with the baking powder. Beat the egg yolks with the sugar. In a separate bowl beat the egg whites until stiff. Add the maraschino liqueur to the egg yolks and mix in well. Add the almonds. Add the bread-crumb mixture alternately with the egg whites; mix lightly to blend. Butter a mold and lightly sprinkle it with sugar and toasted crumbs. Pour the mixture into the mold; place the mold in a pan of water. Bake for 45 minutes in a preheated 350° oven. Remove from the oven, cool, and unmold on a platter. Serve with Sabayon Sauce (see index). Serves 6 to 8.

PUDDING SOUFFLÉ   ✠   POUTIGKA SOUFLE

4 cups milk
1¼ cups sugar
½ cup butter
1 cup flour

6 eggs
3 teaspoons vanilla
1 recipe Apricot Sauce (see index)

    Scald the milk and mix the sugar into it. In a wider pot, melt the butter; add the flour, a little at a time, and stir with a wire whisk to blend well. Add the scalded milk a little at a time, stirring constantly until it is the consistency of a thick cream sauce. Remove from the heat and stir to cool. Separate 4 of the eggs and lightly beat together the 4 yolks and the 2 whole eggs. Add to the sauce, stirring in quickly *in only one direction*. Add the vanilla. Beat the whites in a separate bowl until stiff, and fold them lightly and very gently into the mixture. Butter a mold; sprinkle with flour and sugar. Pour in the soufflé. Place the mold in a pan of water and bake in a preheated 350° oven for about 1 hour. Unmold onto a platter. Serve with the sauce. Serves 8.

WALNUT PUDDING   ✠   POUTIGKA ME KARITHIA

2 cups toasted bread crumbs
1 teaspoon baking powder
5 eggs, separated
1 cup sugar

½ cup butter
½ cup cognac
2½ cups chopped walnuts

    Butter a mold and dust lightly with flour and sugar. Mix the crumbs with the baking powder. Beat the egg yolks and sugar in a bowl until light and fluffy. Melt the butter and add it to the yolks, a little at a time. Add the cognac and the walnuts. In another bowl beat the whites until stiff, and then add them alternately with the crumbs to the pudding, folding in lightly. Pour into a 2-quart mold. Place the mold in a pan of water and bake in a preheated 350° oven for 35 to 40 minutes. Remove from the oven; cool. Turn onto a platter and serve with Sabayon Sauce (see index).

MISCELLANEOUS DESSERTS AND BREADS

HALVAH MORAITIKOS ✠ HALVAS MORAITIKOS

¾ cup blanched almonds
6 cups water
1 cup butter
2½ cups sugar

2 cups farina
2 tablespoons cinnamon
3 tablespoons sugar

Chop all the almonds except 6 or 8. Put the water, butter, and sugar into a wide pot, mix well to dissolve the sugar. Bring to a boil, then add the farina. Stir the mixture rapidly to prevent its sticking and forming lumps. Simmer over a low heat until it thickens, stirring constantly. Add the chopped almonds and half of the cinnamon; stir well. Pour into a buttered pan, spreading the mixture evenly. Cool, and score into squares or diamonds. Put a whole almond on each piece. Bake in 350° oven for 15 minutes. Remove from the oven. Sprinkle with cinnamon and the 3 tablespoons sugar. Cool; cut and serve. Serves 6 to 8.

BAKED HALVAH ✠ HALVAS TOU FOURNO

THE HALVAH
3 cups farina
1 teaspoon cinnamon
1 cup butter
4 eggs, separated
1 cup sugar
½ cup slivered blanched
    almonds

THE SYRUP
2½ cups sugar
3 cups water
1 piece of stick cinnamon
2–3 cloves

Mix the farina with the cinnamon and set aside. Cream the butter in a bowl. In another bowl, beat the egg yolks with the sugar until thick. Add to the butter and beat very well. Beat the egg whites until stiff. Then fold them alternately with the farina into the butter-egg mixture. Add the almonds; mix gently. Put into a buttered pan. Bake in a preheated 350° oven for 45 minutes.

Prepare the syrup by boiling all of the ingredients for about 8 minutes. Remove and discard the cinnamon and cloves. Pour the syrup over the hot halvah. Cool, serve.

HALVAH WITH FARINA 1 ✠ HALVAS ME SIMIGDALI 1
(WITH BUTTER) (VOUTIROU)

½ cup blanched almonds	2–3 cloves
3 cups milk	1 lemon rind
2 cups water	1 cup butter
2½ cups sugar	2 cups farina
3 pieces of stick cinnamon	cinnamon-sugar

Cut the almonds into thin slivers. Put the milk, water, sugar, cinnamon, cloves, and lemon rind into a wide pot; bring to a boil, and boil for 2 minutes. Remove from the heat. Melt the butter in another pot, and brown it until it smokes, then slowly add the farina, stirring constantly with a wooden spoon, until it turns a light golden color. Add the almonds, continuing to brown the mixture very carefully over low heat. Remove from the heat as soon as it is a light-chestnut color. With a slotted spoon, remove the cinnamon, cloves, and lemon rind from the syrup, and once again bring it to a quick boil, then add to the farina. Stir the mixture over low heat until it thickens, then remove from the heat, cover with a clean towel, and let rest for 5 minutes. Pour into a tube pan or other mold, pressing the mixture well into it. Let stand until it is set, and then turn out onto a platter. Dust with a little sugar and cinnamon. Slice and serve.

HALVAH WITH FARINA 2 ✠ HALVAS ME SIMIGDALI 2
(WITH OIL) (LATHIOU)

5 cups water	1 cup excellent oil
2½ cups sugar	2 cups farina or flour
½ cup honey	¼ cup chopped walnuts
2 pieces of cinnamon stick	¼ cup pine nuts
3 cloves	¼ cup raisins
1 lemon rind	

Put the water, sugar, honey, cinnamon sticks, cloves, and lemon rind into a large pot and bring to a boil. Boil for 3 minutes, then remove the cinnamon, cloves, and lemon. Keep the syrup hot over medium heat. Put the oil into a wide pot and heat until it begins to smoke. Add the farina or flour slowly, stirring constantly with a wooden spoon. Cook until it begins to turn golden. Add the nuts and brown them over very low heat, stirring constantly. Be very careful, as the mixture burns easily. When it is the color of chestnuts, add the raisins. Remove from the heat. Add the hot syrup and mix well. Cook over low heat until the farina absorbs the syrup. Remove from the heat and cover with a clean towel. Let stand for 5 minutes. Place in a tube pan or shape into individual mounds by pressing the mixture into a tablespoon and then turning out onto a platter. Sprinkle with a little cinnamon and sugar.

REVANI   ✠   REVANI

1½ cups flour   5 eggs, separated
2 cups farina   1 cup sugar
1 teaspoon baking soda   THE SYRUP
2 teaspoons baking powder   3½ cups sugar
1 cup butter   3 cups water
1 teaspoon vanilla

Sift the flour, then mix it with the farina, baking soda, and baking powder. Cream the butter until very light, add the vanilla, and beat again. Beat the egg yolks in a bowl with the sugar until very thick. Add to the butter, beating in thoroughly. Beat the whites in another bowl until stiff, then fold them alternately and gently, with the flour, into the butter mixture. Pour into a buttered pan and spread evenly. Bake in a preheated 350° oven for 45 minutes.

In the meantime, boil the sugar and water together in a saucepan for 5 minutes. Remove the froth. Pour the hot syrup very slowly and evenly over the hot cake. Cool and serve.

ALMOND REVANI   ✠   REVANI ME AMIGDALA

½ cup chopped blanched   1 teaspoon vanilla
    almonds   5 eggs, separated
1 cup flour, sifted   1 cup sugar
2 cups farina   THE SYRUP
2 teaspoons baking powder   3½ cups sugar
1 teaspoon baking soda   3 cups water
1 cup butter

Mix the nuts, flour, farina, baking powder, and soda together. Cream the butter with the vanilla. Beat the egg yolks in a bowl until very thick, add the sugar, and beat 2 or 3 minutes longer. Add to the butter and beat in thoroughly. Beat the egg whites until stiff. Fold them, alternately with the flour mixture, into the batter. Pour into a buttered baking pan. Bake in 350° oven for about 45 minutes.

Prepare the syrup by boiling the sugar and water in a saucepan for 5 to 8 minutes. Slowly pour the hot syrup over the hot revani as soon as it comes from the oven. Cool, and serve.

APPLE STRUDEL ✠ STROUNDEL ME MILA

THE DOUGH
1 cup (or more) flour
1 teaspoon baking powder
½ cup butter, melted
½ cup Ouzo*
½ cup orange juice
½ cup warm water
flour as needed

THE FILLING
5 cups peeled, sliced apples
½ cup white raisins
½ cup chopped blanched
   almonds
1 cup sugar
1 teaspoon cinnamon

melted butter for brushing the
   pastry
confectioner's sugar

Sift the flour together with the baking powder. Cream the butter in a bowl; add the Ouzo, orange juice, and water, and mix well. Add the flour mixture, a little at a time and as much additional flour as is needed. Knead well to make a medium-soft dough. Roll out on a lightly floured board into a very thin rectangular sheet, almost like tissue paper. Sprinkle the surface with melted butter. Mix together the apples, raisins, almonds, sugar, and cinnamon. Spread along the long side of the dough. Carefully roll up the strudel. Brush the surface with melted butter and place on a buttered baking sheet. Bake in a preheated 350° oven for 30 to 40 minutes. Cool. Cut into slices and serve topped with confectioner's sugar.

NOTE: This can also be made using phyllo* as the dough. Use two sheets of phyllo; brush each one with melted butter. Put one on top of the other, and proceed as above.

LENTEN APPLE STRUDEL ✠ STROUNDEL ME MILA NISTISMO

1 recipe Lenten Skaltsounia
   (see index)
2 cups peeled sliced apples
1 tablespoon cinnamon

¼ teaspoon Ouzo*
¼ cup water
confectioner's sugar
cinnamon for sprinkling

Prepare the skaltsounia pastry and roll it into one large, rectangular sheet. Prepare the filling, and add to it the apples and the cinnamon; mix well. Spread the filling along one long edge of the pastry, then roll the dough over the filling and up to make the strudel. Place it on an ungreased baking sheet and bake in a preheated oven at 350° for 30 to 45 minutes. Meanwhile, mix the Ouzo and water together. Remove the strudel from the oven; cut it into slices. Sprinkle each slice with the Ouzo mixture and dust it with a layer of confectioner's sugar and cinnamon.

PUFF PASTE ✠ ZIMI SFOLIATAS

5 cups flour
2 teaspoons baking powder
1 teaspoon salt

2 cups (approximately) water
2¾ cups butter

Sift the flour with the baking powder and the salt. Place on a marble surface or bread board. Make a well in the middle of the flour and pour in a little of the water. Begin to mix the water into the flour with the fingertips, adding just enough water to make a stiff dough. Do not knead at this point. Shape the dough into a large ball and set it aside in a covered bowl to rest for 30 minutes. While the dough is resting, work the butter in your hands and shape it into a ball. Lightly flour your board. Place the dough in the center and carefully roll with a lightly floured rolling pin into a square about ¼ to ½ inches thick. Place the butter in the center of the dough and bring up the sides of the dough to enclose the butter completely. Lightly flour your hands and begin to work the dough, squeezing it to spread the butter evenly. Shape and pat into a rectangle, and cover with waxed paper; let stand for 10 minutes. Lightly flour the board, rolling pin, and your hands. Place the dough on the board; lightly sprinkle it with flour. Roll the dough into a rectangle (about three times as long as it is wide) about ¼ to ½ inch thick. Fold this over 3 times and lightly press the folds with the rolling pin to join and seal the layers. Let stand for 15 minutes (if it is a very hot day, place in the refrigerator for this time.) Press one finger into a corner of the dough to mark the number of times it has been worked. Again flour the mixing surface lightly and place the dough in the center. Also flour the rolling pin and the surface of the puff paste. Give the dough a quarter turn from its last position and again roll it into a long rectangle, as before. Fold over in three and press lightly with the rolling pin. Let stand for 15 minutes. Repeat this process 3 more times for a total of 6 workings of the dough from the addition of the butter to the end. Remember to give the dough a quarter turn each time. Proceed to make the puffs according to the recipe you are following.

This dough will hold for one day in the refrigerator.

CHOUX ✠ SOU

2 cups flour
1 teaspoon salt
1 teaspoon baking powder

2 cups water
1 cup shortening
6 eggs

Sift the flour with the salt and baking powder. Place the water and the shortening in a pot and bring to the boil. Boil for about 2 minutes, then remove from the heat and add the flour all at once, mixing with a wooden spoon until all the flour is absorbed. Replace the pot on the heat and continue to stir until the mixture leaves the sides of the pot easily. Remove from the heat and allow to half cool. Add the eggs, 1 at a time, working them in with your hands until the dough becomes elastic. Pinch off small pieces of the dough and shape into walnut-size balls. Place on a lightly buttered baking sheet and bake in a preheated 350° oven for 15 to 20 minutes. Makes about 40 puffs. Fill as desired.

EASTER BRAIDS OR TWISTS ✠ TSOUREKAKIA PASHALINA

1 tablespoon mahlepi*
½ cup water
10–12 cups flour
3 packages granular yeast
1 cup warm milk
1 teaspoon salt
2 teaspoons grated lemon peel

1¼ cups butter, melted
5 eggs
1 cup sugar
8 eggs, dyed red (see Easter
    Eggs in index)
1 beaten egg

Boil the mahlepi in the water; strain and set aside. Mix the yeast with the milk and add a ½ cup of the flour, stirring in to make a sticky mass or sponge. Cover with a towel and put in a warm place and let rise until doubled in bulk. Sift the flour with the salt and when the dough has doubled, punch down and add to it about 10 cups of the sifted flour mixture. Blend in the mahlepi and the lemon peel, and then the melted butter. Beat in the 5 eggs and the sugar. Turn out onto a lightly floured board and knead well to make a soft dough. Put into a lightly greased bowl and cover with waxed paper and a thick towel. Put in a warm place and let rise until doubled in bulk, then punch down and knead again on the board. Divide the dough into 4 pieces, then divide each piece into 3 pieces. Roll each of these last pieces into a long rope. Braid three of the "ropes" into a twisted loaf and place on a buttered baking sheet. Make 2 depressions in each loaf, and place dyed eggs in them. Cover the loaves and let them rise in a warm place, again until they are doubled in bulk. Brush with the beaten egg, and bake in a preheated 350° oven for 30 minutes.

NOTE: If you prefer, you can make the loaves smaller. In that case, place 1 dyed egg in the top of each loaf. Or shape the dough into 1 large ring, and place the eggs around it, at spaced intervals. Remove the eggs from the cakes before you slice and serve them; the eggs can be eaten separately.

ST. BASIL'S TWISTS ✠ VASILOPITA TSOUREKI

4 packages granular yeast
1 cup warm milk
10—12 cups flour
1 teaspoon salt
1 tablespoon grated lemon peel
1 tablespoon grated orange peel
1 cup butter

1½ cups sugar
8 eggs
3 ounces blanched almonds, chopped or slivered
1 beaten egg for brushing the top

Prepare the dough as for Tsourekakia Pashalina, above, omitting the mahlepi. Punch down, and place in a well-greased pan, making sure the dough does not more than half fill the pan or it will run over it in the baking. (If necessary, divide the dough in half and bake it in 2 pans.) Cover with waxed paper and a thick towel or light blanket; place in a warm place until the dough again doubles in bulk. Brush the top lightly with the beaten egg and place the almonds on it. Bake in a preheated oven at 350° for about 1 hour. (A smaller twist will bake faster.)

CORN BREAD WITH SYRUP ✠ BOBOTA ME SIROPI

3 pounds corn meal
¾ cup oil
2 teaspoons baking soda
2 cups orange juice
½ cup cognac
1½ cups sugar
2 tablespoons grated orange peel

1½ cups white raisins
water as needed
THE SYRUP
4 cups sugar
3 cups water
1 lemon rind

Sift the corn meal into a ceramic or glass bowl. Heat the oil until it smokes and pour into the meal. Cool slightly, then rub with the fingers to blend well. Make a well in the center of the meal. Dissolve the soda in the orange juice and add it to the meal. Add the cognac, sugar, orange peel, raisins, and as much water as is needed to make a smooth dough. Mix well. Pour the dough into a buttered pan. Bake in a preheated 350° oven for 45 minutes.

Prepare the syrup by boiling the sugar, water, and lemon rind in a saucepan for 8 minutes. Remove from the heat, and pour the hot syrup over the cooled bobota.

GRANITES

ABOUT GRANITES

Granites are delicious iced desserts similar to ices and sherbets, made with fresh fruits or fruit juices, and simple to make. The only tricky part is setting up the correct proportion of sugar to liquids. There is a very easy way to determine this proportion: Float a raw egg, in its shell, in the granite solution. When just about half of the egg is submerged in it, the solution is correct. If you can use a hydrometer or sacchrometer, pour the solution into a tall narrow container, float the gauge in it; if it registers 17, the proportion you are using is correct. A variation of more than 2 or 3 degrees is easily corrected by adding a little more water or sugar, as needed.

To freeze: These ices may be made in an ice cream churn, but they are also easily made in a freezer. Pour the thoroughly mixed ingredients into empty ice cube trays, place in the freezer. Stir the ices every thirty minutes until they begin to set. They will start to set during the first 2 hours. But they will need about 6 hours completely to set. They may be kept in the freezer until ready to use. To serve, scrape or scoop the granites into parfait or other fancy glasses. Serve as is, or with a liqueur poured over them. Or tint with food colors, if you like.

LEMON GRANITE ✠ GRANITA LEMONIOU

5 cups water	1 cup lemon juice
3–4½ cups sugar	2 tablespoons grated lemon peel

Pour the water into a bowl; slowly add to it 3 cups of the sugar; add the lemon juice. Stir well to dissolve the sugar. Test with a hydrometer or raw egg (see introduction to this chapter: About Granites) to see whether more sugar or water is indicated. If you do add more sugar, again stir completely to dissolve it. Add the lemon peel, mixing in well; add food coloring, if you wish. Pour into freezer trays and place in the freezer. Stir the mixture every 30 minutes until it begins to set. This mixture fills about 6 trays and takes about 6 hours to freeze. Serve in parfait or other tall glasses.

ORANGE GRANITE   ✠   GRANITA PORTOCALIOU

4 cups water
3–3½ (or more) cups sugar
3 cups (approximately) orange
   juice

3 teaspoons lemon juice
3 tablespoons grated orange
   peel

Pour the water into a bowl; add 3 cups of the sugar; stir well to dissolve. Add the orange juice, lemon juice, and orange peel. Test with a hydrometer or egg (see introduction to this chapter: About Granites) to check for correct proportions. Freeze in an ice cream churn, or still-freeze in ice-cube trays in the freezer, following the instructions in the introduction.

BANANA GRANITE   ✠   GRANITA BANANAS

10 bananas
4 cups water

1½ cups sugar
⅓ cup lemon juice

Peel and mash the bananas; add 2 cups of water to them. Mix well, then pass through a sieve. Add the sugar, lemon juice, and the remaining 2 cups water. See introduction to this chapter—About Granites—on instruction for checking the proportions and freezing. Freeze in an ice cream churn, or still-freeze in the freezer.

PEACH GRANITE   ✠   GRANITA ROTKALINO

4 cups peaches
4 cups water

1½ cups sugar
⅓ cup lemon juice

Peel the peaches, remove the pits; and mash the fruit thoroughly. Add 2 cups of the water to the pulp, mix well, and pass through a fine strainer. Add the rest of the water, the sugar, and lemon juice. Mix well until the sugar is dissolved. (See About Granites, in the introduction to this chapter, for instruction on how to check the proportions and how to freeze.) Freeze in an ice cream churn, or still-freeze in a freezer.

TYPICAL MENUS

The following menus can be used interchangeably for luncheon or dinner menus. The omission of a dessert and beverage from each is deliberate. Greeks generally end the meal with fruit; coffee and cake are served separately, and a good while after the meal. Refer to the index for special recipes (designated here with a dagger †) that are found in this book.

CAULIFLOWER STIFADO† (KOUNOUPITHI STIFADO)
TARAMA PATTIES† (TARAMOKEFTEDES)
HALVAH WITH FARINA 2† (HALVAS ME SIMIGDALI 2)
FRUIT (FROUTO)

BOILED CABBAGE (LAHANO VRASTO)
BOUREKIA WITH CHOPPED MEAT† (BOUREKIA ME KIMA)
COMPOTE (KOMPOSTA)

PILAF WITH MUSSELS† (PILAFI ME MITHIA)
SALAD, OLIVES (SALATA, ELIES)
FRUIT (FROUTO)

ARTICHOKES BÉCHAMEL† (ANGINARES BESHAMEL)
FRIED POTATOES (PATATES TIGANITES)
CHEESE (TYRI)
FRUIT (FROUTO)

RICE WITH WHITE SAUCE AVGOLEMONO† (PILAFI ME ASPRI SALTSA
AVGOLEMONO)
FRIED EGGS (AVGA TIGANITA)
SAUTÉED CARROTS (KAROTA SOTE)
CHEESE (TYRI)
FRUIT (FROUTO)

POTATO SALAD† (PATATOSALATA)
CHEESE OMELET† (OMELETA ME TYRI)
COMPOTE (KOMPOSTA)

ARTICHOKES WITH CHOPPED MEAT† (ANGINARES ME KIMA)
TARAMA SAUCE† (TARAMOSALATA)
OLIVES (ELIES)
ORANGES (PORTOCALIA)

LAMB FRICASSEE WITH ONIONS AND LETTUCE† (ARNAKI FRICASE ME MAROULIA)
FRIED POTATOES (PATATES TIGANITES)
CHEESE (TYRI)
APPLES (MILA)

SMYRNA MEATBALLS† (SOUDZOUKAKIA)
BOILED RICE† (PILAFI)
RAW SALAD (OMI SALATA)
CHEESE (TYRI)
FRUIT (FROUTO)

CABBAGE DOLMATHES WITH AVGOLEMONO SAUCE† (LAHANO DOLMATHES ME SALTSA AVGOLEMONO)
TARAMA PATTIES† (TARAMOKEFTEDES)
FRUIT (FROUTO)

STIFADO† (STIFADO)
SALAD (SALATA)
CHEESE (TYRI)
FRUIT (FROUTO)

PILAF WITH SHRIMP† (PILAFI ME GARIDES)
SALAD (SALATA)
CHEESE (TYRI)
FRUIT (FROUTO)

CAULIFLOWER KAPAMAS† (KOUNOUPITHI KAPAMAS)
FRIED SALT COD† (BAKALIAROS PASTOS TIGANITES)
SALAD (SALATA)
CHEESE (TYRI)
RICE PUDDING (RIZOGALO)

POTATOES AND SQUASH MOUSSAKA† (MOUSAKAS PATATES KOLOKITHAKIA)

SALAD (SALATA)
CHEESE (TYRI)
FRUIT (FROUTO)

MEATBALLS WITH AVGOLEMONO SAUCE† (YOVARLAKIA AVGOLEMONO)
TOMATO SALAD (DOMATOSALATA)
CHEESE (TYRI)
FRUIT (FROUTO)

SPINACH AND RICE† (SPANAKORIZO)
ANCHOVIES PACKED IN SALT† (SARDELIS PASTES)
OLIVES (ELIES)
HALVAH WITH FARINA 2† (HALVAS ME SIMIGDALI 2)
FRUIT (FROUTO)

CHICK PEA SOUP† (SOUPA REVETHIA)
FRIED SQUID† (KALAMARAKIA TIGANITA)
SALAD (SALATA)
FRUIT (FROUTO)

COUNTRY-STYLE MEAT PIE† (KREATOPITTA HORIATIKI)
SALAD (SALATA)
CHEESE (TYRI)
CRÈME PIATOU† (KREMA PIATOU)
FRUIT (FROUTO)

EGGPLANT "LITTLE SHOES"† (MELITZANES PAPOUTSAKIA)
CHEESE (TYRI)
RICE PUDDING (RIZOGALO)

OKRA IN OIL† (BAMIES LATHERES)
TARAMA SAUCE† (TARAMOSALATA)
OLIVES (ELIES)
FRUIT (FROUTO)

GREEN BEANS IN OIL† (FASOLAKIA PRASINA YIAHNI)
SHRIMP CROQUETTES† (GARIDES KROKETES)
CHEESE (TYRI)
FRUIT (FROUTO)

COOKED-GREENS SALAD† (SALATA HORTA VRASMENA)
FRIED FISH (PSARI TIGANITO)
SVINGI WITH SYRUP† (SVINGI ME SIROPI)
FRUIT (FROUTO)

VEAL WITH MACARONI† (MOSXHARI ME MAKARONAKI KOFTO)
TOMATO-AND-CUCUMBER SALAD† (SALATA DOMATES KE AGOURIA)
CHEESE (TYRI)
FRUIT (FROUTO)

FRIED SQUASH† (KOLOKITHAKIA TIGANITA)
GARLIC SAUCE† (SKORDALIA)
CHEESE (TYRI)
FRUIT (FROUTO)

DRIED BEANS SALAD (FASOLIA HIRA SALATA)
BAKED FISH SPETSIOTIKO† (PSARI FOURNO SPETSIOTIKO)
FRUIT (FROUTO)

CHICKEN WITH PILAF† (KOTTOPOULA ME PILAFI)
LETTUCE SALAD† (SALATA MAROULIA)
OLIVES (ELIES)
ORANGES (PORTOCALIA)

INDEX